THE SONS
OF
CAESAR

PHILIP MATYSZAK

THE SONS OF CAESAR

Imperial Rome's First Dynasty

with 90 illustrations

Thames & Hudson

For Malgosia

FRONTISPIECE The Death of Caesar *by Jean-Léon Gérôme, painted in 1867. Though republicans assassinated Julius Caesar, they could not prevent his family from dominating Rome and her Empire for the next century.*

First published in 2006 in hardcover in the United States of America by Thames & Hudson Inc., 500 Fifth Avenue, New York, New York 10110

thamesandhudsonusa.com

Library of Congress Catalog Card Number 2005906273

ISBN-13: 978-0-500-25128-7
ISBN-10: 0-500-25128-2

Printed and bound in Slovenia by MKT Print d.d.

CONTENTS

N

Temporary conquest
12 BC – AD 9

ATLANTIC OCEAN

BRITANNIA
Camulodonum
Londinium

ENGLISH CHANNEL

Rhine
Elbe
Danube

GERMANIA

Seine
Cenabum
(Orléans)
Lutetia
(Paris)

RAETIA

NORICU

**TRANSALPINE
GAUL**
Alesia
Bibracte

Gergovia

Rhône

**CISALPINE
GAUL**
Mutina
Ravenna
Pisa

**PAN
ON**

IL

SPAIN

Massilia
(Marseilles)

ITALY

CORSICA

■Rome

Gades
(Cadiz)

SARDINIA

Rhegium

SICILY

MAURETANIA

Carthage
Pandateria

NUMIDIA
Thapsus

APPROXIMATE AREAS UNDER ROMAN CONTROL
AT THE DEATH OF THE FOLLOWING RULERS:

Julius Caesar 44 BC

Caligula AD 41

Augustus AD 14

Claudius AD 51

Tiberius AD 37

Nero AD 68

0   500 km

0   300 miles

Tiber

Rome
Bovillae
Aricia
Ostia
Velitrae
Antium Satricum
Arpinum
C A M P A N I A
Capua
Cumae
Baiae
Naples Pompeii
Capri

N

80 km
50 miles

DACIA

BLACK SEA

MOESIA
PONTUS
ARMENIA

THRACE
Byzantium BITHYNIA
MACEDONIA
Philippi
GALATIA
CAPPADOCIA
PARTHIAN
EMPIRE

Troy
ASIA
Pharsalus
Mytilene
Carrhae

ctium
Athens
CILICIA
SYRIA

Miletus
Euphrates

Rhodes
LYCIA &
PAMPHYLIA

JUDAEA

MEDITERRANEAN SEA

Alexandria

AFRICA

EGYPT

JULIO-CLAUDIAN FAMILY TREE

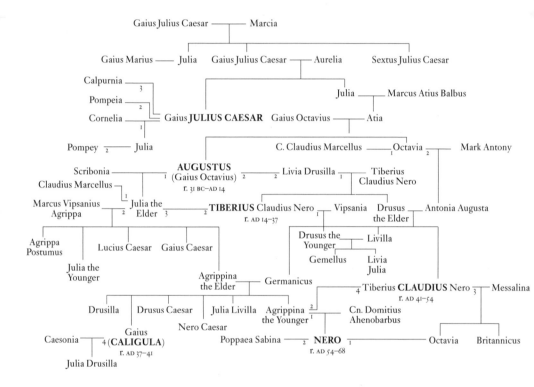

PREFACE

It is no easy thing to overthrow a democracy, and harder yet to replace it with an autocracy. The social institutions of any society possess a massive inertia which, unlike governments, cannot be changed overnight.

In a democratic republic, the organs of state are separate and may even at times work at cross-purposes, with one acting as a balance for the other. In an autocracy these organs must be deprived of their relative autonomy and reorganized with a clear line of command directly to the autocrat. The culture of these institutions must also be changed so that the primary loyalty of those working within them is to the autocrat rather than to those whom their institution serves. If this fails, then the autocrat may develop parallel institutions which gradually take over the necessary functions of state.

The power elites of the state will be disenfranchised no less effectively than the voters. They must either be co-opted into the new system, eliminated or, at the least, give their grudging blessing. Above all, the people need to be brought to accept the new status quo. Since democracy comes from the Greek and means literally 'the rule of the people', it follows that it is the people who have the most to lose. In an autocracy, politicians do not need popularity to win office. Sons and husbands cannot choose in which wars they will be called on to fight, nor do they have any say in the level of taxes which are imposed upon them.

Yet this book is a study of the century in which exactly such a transition took place. A century during which Rome underwent the transition from a Republic (a *res publica*, literally a 'public thing') into a private family possession. A state based upon law and the ballot mutated into a state based upon the diktat of an emperor and the outcome of palace intrigues. This book studies the process of this mutation, not through detailed socio-political analysis, but through the lives of members of a dynasty which was both the catalyst and chief agent of that change.

It will be argued that the Caesars assumed the role once held by the tribunes, as protectors of the people against an oligarchy which had been running out of control. By a mixture of personal charisma and political skill, the Caesars convinced the Roman people to relinquish their democratic rights in exchange for an implicit promise that autocratic rule would be in their interest. Yet at least some of Rome's former oligarchic rulers needed to be co-opted into the imperial project. Caesar failed to do this and paid with his life. Augustus brought the Claudians, perhaps Rome's most powerful aristocrats, into such a tight alliance that the dynasty he created is known as the Julio-Claudian.

It is sometimes forgotten how much history was affected by the longevity of Rome's first two emperors: the Julian emperor Augustus and his Claudian successor Tiberius. The period from Augustus' first consulship in 43 BC until Tiberius' death in AD 37 spans a period of eighty years, while the combined reigns of Gaius Caligula, Claudius and Nero amount to less than half of that. Under the rule of Augustus and Tiberius first Italy, and later the Empire, came to enjoy an unprecedented degree of peace and stability. Though the senate justifiably loathed Gaius Caligula, there are no indications that he, or his successor Claudius, seriously threatened that stability. It was only when, under Nero, the effects of misrule were felt by the common people that the Julio-Claudian dynasty was doomed.

Yet by then it was too late. The social momentum was now unstoppable, and the Empire which the Julio-Claudians had brought about was an accomplished fact, even though there were no more Julio-Claudians to head it. The cataclysm of achieving supreme power destroyed these two great and ancient families. Even as the emperors brought peace and prosperity to their Empire, they wreaked havoc among their own kin. For every emperor assassinated by others – and it is probable that only Augustus and Tiberius died naturally – the Julio-Claudians executed, assassinated and exiled at least half a dozen of their own.

Few families can have compressed such a spectrum of virtues and vices into a few short generations as did that of Caesar and his heirs, yet while the intrigues and follies of Claudius, Caligula and Nero make fascinating history, history they are. It is the first emperors – Caesar, Augustus and Tiberius – who literally changed the history of the world, and whose shadow remains over us today. The Tsars and Kaisers who used the name of Caesar are gone, yet the pernicious example of Caesar and his heirs continues to convince many that an effective autocracy is superior to a dysfunctional democracy.

CHAPTER 1

INTRODUCTION:
FROM REPUBLIC TO EMPIRE

Even those just starting out in politics do not rely on their personal qualities
to do better than the nobility. They [too] use plots, subterfuge and open violence
instead of more honourable routes to military and civil power. As if becoming
praetor or consul was wonderful and magnificent in itself, when in reality
these offices only deserve respect according to the worth of the people
who hold them.

Sallust *Jugurthine War* 4

At the birth of Julius Caesar in 100 BC, Rome had been a Republic for over 400 years. When the last of Julius Caesar's family died in the late AD 70s, Rome was firmly and irrevocably under imperial rule. The history of that transition from republican democracy to military autocracy is also the story of the most remarkable dynasty in antiquity – the Julio-Claudians. So colourful were the lives and personalities of Rome's first emperors that it is easy to become mesmerized by biographical detail and so miss the massive changes that the Julio-Claudians wrought upon Roman society as a whole.

In effect, the Julio-Claudian dynasty hijacked the government of Rome and turned the state into a personal possession. And they did this so effectively that the civil war which followed the death of the last Julio-Claudian emperor was not about whether to restore the Republic, but about who should now rule their Empire. To achieve this, the Julio-Claudians had to overcome the checks and balances built into the Republic by its founding fathers.

The Republic was born when the Roman people deposed the tyrannical King Tarquin. They were determined never again to be ruled by a monarch (Cato the Censor was later to comment that 'kings are carnivorous beasts') and they even went so far as to forbid any king of any nation from setting foot in Rome.

The institutions of the new Republic were carefully crafted to prevent any single person from seizing power. The highest office in Rome was the consulship, and to prevent the consul from getting carried away by his lofty position, the Roman constitution provided not one consul, but two. (Indeed, this may have been the origin of the word consul – the joint heads of the Roman state were linked together like two oxen at the plough: consules, or co-ploughers.) Harmony in office was essential as the veto of one consul automatically overrode the proposal of his colleague. As a further guard against autocracy, the consuls held office only for a year. Repeated consulships were possible but rare, as competition for the post was intense.

Furthermore, the senate could, and often did, find some failure of religious protocol which could obviate a consul's legislation, or even his holding of office. And the tribunes, officials elected to guard the interest of the common man, could not only veto the consuls' actions, but could in theory even have the consuls hauled off to jail.

As in modern democracies, the Roman people as a whole voted to choose their government officials. Unlike most modern governments, the people also voted directly on any legislation. The nearest ancient Rome had to a parliament, the senate, was almost devoid of any constitutional power and relied for its authority on the massive influence and personal power of its members.

Ultimately it was the struggle for that influence and power within the senate which proved Rome's undoing. The self-interest and internecine struggles of the Roman elite alienated the Roman people whose lives and lands they blighted. The cynical contempt of Rome's aristocracy for their own political system proved all too contagious and, even as they accepted the bribes, the electorate came to despise the bribers. The career of the impetuous tribune Clodius (Chapter 2) showed clearly that the people still looked for a lead from the aristocracy, for Clodius was a Claudian, one of Rome's greatest families. Yet such was the contempt for the senate through which the aristocracy exercised its collective rule that the senate house was destroyed in the public disorder that followed

Clodius' death – in short, by the first century BC Rome was ripe for a military coup led by an aristocrat.

The alternative explanation for the Republic's replacement by the military dictatorship of the Caesars, that its institutions collapsed under the strain of running Rome's ever-expanding Empire, is too facile. Firstly, autocracies are not, ipso facto, better at running large states than democracies. Secondly, most of the Roman Empire pretty much ran itself. Given the vast distances and rudimentary bureaucracies involved, it could hardly have been otherwise. The basic component of the Roman Empire was the civitas – a large urban centre and its hinterland. Every large city had its own constitution and acted as a religious and administrative centre for the surrounding countryside. The entire Empire – with some exceptions – could be seen as a mosaic of such city-states co-ordinated from the centre for certain specialized areas (such as paying taxes to a central fund and, above all, maintaining the army).

Thirdly, the institutions of the Republic only changed gradually with the advent of the Caesars, and least of all in those parts directly concerned with administering the Empire. In the Republic, the governor of each province was answerable to the senate. When Rome acquired an autocrat, the machinery of government in the provinces continued largely unchanged, though most governors were now under the direct control of the emperor. As the imperial influence slowly took hold, most administrative changes which did take place were for the worse, as the emperor and a growing bureaucracy gradually centralized power and choked the life from the local political process.

The Julio-Claudians did not change the structure of the state overnight. Even in Rome, elections took place for a while, though they became steadily more meaningless. The praetors continued to dispense justice, though often from basilicas built to glorify the imperial name. The priests performed the centuries-old rituals in the temples, but now the choice of the top priests required the imperial sanction, and many of the sacrifices were for the well-being of the emperor. Thus under the Julio-Claudians, the imperial power ran for a greater or lesser time alongside the republican institutions which it was supplanting. But in one unmistakable way imperial Rome was different from the Republic which preceded it – it had an imperial dynasty.

The sources

The reign of the Julio-Claudian emperors is one of the best-documented periods in all ancient history. Those doing the documenting were well informed, articulate and opinionated, and through them the Julio-Claudian family is brought vividly to life. But these were not impartial, dispassionate reporters. Praise or blame are allocated according to private agendas, and facts are twisted to make their subject appear in a more or less flattering light. Even the most distinguished writers have the Roman penchant for gossip and tittle-tattle which sometimes makes them read like the most unedifying of modern tabloids – and quite probably with even less regard for veracity.

Therefore the ancient historians must be read with caution, all the more when the historian appears to be non-partisan. For example, one of the best sources for the campaigns of Julius Caesar is Julius Caesar himself. Writing in spare, elegant Latin, Caesar pretends to present his campaign notes for future historians. In fact, these 'notes' are masterly works of propaganda which have burnished Caesar's image for two millennia.

Another Caesar who speaks directly to us across the centuries is Caesar's adopted son, Augustus. His *Res Gestae* (Things Achieved) is a stunning assemblage of half-truths, disingenuous misinterpretations, distortions and outright lies. Yet it is also an eloquent testimony to the accomplishments of the man who ended a century of civil wars and established a new world order which endured for hundreds of years.

Among others in the literary cornucopia of sources for the early Caesars we have the letters of Cicero, the poems of Horace and the history-cum-laudation of Velleius Paterculus. Livy – perhaps Rome's greatest historian – would have been invaluable for the lives of Caesar and Augustus, but though his work for this period is lost, it was undoubtedly consulted by the three authors who stand supreme as chroniclers of the imperial Julio-Claudians. These are Cassius Dio, Suetonius and Tacitus.

Cassius Dio, along with Tacitus, is invaluable for putting a framework on the chronology of the period. Yet of all our sources he is the least contemporary. Born in AD 164, he went on to serve as a consul of Rome and as proconsul of the province of Africa before writing his *Roman History* some time around AD 202. The political turbulence and tyrannical emperors of his own times have coloured the whole of Dio's history, yet this ambience holds true for the Julio-Claudian period, which saw its share of tyranny and upheaval. Dio not only describes but also analyzes the transition from Republic to Empire, and is sensitive to nuances of imperial propaganda. Sadly, his work has not come down to us intact, and there are large gaps in the text from 6 BC onwards.

Suetonius was born just as the Julio-Claudians became extinct. He avoided politics and after briefly practising law he held a number of posts in the imperial bureaucracy, including that of chief secretary to the emperor Hadrian. Thereafter he turned to biography. His *Caesares* – the Lives of the Caesars – stands with the works of Cornelius Nepos as the earliest Roman biographies which have survived to our time. Suetonius is scurrilous, gossipy and thoroughly entertaining. For instance, he tells of Tiberius insisting that the electoral roll state, next to the name of a man he had granted Roman citizenship, that 'The emperor was forced to do this by his mother.' Through Suetonius we see what contemporary Romans expected of their rulers in terms of personal conduct, public displays and military prowess.

Where Suetonius is a biographer, Tacitus is a historian. As a senator of the generation which followed the Julio-Claudian era, Tacitus had access to the official records from that period. He used these accurately and conscientiously. Tacitus was capable of shrewd analysis and concise yet detailed reporting, but was also arrogant, acerbic, biased and brilliant – never short of a brusque put-down or wounding epigram. Tacitus judged emperors by their relationship with the senate, and in this regard the Julio-Claudians fell far short of the more relaxed regime of his own time. We are particularly indebted to Tacitus for his *Annales* – a history of the reigns of Tiberius, Gaius Caligula, Claudius and Nero.

Leaving aside the literary texts, we have a wealth of supplementary material, with archaeology constantly contributing new findings from across Europe. Where the *imperium* (Roman power) directly touched an individual or city, it was not uncommon for a record of the occasion to be engraved on stone. The decrees, and even the speeches of emperors and governors, have been found from Cardiff to Baghdad, telling us how the emperors wanted to be seen by their subjects, and what those subjects expected of their emperor.

It is possible still today to stand on the grounds of Domitian's palace on the Palatine hill of Rome, to look over the forum and see the Via Sacra where the legions marched towards the senate house in a Roman triumph. Sculptures and friezes tell us of the dress and social hierarchy of the Romans of the early Empire. Mosaics show farming and hunting scenes, parties and banquets, while tombstones tell of family relationships, offices held and age at death.

We have so much evidence for the period that the profession of prosopographer has developed – a specialist who attempts to trace the career of individual Romans from inscriptions, official records, tombstones and casual references in the literary sources. For example, we know from historians that Julius Classicianus was procurator in Britain directly after the revolt of Boudicca in AD 60 while Nero was emperor. After his death Classicianus' ashes were placed in a small tomb which was found in modern times near Tower Hill in London, bearing the inscription

To the spirits of the departed and Gaius Julius Alpinus Classicianus, son of Gaius, of the Fabian voting tribe, […] procurator of the British province. His wife Julia Pacata Indiana, daughter of [Julius] Indus [made this].

Coins carried imperial ideology to the people of the Empire, and the messages on the coins, short and cryptic as they are, tell us much about the policy of the emperors who ordered those coins struck. From the metal content of the coins we can make some assumptions about the economic health of the Empire and ascertain whether Gaius Caligula and Nero were as ruinously profligate as their detractors claimed.

Archaeology has proved to be a guide to the accuracy of our written sources. Tens of centuries after the battles described by Tacitus and Livy, it has been possible to return to those lost battlefields; excavations there have shown that in general our ancient historians were accurate reporters of fact. Their opinions and interpretations of those facts are of course another matter.

CHAPTER 2

FAMILY FORTUNES

In the same way [as a master owns his slaves] are our children in our power, so long as they are children born of a properly legal marriage. This absolute power over our children is a phenomenon peculiar to Roman citizens: there are almost no other people in the world who have the same degree of power over their sons that we have.
(The jurist Gaius on the power of Roman fathers over
their children – *patria potestas) Institutes* 1.56

Background to Empire – Roman Political Dynasties

At the start of the Julio-Claudian story, Rome was a democracy. However, it was certainly not a democracy in which all men were created equal. The vote was only given to free males, and even then the constitution was biased towards those with the greatest wealth and property. The state and its political offices were dominated by a tightly knit group of families who used the ballot box as an instrument of dynastic power along with money, patronage and judicious marriages. However, though dominated by its aristocracy, Rome had the essential ingredient of a constitutional democracy. Power was ultimately derived from political office to which the holder was elected by the people.

The story of the Republic is the story of the interaction between Rome's great dynasties and democracy. Each was changed by the other, and the process shaped the Julio-Claudian clan which eventually brought the interaction into the imperial era.

An elite Roman family judged success by political power. Power came through the ballot box, and elections were won by a mixture of public perception and the application of money. It was vastly expensive to embark on a political career, yet senators squandered huge sums to secure even the lowliest of state offices, simply because the rewards were so great. Political office meant power, and power could be converted back into money. For example, a praetorship in Spain saved the young Julius Caesar from bankruptcy, and Pompey's wars in Asia Minor made him the richest man in Rome.

Legislation could be equally lucrative, and not simply because of bribes from the interested parties. All legislation produced winners and losers, and those who benefited from a particular law felt personally indebted to the person who passed it (which is why Roman laws tended to bear the name of the legislator who proposed them). One reason that the Gracchus brothers – the powerful second-century BC social reformers – were opposed by the senate was that the oligarchs feared the constituency of supporters the brothers would obtain from their reforms and building projects. As well as providing contracts for favoured clients, building projects put the family name before the voters and were an eternal advertisement for that family's name.

In the last days of the Republic it was vital to keep the family name before the electorate. A family which was not favourably remembered was a family whose members were not regularly elected. This could easily lead to a slide into insignificance which was immensely difficult to reverse. During the early imperial era, when the legitimacy of autocratic rule was still in doubt, the Julio-Claudians advertised themselves as Rome's first family, and deserving of their extraordinary prestige and powers. They also took a very dim view of other members of the nobility who tried to impress the public favourably, and thus set themselves up as potential rivals.

All members of a noble family benefited from one of the clan doing well, and not just through improved marriage and electoral opportunities. Roman magistrates were expected to use patronage, bribery, favouritism and nepotism – this was not corruption, because corruption suggests an alternative system to be corrupted. In Rome this was the system, and it allowed family members to promote the ambitions of their kinsfolk. Roman generals often took their sons on campaign with them (according to legend Scipio Africanus saved his father's life during one of the early clashes with Hannibal), and ex-consuls unhesitatingly pulled strings to place their relatives in the best jobs. Thus the high commands bestowed upon relatives of a Julio-Claudian emperor were merely the continuation of republican business as usual.

It helped that the Romans had direct ideas about heredity. A child was not a chip off the old block as much as an extension of the block itself. The Romans felt they knew what they were getting in a Fabius (an able soldier), a Domitius Ahenobarbus (someone undiplomatic and fearless) or a Claudius (an arrogant, but usually capable, administrator). The orator Cicero (plate 2) was acutely aware that he came from an undistinguished family. He once said, 'When I was a candidate, I had no ancestors to recommend me to you. If I am guilty of any fault, I will have none of their images to intercede with you on my behalf.'

The 'images' were those of distinguished ancestors. When a noble Roman who had done good service to the state died, his heirs were allowed to make a wax mask of his face (the *ius imaginum*). These masks were displayed in every aristocratic home, reminding visitors of the debt which Rome owed to that family.

Cicero made this absolutely plain in a speech attacking a nobleman called Calpurnius Piso:

You crept into office by mistake, on the recommendation of those smoke-stained family images…. When you were made quaestor, even men who had never seen you were prepared to bestow that honour on your name. You were made aedile; it was as a Piso, not you who bear that name, whom the Roman people elected. In the same way, it was your ancestors, not you, who were given the praetorship. They were dead, but everyone knew of them.

Cicero *In Pisonem* I.I & I.2

Thus (to quote Cicero again) some men were 'made consuls in their cradles'.

Education and upbringing could only go so far in changing a man's basic nature. 'You can produce a stunted oak or a luxuriant weed', Plutarch brutally explains, but you have an oak and a weed nonetheless. One's basic nature was inherited, but a Roman might choose to adopt a kindred spirit from the next generation. Adoption was common among the great families of Rome (though it was never practised by the Claudians of the Republic). Partly the reason was political. Even for an elite family an electoral campaign was prohibitively expensive, and very few families could afford to put more than one or two sons through the *cursus honorum* – the ladder of offices culminating in the consulship of Rome. Therefore a family with surplus sons might choose to put some out for adoption.

An adopted son benefited in two ways – the electorate remembered the virtues allegedly inherited from his ancestors, and the public endorsement of his adoptive family. Both factors became crucial in imperial adoptions, which were the principal means of succession among the Julio-Claudian emperors. Elections were not an issue, but credibility with senate and army was vital to the success of each new regime.

A final aspect of adoption is the peculiarly Roman institution of *patria potestas* which gave a Roman father literally life and death powers over his children. While in most other ancient societies a child attained some degree of autonomy after coming of age or getting married, a Roman father's powers over his male children were only restricted if the son held a magistracy or was doing military service. Women passed into the *potestas* of their husband on marriage if they married with the ancient *cum manu* formula (in the *manus*, or hands, of her husband), as many patrician families did. Generally, though, women stayed in *patria potestas* which meant that Roman fathers (including Roman emperors) could order their daughters to divorce spouses who displeased them.

1 *The right to produce masks of one's distinguished ancestors (the* ius imaginum*) was limited to the aristocracy. The style of this man's toga suggests the Augustan era, but his head was added later. It was not uncommon in Roman times for sculptors to make only a body whilst a skilled portrait sculptor worked on the head.*

Social pressure had a very strong role – disobeying a parent was impious and truly shocking behaviour. Thus adoption into a household tied the adoptee closely to the head of the family, putting him into a situation where public dissent was well-nigh impossible. And as will be seen in later chapters, an adopted son could even legally be killed by a father who was prepared to accept the consequent social outrage. In short, adoption was not only a public declaration by the adopter that he and his new son shared the same values and aspirations, it was also an unconditional pledge of loyalty and obedience from the adoptee. Since the Julio-Claudian emperors seldom produced sons, they generally used the advantages presented by the process of adoption to designate their successors as such.

Another area of family life inextricably entangled with both republican and imperial politics was marriage. Among the Roman elite, marriage was a dynastic affair in which love played little part. Cicero's ex-slave and literary executor Tiro indignantly denied that Cicero married his second wife for love. The great statesman was above such emotional frailties. No, the girl was rich, and Cicero needed the money.

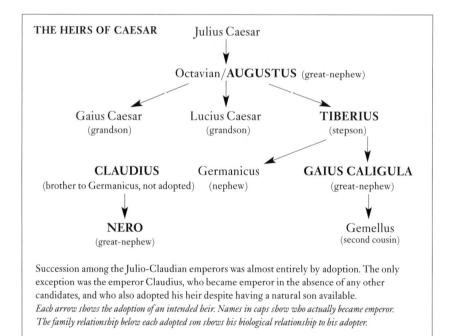

THE HEIRS OF CAESAR

Julius Caesar

Octavian/**AUGUSTUS** (great-nephew)

Gaius Caesar (grandson) Lucius Caesar (grandson) **TIBERIUS** (stepson)

CLAUDIUS (brother to Germanicus, not adopted) Germanicus (nephew) **GAIUS CALIGULA** (great-nephew)

NERO (great-nephew) Gemellus (second cousin)

Succession among the Julio-Claudian emperors was almost entirely by adoption. The only exception was the emperor Claudius, who became emperor in the absence of any other candidates, and who also adopted his heir despite having a natural son available.
Each arrow shows the adoption of an intended heir. Names in caps show who actually became emperor. The family relationship below each adopted son shows his biological relationship to his adopter.

A marriage generally indicated a political alliance between the groom and his father-in-law. A Roman bride might be in her husband's house, but she remained very much 'daddy's girl' (as can be seen in contemporary Roman comedies, where wives in difficulty immediately send for their fathers). If the alliance between father and son-in-law broke up, the marriage rarely survived. The bride's dowry was returnable after a divorce, and this could be a very substantial sum.

One view of a Roman political marriage is that, in return for political support, the father-in-law sponsored the husband's career – not least by the giving of a dowry to defray electoral expenses. The wife was not only mistress of her husband's house, but also guarantor of that loan. She was in charge of the slaves, who had the run of the household, and since a Roman politician's office was his home, there was little he could do of which his wife was unaware. A Roman husband could keep secrets from his wife, but he could not avoid her knowing that he was hiding something, which was itself grounds for suspicion. Given the close and continuing ties between a Roman wife and her father, this meant that the father could effectively monitor his son-in-law's behaviour and contacts.

Naturally, married couples could and did fall in love, but this was more a happy side-effect than the point of the whole business. In fact, Roman law explicitly forbade husband and wife from exchanging expensive presents, lest their families be impoverished through the 'mutual pillage' of their assets. In many ways the Julio-Claudian emperors were republican Roman senators writ large. They shared the same dynastic concerns, were determined that their clan should be the foremost in the state, and they wanted the next generation to make marriages which were politically advantageous, fruitful and happy – strictly in that order of priority.

The Julian Clan

The first Roman emperors were called Caesar because they were all – by birth or adoption – members of the family of Julius Caesar. But though of great antiquity, the Caesars were by no means the greatest family in Rome until Gaius Julius Caesar seized power and made himself dictator for life. Early in his *imperium* (period of rule), Julius Caesar's successor, Augustus, married into the family of the Claudians. This family, though in relative decline, was arguably the greatest in Rome. The dynasty which resulted from this union is generally known by the combined name of Julio-Claudian, and any study of the Julio-Claudian emperors must begin with the families which produced them.

Upon Aphrodite herself Zeus cast sweet desire to be joined in love with a mortal man, with the purpose that, very soon, not even she should be innocent of a mortal's love; for otherwise laughter-loving Aphrodite would one day softly smile and mock all the gods that she had joined in love with mortal women who gave to the deathless gods sons who were fated to die, and that she [Aphrodite] had mated goddesses with mortal men.

    Homeric Hymn 5

So, legend says, the enchanted Aphrodite lay with Anchises the Trojan and bore him a son, who was named Aeneas. When evil times came to Troy, Aeneas and his countryman Hector battled against the Greeks led by Agamemnon and Achilles. Homer tells how the Trojans were deceived by the wooden horse of Odysseus, and how, after the Greeks had sacked Troy, Odysseus wandered for years on his long journey home, tormented by the vindictive Aphrodite.

Troy too produced a wanderer. Aeneas escaped the burning city carrying old Anchises on his back, and with his son Ascanius clinging to his thigh. This Ascanius, sometimes called Iulus, was claimed by the Julians as their progenitor, tracing their ancestry through him to Aphrodite, or Venus as the Romans called her. It was perhaps this Ascanius who founded the city of Alba Longa when the weary Trojan refugees finally settled in Italy.

2 *This denarius coin shows Aeneas, the founder of the Roman race, fleeing Troy with his father on his shoulders. Aeneas was the child of Venus and, because the Julian family traced their ancestors to Aeneas, Julius Caesar and his family could claim to be descended from the gods.*

3 (opposite) *Romulus, Remus and the she-wolf. Despite being one of the most famous images of ancient Rome, none of this sculpture (called the Capitoline Wolf) is in fact Roman. The she-wolf is Etruscan and dates from about 500 BC, while the children beneath were added 2,000 years later during the Renaissance.*

We will not discuss the question (for who can speak decisively about a matter of such extreme antiquity?) – whether the man whom the Julian house claim, under the name of Iulus, as the founder of their name, was this Ascanius or one older than he, born of Creusa, whilst Troy was still intact, and after its fall a sharer in his father's fortunes. This Ascanius, wherever born, or of whatever mother – it is generally agreed in any case that he was the son of Aeneas…built a new city at the foot of the Alban hills, which from its position, stretching along the side of the hill, was called 'Alba Longa'.

Livy 1.3

From Alba Longa some 300 years later, two young men raised by a she-wolf – Romulus and Remus – set out to found a new city on hills about the river Tiber. Perhaps there were some members of the Julian clan among Rome's founders, for a Julius Proculus claimed to have spoken to the spirit of Romulus shortly after his death. This is the first mention of a Julian in Rome, and it confirms the tradition that the Julian family was both extremely old, and intimately connected with the fortunes of Rome.

The same tradition asserts that the bulk of the Julian family remained in Alba Longa until the city was absorbed into the Roman body politic by King Tullus Hostilius. The historian Dionysius of Halicarnassus mentions the Julians among the leading families who were resettled in Rome,

but an alternative tradition suggests that some of the family moved to nearby Bovillae (modern Frattocchie). Centuries later, the emperor Tiberius dedicated a small temple to the Julian family in Bovillae together with a statue of Augustus. The Bovillae connection has been strengthened by the discovery of an altar of great antiquity in the town where sacrifices were made according to the Alban rite.

In the decades following the destruction of Alba Longa, Rome came strongly under the influence of the Etruscan civilization to the north, and the Etruscan kings of Rome completed the city's transformation to a fully fledged city state. The Etruscan kings were overthrown by Lucius Brutus the liberator, and a Republic was established. The great dynasties of the early Republic were not Julians but Valerians, Horatians and Claudians. The leading branch of the Julian family, bearing the name Julius Iullus, did however produce a series of consuls in the early fifth century BC. Also a certain Gaius Julius appears as one of the decemvirs (ten men elected to draw up a code of laws) who tyrannized Rome in 451 BC. Another Julius, consul in 431 BC, dedicated a temple to Apollo, a god to whom the Julian clan felt a particular attachment.

Other branches of the Julians were called Libo, Mento and Bursio, though the only record of this last branch is a single mention on a coin of the late Republic. In the year 208 BC, while Hannibal was devastating Italy during the Second Punic War, we find the first mention of a Julius Caesar. This Caesar was a praetor, the rank just below consul, and he governed the province of Sicily.

Even the Romans were unsure of the origin of the word 'Caesar'. One theory was that it came from *caesus* meaning 'cut', and it was suggested that the first Julius Caesar had been cut from his mother's womb in a difficult birth. If the Caesars did not get their name from this operation, they may instead have given it, since it is

4 *Silver denarius of the late Republic stamped with the name of L. Julius Bursio, another branch of the Julian clan. The head is not Bursio, but a deity with the winged cap of Mercury and Poseidon's trident. The other face of the coin shows winged Victory riding a chariot.*

possible that a Julius Caesar of the second century BC originated the leg-islation that allowed the cutting of a baby from the mother if it was apparent that the mother was going to die in childbirth anyway. Julius Caesar the dictator was not, as many people believe, born by Caesarian section. Had he been, his mother would not have survived the birth, and in fact she lived for many years afterwards.

We can also probably discard the etymology which claims that Caesar is from the ancient Moorish for 'elephant', the name relating to the heroism of an early Caesar in killing one. This is unlikely, not least because later Caesars would have made much of the story were it true. A more probable candidate is the word *caesaries*, someone with thick, curly hair. (The Roman habit of turning a physical characteristic into a surname can be seen with the Claudians, a branch of whom were called Pulcher or 'pretty'.)

During the early second century BC, a number of Julius Caesars rose to the praetorship. Their first known consul appears in the person of Sextus Julius Caesar, elected for 158 BC. It may be that the rise of the Cae-sarian family can be indirectly attributed to Hannibal. Rome suffered horrendous casualties during the Second Punic War, with up to one adult male in three dying during the fifteen years of warfare. The Roman aristocracy led from the front, and bore a disproportionate number of these casualties, diminishing the families of subsequent generations and allowing others to rise in their place. Even without the attrition of warfare, most aristocratic families rose and fell depending on the ability of individuals or the whims of the electorate.

Throughout the second century BC, the Julians stressed their connec-tion with Venus, their legendary ancestor. While in charge of the treasury in around 130–125 BC, a Julius Caesar issued coins with Venus as a motif, as did another Caesar in 105 BC.

The fortunes of the Julius Caesars received another boost when a daughter of that house married the up-and-coming Gaius Marius after his successful campaigns in Spain in 113 BC. The ancient and honourable Julian name, combined with the financial and political clout of Marius, helped another Julius Caesar, called Lucius, to become consul in 90 BC and censor the following year. The censorship had less real power than the consulship, but it was the most prestigious rank to which a Roman could aspire. That a Julius Caesar now held this post showed that, by the start of the last century of the Roman Republic, the Caesars were a power in the land.

The Claudians

The origins of the Julian family are lost in myth and legend. But the Claudians came to Rome through pragmatic power politics and continued in the same brutal and uncompromising style thereafter. From the day of their arrival until the death of the last of their clan, the Claudians were one of Rome's leading families. Every generation saw at least one Claudius rise to the consulship, and by 49 BC few could have predicted that this wealthy, numerous and well-connected clan could rise any higher, or that it was doomed to perish within a few generations.

The Claudians were originally Sabines, a people with whom the Romans had an ambiguous relationship. Almost as soon as Rome was founded, the Romans kidnapped a large group of Sabine women to be their brides (the notorious Rape of the Sabines). After a brisk war, many Sabines threw in their lot with the Romans. But the Claudians remained with those who alternately allied themselves with and fought against Rome throughout the regal period.

Rome became a Republic in 509 BC. With another war against the Sabines imminent, Valerius Poplicola, one of the Republic's first leaders, pulled off the diplomatic coup of persuading Attus Clausus, the leader of the greatest family in the city of Regillus, to move himself and his 400-strong clan of family and dependants to Rome.

Clausus, now called Appius Claudius, was controversial and reactionary. As consul in 495, he opposed reforms giving the poor farmland and debt relief. So violently did he fall out with the plebeians that he was largely responsible for their first attempt to secede from the state altogether.

---

5 *Constructed in the late third century BC, the famous Appian Way is still used by walkers and cyclists today. St Peter travelled up this road to Rome, and Clodius (one of the descendants of the Appius Claudius who built the road) was murdered on it while returning to the city.*

His son was in the same mould. As a general he had modest success against Rome's enemies, but infuriated his troops to the point of mutiny. Brave well past the point of pig-headedness, he once harangued a hostile crowd in the forum, oblivious of personal danger, until his fellow consul had him dragged away for his own safety.

In the 450s BC the Romans experimented with a form of government called the decemvirate, in which a panel of ten men codified the laws of the state. This came to an end when an Appius Claudius established himself and his nine colleagues (including, as we have seen, one Julian) as tyrants who were finally overthrown in a popular revolution. We cannot be sure of the truth of this story, but the Romans were already dividing this extraordinary family into the 'good Claudians' and the 'bad Claudians'.

If Appius Claudius the Decemvir was a bad Claudian, then Appius Claudius Caecus, the censor of 312 BC, exemplified what was good about the family. Though typically contemptuous of Roman democratic sensibilities, Appius Claudius Caecus governed well and built the road from Rome to Capua which still bears the name of the Appian Way. When Pyrrhus, a warlike successor of Alexander the Great, invaded Italy, Appius Claudius Caecus rallied resistance and forced Pyrrhus to retire with heavy losses. Appius Claudius Caecus was one of the first writers in the Latin language, though his works have not survived.

During the First Punic War, 264–241 BC, a particularly incompetent Appius Claudius commanded the Roman navy. Just before a major battle (perhaps prompted by Claudius' more capable subordinates) the sacred chickens refused to eat – a very bad omen indeed. But Claudius would not to be denied his battle. 'So let them drink', he said, and had the birds thrown overboard to drown. The sacred chickens were soon followed by most of the Roman fleet and thousands of unfortunate Roman sailors. Claudius' sister added insult to injury shortly afterwards. She stunned the crowds delaying her return from a public spectacle by announcing that her brother needed to lose a few more fleets to cull the plebs to a more manageable number.

Yet during the Second Punic War of 218–202 BC it was a Claudius of the Marcellan line who led the resistance to Hannibal. His aggression combined with the defensive skill of Fabius Maximus so that the pair were called 'the sword and shield of Rome'. Hannibal himself commented, 'I look on Fabius as a schoolteacher, for he punishes my mistakes; but I see Marcellus as a rival, for he seeks to harm me any way that he can.' Marcellus died in action in 208 BC, one of many Claudians who perished in their country's service.

After the defeat of Carthage the Claudians, though rich and powerful, were no longer the force they had been in the early Republic. In early Rome, the patricians had made up the aristocracy, and the plebeians the commonalty, but in the later Republic the title of patrician meant much less. The Gracchans and Metellans were plebeian families, but were now considered no less aristocratic for the fact. Even the Marcellans, one of the most distinguished branches of the Claudian family, were plebeian.

During the final crisis of the Republic, three Marcellan Claudians, two brothers and a cousin, held successive consulships between 51 and 49 BC. Though all disliked Caesar, Gaius Marcellus, the consul of 50 BC, equally disliked Pompey and sat out the civil war in Italy. This Gaius (his cousin, the consul of 51 BC, was another Gaius Claudius Marcellus) married Octavia, the sister of Octavian, Caesar's heir, and thus brought together the Julian and Claudian lines even before Octavian adopted a Claudius Nero as his heir.

Although a Claudius Nero had served with Marcellus against Hannibal and distinguished himself at the battle of the Metaurus in 207 BC, until Tiberius' adoption by the emperor, the Claudian Neros had been a relatively undistinguished branch of the family. The last Nero to be consul had held office in 202 BC.

While Cicero was in the East in the 50s BC, he met a young Claudius Nero called Tiberius. Cicero was so impressed by Tiberius Claudius (who later commanded the fleet in Caesar's Egyptian campaign) that he offered his daughter in marriage. When it turned out that Cicero's daughter in Italy had already arranged a fiancé for herself, Tiberius Claudius instead married a kinswoman called Livia.

Livia was born in either 59 or 58 BC. Her father was Marcus Livius Drusus Claudianus, descended through the line of the Pulchers, the senior Claudian family. Since Livia's marriage brought together the bloodlines of the Claudius Neros and the Appius Claudius Pulchers, Tiberius, her son from that marriage, could justifiably claim a pedigree worthy of adoption into the imperial family.

Despite her Claudian antecedents, Livia was technically a Drusus, since her father had been adopted into that clan (which explains why so many of the following generations of Julio-Claudians were named Drusus, including the brother of Tiberius himself). The Drusus name had its own resonance, since a Livius Drusus had been a reforming tribune of 91 BC who was still fondly remembered by the Italian people.

However, in the years preceding Caesar's march on Rome, it was not the Claudius Neros, nor, for all their political clout, the Marcellan Claudians, who shocked, titillated and occasionally threw Rome into chaos. That was the role of the youngest and wildest of the great Claudian clan – the children of the Appius Claudius Pulcher who was consul in 79 BC.

Appius Claudius Pulcher's daughters, being of the Claudian house, were called Clodia, Clodia and Clodia. This confusion of Clodias, each with a propensity for scandal and amorous adventure, presented both contemporary Romans and later historians with immense difficulty in determining which Clodia was doing what with whom at any given time. (It was one of these Clodias, under the pseudonym of Lesbia, to whom the poet Catullus declared in verse his burning love and subsequent abject heartbreak.)

The oldest Clodia married a Metellus, the Metellus family being perhaps the most powerful dynasty in Rome at the time. She and Cicero loathed each other, and Cicero gleefully slandered her for her many and complex love affairs. Another Clodia married the general Licinius Lucullus, and the third married Marcius Rex, scion of an aristocratic family with which the Julians also had close connections.

All of the Clodias' husbands had been consuls of Rome, and achieving the same was automatically expected of the Clodias' brothers. Appius, the eldest, was a conservative and cultured gentleman who often corresponded with Cicero. He was consul in 54 BC and censor in 50 BC – the last patrician to hold that office in the Republic. His brother Gaius reached the praetorship in 56 BC, and then served in the province of Asia until 53 BC. On his return to Rome, Gaius fell foul of the extortion courts and was condemned. Thereafter Gaius dropped out of politics and lived the life of a cultured Roman gentleman. The youngest of the family was Publius.

Publius Appius Claudius Pulcher, known to historians and contemporaries alike as Clodius due to a mutation of the Claudian name, knew that he would be accounted a failure if he reached anything less than the consulship. Driving ambition and aristocratic pride marked his career from the start.

As with most young aristocrats, that public career started with military service abroad; in this case, serving with the army of Lucullus in Asia Minor. When Clodius felt that his commander-in-chief and brother-in-law was not giving him the respect he was entitled to, he began inciting his troops to mutiny (not a difficult task, since Lucullus' troops were already rebellious).

Ejected from service with one brother-in-law, Clodius took himself to another, Marcius Rex, the proconsul of nearby Cilicia, on the south coast of modern Turkey. In the late 70s, Cilicia was infested with pirates – as Julius Caesar discovered (p. 43). Put in charge of the local fleet, Clodius commanded so unsuccessfully that he was finally captured by the pirates he was meant to be suppressing. Fortunately for him, the last thing the pirates wanted was a feud with the Claudian family.

Released by the pirates, and after further escapades in Syria and Gaul, Clodius returned to Rome in the mid-60s BC. He was deep in debt and had a reputation for being wild and dissolute, a reputation which was about to get much worse.

In 62 BC Clodius attended a religious ceremony at the house of Julius Caesar, who was then the Pontifex Maximus (p. 49). This ceremony was the rite of the *Bona Dea* (the 'Good Goddess') which was celebrated only by women. Clodius was discovered among them disguised in a veil and a dress. His presence was either a high-spirited prank, or for a romantic assignation – perhaps even, rumour afterwards alleged, with Caesar's wife Pompeia. The entire power of the Claudian clan was needed to save its scapegrace scion from disgrace. Though Cicero shattered Clodius' alibi, the jury was bribed, blackmailed and intimidated into a 'not guilty' verdict.

Clodius, who had recently been elected to a quaestorship, hurried to take up his official duties in Sicily. When he returned to Rome the following year, he announced his intention to become a tribune.

However, tribunes were the guardians of the common people against the aristocracy and Clodius was from the aristocracy of Rome's aristocrats, and ineligible for the position. Consequently Clodius wanted to get adopted into a plebeian family by a process called *adrogatio. Adrogatio* was a complex public process easily derailed by vested interests, and at that time the vested interests which counted were those of the triumvirs, Crassus, Pompey and Caesar. These three had no desire to see a rival gain power and constantly frustrated the adoption.

Then Cicero antagonized the triumvirs with an ill-judged speech and, knowing of the powerful antagonism between Cicero and Clodius, the triumvirs decided to let Clodius off his leash. Within hours Clodius was campaigning for the tribuneship as the adopted son of a plebeian nonentity called P. Fronteius. The Roman people, who liked their demagogues as aristocratic as possible, had no hesitation in electing him.

Clodius entered office in 59 BC. His first measures were balanced and careful. The senate muttered when Clodius ordered further corn distributions to the people, but they heartily approved of Clodius' proposal that the censors could not strike from the senatorial roll anyone whom the senators themselves had not condemned. Then, building on the precedent set by Caesar's trial of Rabirius (p. 47), Clodius proposed the punishment of anyone who had put Roman citizens to death without trial – starting with Cicero who had executed some conspirators on his own authority (see the Catiline case, p. 48).

The man who had shown the most steadfast courage in that affair [Cicero] now lost his nerve completely when brought to task. He put on humble, filthy clothes [traditional behaviour for a Roman in distress] and begged help from those he met in the streets…all this panic about his own case from a man who had been conducting cases for others for most of his life!… Clodius scornfully put an end to Cicero's supplications in the streets whereupon Cicero fell into despair, and like a latter-day Demosthenes took himself into voluntary exile.

Appian *Civil Wars* 2.16

Clodius had Cicero's house in Rome destroyed, and built a temple to the goddess Liberty on the site. Then the Claudian tribune proved he was no minion of the triumvirs by turning on Pompey, using his power of demagoguery so effectively that Pompey was sometimes penned into his house for days at a time by the hostile mob.

Pompey fought back, and riots and public tumult became everyday occurrences throughout the streets of Rome. By 57 BC Pompey had secured the support of two influential tribunes – Milo and Sestius – and his professional thugs were winning the battle in the streets. The senate had tired of Clodius' antics and overwhelmingly agreed to recall Cicero from exile.

Cicero turned his oratory against Clodius with venom:

I never had any illusions about him – nothing good can be expected from someone who has been from his earliest youth a servant to the lowest and least discriminating of human vices. Who had given every part of his body to impure and intemperate urges and worked as hard at bankrupting himself then as he did the state later, and then supported himself in his destitution by turning his house into a brothel.

Cicero *On his Restoration to the Senate* 5.1

Though Cicero enthusiastically promoted the rumour that Clodius was having an incestuous affair with his sister Clodia, the ex-tribune retained enough support to be elected aedile for 56 BC. This proof that Clodius had not lost momentum made the praetorship a clear possibility in 52 BC. Hastily Clodius patched up relations with Pompey, and courted other high-ranking senators.

While returning from a visit out of town, Clodius encountered his enemy Milo *en route* at Bovillae on the Appian Way. A fracas broke out between their supporters in which Clodius was wounded then, once his entourage had been driven off, lynched. Ironically, he was killed beside a shrine to the *Bona Dea*, the goddess whose rites he had once profaned.

Clodius was given the funeral he would have wanted. The mob attacked Milo's house, and then carried Clodius' body to the forum. There he was cremated on a pyre allegedly made from benches taken from the senate, in a blaze which destroyed the senate house itself.

Nothing could show more clearly that while the senate had lost touch with the common Roman people, individual aristocrats could gain a devoted following. Clodius taught the Julio-Claudians that popular support could trump senatorial hostility. The lesson was well learned. The senate at best tolerated and at worst hated the imperial Julio-Claudians, yet the dynasty ruled Rome until Nero lost the support of the common people.

CHAPTER 3

JULIUS CAESAR: FROM A RENEGADE TO A GOD

When his route took him to the Rubicon...he stopped, gazed at the stream, and considered the evil that his crossing this river with his army would bring. Pulling himself together, he told his audience, 'My friends, if I cross this river it will be a disaster for humanity. If I do not, it will be a disaster for me.' Thereupon he rushed across like a man possessed, shouting the famous phrase 'Let it be so! The die is cast.'
Appian *Civil Wars* 2.35

Probably more has been written about Gaius Julius Caesar (100–44 BC) than about any other single person in antiquity. Caesar was a soldier, a politician, a writer and an orator. As an orator he roused the Roman populace with speeches so emotive and lucid that Cicero, the greatest orator of the day, commented, 'There are those who cannot match him, even if they have given a lifetime to the study of this subject.' As a writer, he has left us with a priceless description of his campaigns, written in clear forceful Latin that has delighted military historians and classicists alike. Caesar the politician rose to hold the highest offices of state, and founded a dynasty that ruled Rome for a century. As a soldier Caesar campaigned in Africa, Europe and Asia Minor, winning victory after victory.

Yet historians, both ancient and modern, are ambivalent about Caesar. While acknowledging his brilliance as a general, they deplore the hundreds of thousands of lives he sacrificed for his political ambitions. As a politician, Caesar overthrew the already dysfunctional Roman Republic and replaced it with a military dictatorship. And, for all that has been written about him, Caesar himself remains an enigma. To understand him better, we have to understand both the society and the times in which Caesar lived.

O tempora! O mores! 'Oh, the times, the morals!', lamented Cicero of the standards of his day. In the centuries after the founding of the Roman Republic in 509 BC, the elite of Rome had constantly jostled for power and influence. Yet these struggles had been fought in elections and law-suits, with fines and banishment awaiting the losers. All this changed a generation before Caesar's birth. Two brothers of Rome's noble Sempronian house, Tiberius and Gaius Gracchus, tried to force through reforms which were necessary and long overdue.

These reformers met with passionate resistance from short-sighted and reactionary senators and, though most of the proposals of the Gracchus brothers eventually became law, both brothers lost their lives in the struggle. They were not alone – hundreds died in the riots and persecutions as, for the first time in centuries, Roman fought against Roman. As one ancient writer put it, the career of the Gracchus brothers had 'thrown daggers into the forum' and, to the already ungentle processes of Roman public life, was added the risk of riot, political purges and death.

Some thirty years after the death of the Gracchus brothers, Gaius Julius Caesar was born on the fifth day before the Ides of Quintilis in the consulship of Valerius Flaccus and Gaius Marius (for the latter, see below). Two millennia of revisions to the calendar have made the exact date uncertain in modern terms, but it was probably 13 July 100 BC. It is because Julius Caesar was born in this month that Quintilis was later renamed in his honour (modern July). By an interesting coincidence Caesar's birthday fell on the principal day of the games to Apollo, the Julians' preferred deity.

The year of Caesar's birth marked another stage in the Roman Republic's long slide into anarchy. The tribune Saturninus, a man with the populist approach of the Gracchus brothers but none of their idealism, was arrested and stoned to death in the senate house of Rome while his ally, the praetor Glaucia, was dragged into the street and lynched while still wearing his robes of office.

Another significant fact of that year was that one of the consuls was Gaius Marius. Marius too had once been a populist tribune venomously opposed to the privileged elite of the senate (he had once threatened to arrest a sitting consul). Now Marius was himself a consul. He had reached this position only because he had come to understand that aris-

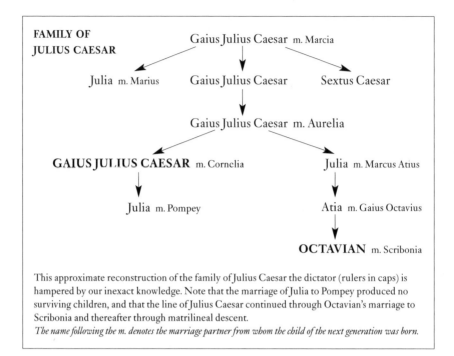

FAMILY OF JULIUS CAESAR

Gaius Julius Caesar m. Marcia

Julia m. Marius   Gaius Julius Caesar   Sextus Caesar

Gaius Julius Caesar m. Aurelia

GAIUS JULIUS CAESAR m. Cornelia   Julia m. Marcus Atius

Julia m. Pompey   Atia m. Gaius Octavius

OCTAVIAN m. Scribonia

This approximate reconstruction of the family of Julius Caesar the dictator (rulers in caps) is hampered by our inexact knowledge. Note that the marriage of Julia to Pompey produced no surviving children, and that the line of Julius Caesar continued through Octavian's marriage to Scribonia and thereafter through matrilineal descent.
The name following the m. denotes the marriage partner from whom the child of the next generation was born.

tocratic allies were essential to his political career. Accordingly, he had married into the highly pedigreed but otherwise undistinguished Julian family. The Julia he had married was an aunt of Gaius Julius Caesar, who was thus born with a consul of Rome for an uncle.

Marius was not the young Caesar's only distinguished relative. His mother was Aurelia, of the family of M. Aurelius Cotta, a man who had been consul in 119 BC, and whose family was a rising power in the state. Caesar's own father was just ascending the rungs of the *cursus honorum*, and was probably quaestor at the time of Caesar's birth.

We have little information about the first decade of Caesar's life. The history of Livy and the biography of Suetonius are both missing for this time, and as a result we are not even certain of the exact descent of Caesar's father, nor which of an earlier generation of Caesars could claim him as a great-grandson.

Like all noble children Caesar learned Greek, but he possibly also learned some Gallic from a tutor who seems later to have opened a school of rhetoric in Rome, which Caesar occasionally patronized even as a grown man. A casual mention by another historian suggests that he had a showy trick of riding a horse with his hands held behind his back (not easy in an age before the invention of stirrups) and, though not particularly robust, he was good at sports requiring endurance.

As Caesar entered his second decade, Rome underwent a further convulsion. The Italian allies of Rome, too long exploited and ignored, rose in revolt in 90 BC, and for a while the very survival of Rome was in doubt. Another Caesar, Sextus Julius Caesar, played a leading role in the war, both as a commander and as a legislator. His proposal that citizenship should be granted to those rebels who laid down their arms took the sting from the revolt. Sextus died campaigning against diehard rebels soon afterwards, but his career added to the growing lustre of the Julian name.

Caesar's uncle Marius fought in the war and won some victories, but he was eclipsed by his young rival Sulla. This rivalry flared up again in 88 BC when Marius manoeuvred Sulla out of the command of a campaign in the East. In response, Sulla led his army against Rome and Marius – the first time a Roman general seized power by military force. Marius fled for his life and Sulla, after briskly restoring order, set off on the Asian campaign that had been the whole point of his coup.

With Sulla safely abroad, the struggle between his supporters and opponents escalated into a full-scale civil war. Marius joined forces with Lucius Cinna, the leader of Sulla's enemies, and eventually he and Cinna captured Rome. With Cinna either unable or unwilling to prevent him, Marius then launched on a bloody purge of everyone who had ever opposed him. As a nephew of Marius, the young Caesar was safe, but the purges took the lives of kinsmen C. Julius Caesar Strabo, and of L. Julius Caesar, an orator and man of letters. Their heads were placed on spikes in the forum, an image which must have powerfully coloured Caesar's opinion of politics.

In Caesar's sixteenth year his father died. Julius Caesar *pater* had just completed a successful praetorship and a foreign posting. He was in Pisa, probably in 84 BC, when one morning he bent to tie his bootlaces and expired, possibly from heart failure. This is worth noting, since it shows that Caesars were unexpectedly dropping dead even before wild rumours and gossip surrounded every unexplained death in their household – in the ancient world, death from natural causes could unexpectedly take people of any age or social status.

Now officially head of a family that included his two sisters and his doting mother, Caesar renounced an earlier engagement to the wealthy heiress Cossutia and attached himself more closely to the new regime by marrying Cornelia, Cinna's daughter.

There are suggestions that Caesar was appointed to a priestly office, perhaps even that of *flamen dialis*, a prestigious and ancient priesthood. In Rome religion and politics were inseparable, and politicians were often priests. But it is doubtful that Caesar would have wanted to be *flamen dialis*, since the office was surrounded by so many rituals and taboos that it effectively disqualified the holder from any other function. Nevertheless, Cinna may have pressed Caesar to take the post to show the populace that even in those turbulent times, the timeless rituals of Rome were still respected.

Any arrangements were cancelled by the death of Marius and Sulla's return to power. Sulla was accompanied by two henchmen with whom Caesar later became very familiar. These were Gnaeus Pompey, whose opportunism and brutality had already earned him the title of *adulescentulus carnifex*, 'the butcher boy', and Marcus Licinius Crassus, who was busily enriching himself with the property of Sulla's enemies. At that time, Caesar was certainly numbered among those enemies, especially as he refused to divorce Cornelia, whom Sulla had already stripped of her inheritance and estates.

Though suffering from a violent attack of fever, Caesar was forced to disappear from public view, finding a new hiding place every night, and bribing householders to protect him from Sulla's informers.
Suetonius *Life of Caesar* 1

Eventually Caesar was hunted down, and his mother mobilized all her resources to save him. A stream of aristocrats appealed to Sulla, including M. Aurelius Cotta, who was both a kinsman of Caesar's and a Sullan partisan. Sulla too had some connection with the Julian family, for his first wife (now deceased) had also been a Julia. Sulla finally gave way to the combined pressure of Aurelia's kinsfolk and their allies, saying,

All right then, you have made your point. Take him! But mark my words – you are saving the very man who will be the ruin of everything you and I have fought for and hold dear. There are many Mariuses in that Caesar.

Suetonius *Life of Caesar* I

Appian tells a different story with the same theme. In 80 BC Sulla, while completing his second consulship, announced that he was resigning the dictatorship. In a stunning piece of political theatre he dismissed his lictors and walked home from the forum as a private citizen. No one raised a hand against him.

The people simply looked on in astonishment. But on his way home, a young lad started to shout abuse at him. No one stopped this youth, who followed Sulla to his door, heaping curses on him. And Sulla, whose towering rages had overcome the greatest of men and nations endured it all calmly. But as he went into the house he commented, either through an inspired insight or through his own natural sagacity, 'That young man will make it impossible for anyone who ever holds powers such as mine ever to give them up.' And in this the Romans were to discover he was correct, for when Caesar held such powers, he never laid them down.

Appian *Civil Wars* I.105

Such stories are related by historians with foreknowledge of what was to come, and must be regarded with considerable scepticism. In fact, whatever Appian may imply, it is unlikely that the youth he refers to could have been Caesar, for the latter had wisely decided to absent himself from Rome for a while. In any case, in reality the young Julius Caesar was then so unimportant as to be almost a nonentity. It is highly improbable that Sulla lost any sleep on account of this precocious young man.

6 *Gnaeus Pompey. Originally a brutal henchman of Sulla, Pompey went on to become a great general, then a political ally, and finally an enemy of Julius Caesar.*

Political life in Rome slowly returned to normality, a process speeded by Sulla's retirement. But Caesar had started his career by seeing the bloody murders of dozens of senators and hundreds of lesser aristocrats in a state-sanctioned terror. Little wonder that in later life Caesar felt that he had to succeed or die.

Caesar – Early Career

Though Sulla was retired, his regime was very much alive, and Caesar was a known opponent of that regime. Accordingly, in 81 BC, Caesar decided to absent himself from Rome for a while and took a posting in the eastern Mediterranean where Minucius was besieging Mytilene, the principal city of Lesbos. Because Lesbos is an island, Minucius needed a fleet; King Nicomedes of Bithynia, a Roman client king in Asia Minor, was selected to supply one. Caesar was sent to expedite arrangements.

Nicomedes made Caesar very welcome, and the two became close friends. Caesar spent more time with Nicomedes than his mission warranted, and then chose to return once more on private business. Certainly the cultured court of an Eastern monarch was a fascinating experience, and the friendship of the king was flattering for the young Caesar, who was then, after all, a minor aristocrat out of favour in Rome. Nevertheless, the nature of Caesar's friendship with Nicomedes became a source of malicious gossip. Rumours that this had been a homosexual affair haunted Caesar for the rest of his career.

Eventually parting from Nicomedes, Caesar returned to play a distinguished role at the fall of Mytilene. His bravery in storming the walls led to the award of a civic crown – a mere garland of oak leaves, yet one of the highest awards the Roman state could bestow. Caesar then campaigned in Lycia and Cilicia (on the south coast of modern Turkey), under P. Servilius, until word reached him in 78 BC that Sulla had died and it was safe to return to Rome, his family and his infant daughter.

In Rome Caesar found that not his war record, but his relationship with Nicomedes, attracted most attention. When Caesar was reporting to the senate the gifts which Nicomedes had bestowed, one senator commented, 'We all know what he gave you – and what you gave him.' Whatever the true nature of the relationship, it moved the young Caesar to pen verses that Augustus later went to some trouble to keep from becoming public. It also added to Caesar's later reputation as 'every woman's man, and every man's woman'.

Caesar's next step into politics was to prosecute the senator Dolabella for extortion while he had been governor of Macedonia. That this was an acceptable manner for a young Roman to make his debut says much about the cut-throat nature of even 'normal' Roman politics. Caesar's prosecution failed but gained him a reputation for eloquence. To further hone this eloquence, and to escape the vengeful Dolabella, Caesar left Rome to study rhetoric in Rhodes.

Near Miletus, Caesar was captured by pirates. This was not an uncommon occurrence in the ancient Mediterranean. Always jealous of the power of others, the Romans had destroyed the naval capacity of the Rhodians, and since they themselves were poor sailors with little interest in policing the seas, corsairs now swarmed from the unguarded coast of Asia Minor, occasionally even to raid Italy itself. Plutarch takes up the story:

When the pirates demanded twenty talents for his ransom [a very substantial sum even for a wealthy senator], he laughed at them for not knowing who their captive was, and suggested that they should ask for fifty…then he took part in the sports and exercises of these most murderous of villains without the slightest concern, and if they showed no respect for the poems and speeches which he practised upon them he would laugh, call them illiterate barbarians to their faces, and threaten to have them all hanged.

Plutarch 2

This tale is probably an invention by posterity, as is the suggestion that Caesar exclaimed that Crassus would be delighted by his capture. Caesar was still too obscure and unimportant either for the pirates to know him, or for him to matter much to Crassus. However, Caesar demonstrated his talent for organization and energy the moment he was ransomed and released in Miletus. Raising a fleet, he caught his former captors and their fleet in their hideaway. He reclaimed his ransom, and handed the pirates over to the local administrator. This man did nothing immediately, as he hoped the pirates might exchange more booty for their lives. Caesar promptly had the pirates crucified by his own authority. This showed aspects of Caesar's character which became more apparent later – speed and decisiveness in action, contempt for established authority and ruthlessness towards non-Romans (though Caesar was not completely merciless: he did have the pirates' throats cut before he nailed them up).

Caesar was fated never to complete his studies of oratory. No sooner had he arrived on Rhodes than war between Rome and the Pontic king Mithridates flared up in Asia Minor. Caesar crossed to the mainland, raised a force from local cities, pushed back the enemy and secured the immediate area. Then he returned to Rome, taking care to charter a boat fast enough to outrun the keenest pirate.

Caesar's uncle Cotta, the consul of 74 BC, had died while holding a provincial command in Gaul, and Caesar, now twenty-seven years old, was elected *pontifex* in his place. The *pontifices* held the chief priestly offices in Rome, and election to their college was a keenly contested honour. That Caesar achieved it at a relatively early age is a testament to the political clout of his mother's family.

Caesar resumed the life of an aspiring Roman politician. He was elected military tribune for 72 BC, and enthusiastically joined in prosecuting the official who had failed to crucify his pirates. Caesar also campaigned for the recall from exile of his brother-in-law Cinna, although this family connection was to be severed by the death of his wife Cornelia. In 69 BC Caesar became quaestor. Soon afterwards his aunt, the widow of Marius, died. Caesar's funeral oration was a eulogy of his clan:

On her mother's side, my aunt was descended from kings, on her father's side, from the immortal gods. The family of Marcius Rex is of the line of King Ancus Marcius, and the Julians are descended from Venus. Her line has the honour of kings, who are the greatest of men, and gods, who command even kings themselves.

Suetonius *Caesar* 6

Though statues of Marius were forbidden in Rome, Caesar delighted the old general's supporters by displaying his image in the funeral procession. Diplomatically, he then mended his bridges with the Sullans by taking Sulla's granddaughter Pompeia as his new bride.

In the year after his quaestorship, Caesar was assigned to duties in Spain. There is a story that while in Gades (modern Cadiz) he came across a statue of Alexander the Great, and was deeply affected by the thought that this Macedonian had conquered much of the known world by the age of thirty-three, while Caesar, who was almost the same age, had achieved almost nothing of note. While returning to Rome, Caesar stirred up considerable agitation among the peoples north of the river Po by giving his support to their campaign for Roman citizenship. This move increased his political standing in northern Italy even as it alarmed the senate, which kept two legions from going to campaign in Asia Minor until the unrest died down. Once again Caesar became an object of suspicion among the oligarchy.

'I worry about him, and then I see him delicately scratching his immaculate coiffure with a single finger, and I find it impossible to imagine that this delicate fop could be a menace to the state,' confessed Cicero.

The immaculate coiffure was not much longer for this world, for Caesar was afflicted by a receding hairline which, like millions of men through the following millennia, he attempted to conceal by brushing the remains of his hair across the empty expanse. As to the rest of his appearance,

He was finicky in his personal grooming; always neatly trimmed and barbered, and some have alleged that he depilated other parts of his body…. They say too that he always dressed distinctively. He wore the *latus clavus* with fringed sleeves down to his wrists, and always wore a belt, albeit loosely.

Suetonius *Caesar* 45

7 *Julius Caesar. As his receding hairline and lined face show, this bust depicts the dictator in later life. He exudes an air of poised self-confidence in his role as foremost commander of men.*

The *latus clavus* was a tunic with a wide purple stripe which indicated that the wearer was a senator. The long fringed sleeves were an affectation, as was the belt, which was not usually worn with this garment. Caesar's lifestyle became famously lavish and extravagant. Though no gourmet, he understood that sumptuous meals and entertainments impressed both his peers and the public. Plutarch tells that even before he held any public office, Caesar was 1300 talents in debt. Those who disliked Caesar hoped that he would ruin himself through his extravagance, but Caesar was less of a spendthrift than he appeared. 'In reality he was buying things of the greatest value at a small price,' Plutarch comments.

For example, Caesar had himself appointed Curator of the Appian Way. There was a small state budget for maintaining this road, but Caesar far exceeded it, paying personally for numerous improvements. These were duly recorded on the milestones of the road leading to Rome, so that those entering the city (for example to participate in the elections) were reminded at every mile of Caesar's generosity and public spirit.

At this time Caesar was a protégé of old Crassus, the former henchman of Sulla who had since leveraged his ill-gotten gains into the greatest fortune yet amassed in Rome. Crassus knew the importance of money in a senatorial career, and skilfully used his to fund impecunious but promising young politicians. This strategy took Crassus to the height of power in Rome, and was also employed by Caesar once he had enriched himself in foreign wars.

Caesar's next step along the *cursus honorum* was as aedile for 65 BC. This office involved maintaining order in the city, supervising its buildings, bars and brothels, and giving the ever-increasing population a steady supply of grain and water. To these routine administrative tasks was added the organization of the public games and spectacles, which today are remembered as among the most striking features of life in ancient Rome.

Caesar's colleague was Marcus Calpurnius Bibulus, who found sharing public office with Caesar an unrewarding business. He commented that the temple in the forum was properly called the Temple of Castor and Pollux, but everyone referred to it as 'Castor's', just as everyone referred to the aedileship of Caesar and Bibulus as Caesar's.

Although his father had died almost twenty years before, Caesar now staged gladiatorial games to mark his passing and (not incidentally) further to outshine his colleague, who was also a rival for the next post in the *cursus* – that of praetor. Caesar's games were of unprecedented style and splendour. Three hundred and twenty pairs of gladiators were due to take part, all wearing silver armour – though the senate may have intervened to prevent this particular extravagance.

Caesar gave greater offence to the senate by restoring the statues of Marius, arguing disingenuously that recognizing his uncle's merits would help to heal the wounds of the civil war. The senate gave way, not least because Caesar's actions were enormously popular with the people. One senator, Lutatius Catulus, commented ironically that Caesar had stopped trying to undermine the state; now he was going for it with battering rams.

In fact, the undermining of Sulla's regime was going on apace. Caesar arranged for the elderly senator Rabirius to be tried for involvement in the lynching of the tribune Saturninus in 100 BC. Saturninus had been killed while the senate's famous 'last decree' was in force, and it was this, the *senatus consultum ultimum*, which was really on trial. The decree allowed the consuls to 'see that the state came to no harm' and tacitly authorized any action taken to ensure this. The fate of Rabirius warned that senators were answerable for their conduct even after a *senatus consultum ultimum*. The trial suggests that Caesar might even then have considered that he might one day be on the receiving end of such a decree.

Caesar became praetor elect and, typically, pushed his good fortune even harder. The most senior priest in Rome, the Pontifex Maximus, had just died. The vacancy for the office was contested by two of Rome's most distinguished senators, Servilius Isauricus and Lutatius Catulus. Both were appalled when Caesar threw his hat into the ring. Catulus, well aware of Caesar's financial straits, offered Caesar a substantial bribe to withdraw. But Caesar knew that his praetorship would ensure a profitable foreign command to ease his debts. He also knew that he had a good chance of victory, since he had been instrumental in overthrowing the Sullan system of senate-appointed priesthoods and making them elective once more. The stakes were high. On the day of the election Caesar told his mother that she would see him that evening as Pontifex

Maximus or not see him at all, as defeat would surely be followed by exile.

In the event, Caesar won his priesthood, along with a prestigious official residence on the *Sacra Via* (Rome's most distinguished thoroughfare), the guardianship of Rome's Vestal Virgins, and the undying enmity of Catulus and Servilius Isauricus. How dangerous this enmity might be became plain soon afterwards.

All Rome was aware that Cicero had begun a feud with Sergius Catiline, a patrician desperately ambitious to restore the fortunes of his house. Catiline resembled Caesar in many ways. His family, though noble and ancient, was not of the first rank in Rome. Catiline too needed the profits of high political office to pay off his creditors, and he too courted popular opinion while living beyond his means. Cicero was originally neutral towards Catiline, and even once considered defending him in court. But as the extent of Catiline's ambition became clear, Cicero came to see him both as a personal rival and as a danger to the Republic. Goaded by Cicero's oratory, Catiline moved from idle table talk about overthrowing the government to seriously plotting a Sullan-style coup.

Catiline was betrayed at every turn, denounced by Cicero and driven from Rome, whereupon he raised an insurrection in the countryside. Cicero promptly arrested Catiline's co-conspirators in Rome, and the senate debated what should be done with them. As praetor elect, Caesar was entitled to speak, and he argued against the death penalty. In this he was supported by a praetor called Tiberius Claudius Nero, an ally of Pompey, who was by now the most powerful man in the state.

Opposing Caesar was a newly elected tribune called Marcus Cato (great-grandson of Cato the Censor), who had a reputation for uncompromising idealism and stoic virtue, and he used his considerable oratory to swing the senate round to executing the conspirators. Cato also suggested that Caesar's defence of the conspirators might be due to his own complicity in the plot. (It did not help that Catiline had been suspected of an abortive conspiracy in 66 BC in which Caesar had been implicated.) Both Caesar and Crassus were suspected, but it was dangerously unwise to accuse Crassus (the only person who did so died mysteriously a day later), so Caesar bore the brunt of senatorial animosity. Only the physical intervention of Cotta, the ex-consul, and Cicero himself prevented

Caesar from being cut down where he stood (Cicero was later bitterly reproached for this misplaced humanitarianism). Some time later Catulus offered a bribe to Cicero if he would testify against Caesar. Instead Cicero confirmed that Caesar had given him useful assistance in uncovering the plot, so this attempt also came to nothing.

Catulus and Servilius were powerful enemies. When Caesar supported the tribune Metellus against those who had voted to execute the conspirators, the pair persuaded the senate to suspend Caesar from his praetorship. Caesar at first ignored the edict, but when the senate sent soldiers to insist, he quietly surrendered his symbols of office and went home.

This was politically adept, for the Roman people were incensed that the senate had deposed a man whom they had elected, and who had done nothing illegal. Large crowds gathered outside Caesar's house, and might have become unruly had Caesar himself not urged restraint. Since Caesar's house was almost literally a stone's throw from the senate, that august body felt it diplomatic to restore Caesar to his office immediately.

Caesar's eventful praetorship had one more scandal to offer. Towards the end of the year, Caesar was ejected from his house by his wife Pompeia. This was so that she and other noble ladies could celebrate the rites of the 'Good Goddess' (the *Bona Dea*) without the profane presence of males. Unfortunately the previously discussed young aristocrat of the Claudian house, Publius Clodius, was caught on the premises disguised as a woman (p. 33). Rumour suggested that the paramour whom Clodius had intended to seduce was Pompeia herself.

As already mentioned, Clodius was prosecuted for sacrilege, but those jurors not intimidated by the Claudian name were bribed into handing down a 'not guilty' verdict. Catulus, sitting as judge, saw another opportunity to embarrass Caesar pass him by, and solicitously asked the jurymen if they required an armed escort to see their new-found wealth safely home. So dubious was this acquittal that Caesar divorced Pompeia anyway, proclaiming that 'Caesar's wife must be above suspicion'.

After his praetorship Caesar was due for a potentially profitable command in Spain but, not for the last time, his enemies tried to thwart him. They found ready allies in creditors worried about Caesar going beyond their reach before paying at least an instalment of his massive debts. Caesar himself had commented that he needed 25 million sesterces before he could become simply penniless. Caesar's military career might have ended before it had begun had not Crassus come to his protégé's rescue with a timely loan, allowing Caesar to depart with his creditors at least staved off for the moment.

By some reports, Caesar's command in Spain began by doing very little for the people he was governing, being of some advantage to Rome, and mightily benefiting Julius Caesar himself.

He neglected the performance of public affairs, the administration of justice and everything of this sort, because he could see no advantage in it for himself. Instead he gathered an army and attacked the independent Spanish tribes one by one.

Appian *Civil Wars* 2.1.8

There was also a suspicion that those tribes whom Caesar fell upon most ferociously presented not the greatest threat, but the greatest chance of booty.

Both as a general and as a politician Caesar showed himself of questionable integrity. Some have written in their memoirs that when Caesar governed Spain he asked for money from Rome's allies to pay his personal debts, and he attacked and sacked some Lusitanian towns although they had surrendered to his terms and opened their gates to him. Also in Gaul…he sacked towns more for plunder than because of any wrongdoing on their part.

Suetonius *Caesar* 53

Nevertheless, once the powerful and troublesome Callaici and Lusitanian peoples had been cowed, Caesar demonstrated a rare talent for administration. Plutarch comments admiringly on Caesar's legislation on debt in the province, but before the provincials had come to terms with this new aspect of their governor, Caesar was gone again, leaving his province early to stand for the consulship in Rome.

Caesar found a dilemma awaiting him at Rome. Generals commanding armies were forbidden from entering the city, a prohibition made even more understandable after the events of 88 BC (p. 39). However,

Caesar was entitled to a triumph for his successes over the Spanish tribes, and triumphs could only be celebrated by commanders holding office. Caesar's request to stand for the consulship *in absentia* was quashed by Cato, whose animosity towards Caesar had become distinctly personal.

Caesar was a supporter of Pompey, who had put Cato's father to death, and Caesar was having an affair with Cato's stepsister Servilia. During the Catiline affair, Cato had seen Caesar receive a note whilst the senate was sitting. Assuming the message was from a conspirator, Cato insisted it be read aloud. The message was an amorous note to Caesar from Servilia. On discovering this, Cato flung the letter at Caesar saying 'take it, you drunkard', an interesting accusation since Cato drank heavily, whilst Caesar was notoriously abstemious.

Forced to choose between a prospective consulship and a certain triumph, Caesar typically opted for the former, even though a triumph was one of the greatest honours a Roman citizen could achieve. Caesar chose as running mate a certain Lucceius, whose deep pockets would assist in bribing key parts of the electorate. This was enough to swing Caesar's enemies solidly behind the other candidate, Calpurnius Bibulus, Caesar's former colleague as aedile. Even Cato contributed to Bibulus' war chest of bribes and consequently Caesar and Bibulus were both elected as consuls for the year 59 BC.

Consul, Triumvir and General

'Now I'm going to ride on your heads!' remarked Caesar to the hostile faction in the senate. His coarse idiom was readily understood, and someone remarked that this would be a difficult feat for a woman. Caesar was by now used to snide comments about his relationship with Nicomedes, and responded equably that some remarkable queens had ruled in the Middle East, Queen Semiramis being a good example.

Caesar's affability was as much political calculation as his natural good nature. He wanted another profitable command after his year in office, and so he needed the senate on his side. Caesar also wanted legislation giving land to the veteran soldiers who had recently returned from the East. This legislation not only addressed an urgent problem, but would greatly benefit Pompey, whose ex-soldiers they were, and Caesar owed a debt to Pompey for help with his electoral campaign. Aware of the fraught relations of Pompey with the senate, not to mention his own unpopularity, Caesar carefully made the legislation as reasonable as possible, and further offered to make any improvements the senate suggested.

Led by Cato, the senate obstinately refused even to consider the bill. Caesar ordered Cato to be arrested for holding up proceedings and was outraged when a goodly number of senators trooped out in sympathy. 'I prefer Cato's company in prison to yours in the senate,' one senator informed Caesar as he departed.

If Caesar could not win over the senate, he had other recourse. He turned on the one hand to the people, and on the other to Crassus and Pompey. Crassus, Caesar and Pompey, already collaborators, now worked so closely together that their enemies dubbed them 'the three-headed monster'. Later historians call this alliance the first triumvirate, though contemporary senators had less printable epithets to offer.

At the *contiones* (public meetings before major legislation) Crassus spoke in favour of the bill. Pompey announced that if any man took up the sword to oppose it, he would take up his shield. This barely veiled threat from Rome's most powerful citizen gave pause to any who hoped to bring the fate of the Gracchus brothers upon Caesar; and Pompey packed the meetings with his former soldiers in case someone tried anyway.

Caesar urged Bibulus, his fellow consul, to support him. Naturally he failed. Bibulus announced to the crowd, 'You will not get the law this year, even if everyone wants it.' The arrogance of this statement, the blithe assumption that the popular will could be overridden and above all, the identification of Caesar with that popular will, handed Caesar a propaganda gift which is potent even today, and it shows the selfish pig-headedness into which much of the senate had lapsed.

To block the law, Bibulus took to observing the skies. On the day of the ballot he sent word that he had seen lightning. This sign of the disfavour of Jove meant that the vote had to be postponed. Bibulus knew that Caesar would ignore him, but he was laying the grounds by which Caesar's legislation could later be overturned. Bibulus spent much of his consulship closed in his house, observing the skies, and periodically issuing polemics fulminating against his fellow consul. Caesar ignored him, not least because as Pontifex Maximus, he had the last word on whether any omen observed by Bibulus was valid. He went his own way, causing wits to comment that Rome was under the consulship of Julius and Caesar.

When the aged general Lucullus objected to Caesar's high-handedness, Caesar gave him so effective a tongue-lashing that Lucullus ended by not only withdrawing his objections, but abjectly begging for mercy. When Cicero made a speech complaining about the state of affairs, Caesar immediately made it possible for Cicero's enemy Clodius to become tribune and drive Cicero into exile.

Rome was effectively under the rule of the triumvirs, and Caesar had cemented his alliance with Pompey in the traditional Roman way – by giving him his daughter Julia in marriage, probably in May 59 BC. Cicero wrote to his friend Atticus:

So the whole of Rome is subdued. I thought it might be. Well, out in the countryside they are certainly not. The very fields hate this tyranny. Come to Formiae and, by God, I tell you you'll hear protests, indignation and hatred of our Great Friend [Pompey], whose nickname is as out of date as that of Crassus the rich!
Cicero to Atticus 2.13

Though Crassus was still immensely wealthy, Pompey's Eastern campaigns had made him wealthier still. But wealth was not everything. Crassus, with his influential connections, was the one triumvir whom neither demagogues nor oligarchs dared attack. Plutarch tells of the tribune Cornelius, who excused his deference to Crassus by remarking 'that one has straw on his horns' (which was used in the market to indicate a dangerous bull).

The members of the senate were certainly prepared to lock horns with Caesar. Using their prerogative to choose the area of command (*provincia*) for the outgoing magistrates, they assigned to Caesar the care of rural Italy and its woodlands. Caesar again turned to the people, and the tribune Vatinius passed a law giving Caesar command in Cisalpine Gaul and Illyricum (modern Balkans). Furthermore, this command was to last four years. Command of two of Rome's most volatile provinces made military glory and rich plunder almost certain, and if no one else wanted a war, Caesar was quite prepared to start one for himself.

With his immediate future assured, Caesar turned to revenge on the senate. He needed to be nothing other than completely fair and impartial in his *lex Iulia de repetundarum*, a law so well crafted and effectively designed to block exploitation of provincials by senatorial governors that it stood for generations. It also split the idealistic Cato from his more self-interested allies in the senate, which undoubtedly afforded Caesar no little amusement.

As consuls for the following year Caesar supported Gabinius, an ally of long standing, and Piso, who was made an ally by Caesar's marriage to Piso's daughter Calpurnia. Caesar also packed the college of tribunes with his partisans. His foresight was rewarded when that college blocked the enquiry into his consulship which Caesar's enemies convened almost the day he laid down his office.

In Caesar's consulship the senate had been excluded from the political process as it had not been since the tribuneship of Gaius Gracchus. If Caesar abused his office, his enemies cynically manipulated revered institutions and customs to the same effect. Now that Caesar was proconsul in Gaul (the senate had been cowed into awarding him command in Transalpine Gaul to go with the powers given to him by the popular vote), it remained to be seen whether the storm he had raised would blow over, or if the reckoning had merely been postponed.

Illyricum was peaceful, partly because the neighbouring province of Macedonia was governed with exceptional competence by Octavius, a relative of Caesar and the father of Caesar's eventual heir Augustus. So Caesar went to Gaul where a threat was looming from the migration into that country by the Helvetii, a people from the area of modern Switzerland. In any case, the proximity of Gaul to Rome allowed Caesar to intervene in senatorial affairs with threats or bribes as appropriate. As Plutarch comments,

Throughout his stay in Gaul, Caesar either used the arms of Roman citizens to subdue the Gallic peoples, or the money of the Gallic peoples to win the submission of Romans.

Plutarch *Caesar* 20

The Helvetii wanted to migrate across the northern neck of Caesar's province. Because they had little to gain from fighting the Romans, they sent envoys to ask for free passage. Caesar told them that he needed time to consider, and frantically began to muster troops and fortify the eastern border along the Rhône (some of these earthworks were discovered in 1860 by engineers of Napoleon III).

When Caesar returned a refusal to the Helvetii, they attempted to cross in any case, but Caesar's defences were now secure enough to withstand them. This setback caused the Helvetii to re-route their migration through the lands of the Sequani (after whom the modern Seine is named). Caesar claimed that the passage of the Helvetii across the lands of a friendly tribe was sufficient cause for military action.

After a series of diplomatic and military manoeuvres, Romans and Helvetii met in battle at Bibracte – Le Mont-Beuvray in modern Burgundy. This was Caesar's first large-scale battle, and he showed his instinctive grasp of morale by having his horse led away before the battle. This meant that no matter what happened, Caesar would share the fate of his men. Caesar positioned legionaries so that the Helvetii had to charge uphill at them. This helped the Romans withstand the initial charge, after which they forced the enemy back to a nearby hill. The Helvetii fortified this with their wagons, but the legionaries broke the barricade and routed the Helvetii in an assault that lasted long into the night. So ferocious and exhausting was the battle that it was three days before Caesar could follow up his victory.

The Helvetii surrendered, having lost almost two thirds of their numbers. Caesar ordered them to return to their native land, which he did not want to see occupied by the Germans. Discovering that the Helvetii were short of corn, Caesar ordered supplies from friendly tribes. This diplomacy encouraged the Gauls to believe that Caesar might help them against a yet more serious threat – an incursion of the Germans under King Ariovistus.

Ariovistus had earlier been designated a friend and ally of the Roman people, partly at Caesar's instigation. Now Caesar reversed that policy and ordered Ariovistus to abandon his conquests in Gaul. Ariovistus replied that the dictator had no business telling him what to do, and if Caesar did not withdraw to his province, Ariovistus would destroy him.

The German king added that killing Caesar would make him very popular in certain quarters in Rome.

A personal meeting between the two men failed to resolve their differences. When Caesar began to prepare for war, some of his own officers objected. Roman Gaul was not threatened, so why was Caesar risking Roman lives in a war with a friend and ally? Caesar replied that Ariovistus in Germany was a friend, but Ariovistus in Gaul was a threat. If no one else would follow him, Caesar would march with only the tenth legion, a unit with which he had already forged a special bond.

The army was won over. There were further attempts at negotiation, partly because Ariovistus wanted to delay until the new moon, which his soothsayers had predicted would aid his cause, but supplies were low, and he was eventually forced to do battle. After a fierce struggle in which the son of Crassus distinguished himself, the Germans were forced back to their wagons, and from there in rout to the river, 15 miles (24 km) away. Caesar turned his cavalry on the fugitives, and they spared neither the wounded nor women and children. Ariovistus escaped, but lost a daughter and both his wives.

With his battles won and the campaigning season over, the Gauls may have hoped that Caesar would accept their grateful thanks and retire to his province. However, it soon became apparent that the Romans now felt that they had a right to a military presence in Gaul, and the winter of 58–57 BC was full of frantic tribal diplomacy as the Gauls tried to work out what to do about it. Caesar had no doubt of what would happen next, and spent the winter raising and training two more legions – the thirteenth and fourteenth, for which he asked from the senate neither permission nor funds.

Caesar's first campaign was against the Belgae. There were some tense moments, for example when the Romans were caught off guard at the river Sambre, and Caesar was hard put to save his army from total destruction. But overall, and not least financially, this campaign was a great success for him. For example, after a single engagement against the Aduatuci, Caesar sold 53,000 people into slavery, as well as possessing himself of their worldly goods.

Much of this money went back to Rome where Caesar was buying himself a following in the senate. As a protégé of Crassus, Caesar knew

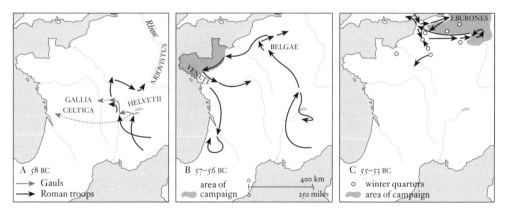

8 *Gallic campaign maps. Caesar's opening campaigns were fought not against Gauls, but against marauding Helvetii and Germans. It was only when the Gauls realized that their 'rescuer' intended to remain as an occupying power that they attempted to eject him by force.*

that sponsoring rising talent gave useful protection against the crises of Roman political life.

Caesar also planned a propaganda coup by invading Britain, which was a strange, distant and semi-mystical place in Roman popular imagination. Britain was believed to be rich in furs, pearls and gold and, more prosaically, in tin and lead. Caesar's intention to control the source of these valuable materials upset the Gallic maritime tribes, especially the Veneti, who were deeply involved in trade with Britain. The subsequent campaign against the Veneti was fought partly at sea, and Caesar's sailors found fighting ocean-going ships a disconcerting experience. For a start, these enemy ships were more strongly built.

> We couldn't damage them by ramming, and they were so high-sided that it was difficult to throw spears or grapnels at them. When the wind picked up strongly, they ran before it, riding the storm easily, and when the tide went out they rested on sandbanks without fear of jutting rocks. Yet all those things were causes of great dread to our ships.
>
> Caesar *De Bello Gallico* 3.13

Fortunately for Caesar, the decisive battle was fought in a dead calm where Roman oarsmen had the advantage. The Veneti were forced to surrender, whereupon Caesar put their leading councillors to the sword, and sold the rest of the population into slavery. Defeating the remaining maritime tribes took the rest of the year and, before Caesar could return to his planned invasion of Britain the following year, trouble developed with another German incursion over the Rhine.

Caesar briskly marched to confront the invaders. A truce was declared for negotiations, but was promptly broken by ill-disciplined German cavalry. A deputation of German leaders went to Caesar to explain what had happened, but Caesar seized the emissaries and launched his army against the leaderless and unsuspecting tribesmen. The Germans were soon defeated, and Caesar was not in a merciful mood.

A crowd of women and children began to flee in all directions, and Caesar sent his cavalry in pursuit.... When the Germans reached the junction of the Meuse and the Rhine, there was no hope of escaping further, and a great many of them had been killed already. The remainder threw themselves into the water, and there, for the most part perished from terror, exhaustion and the force of the current. The Romans did not lose a man....

Caesar *De Bello Gallico* 4. 14–15

The Romans were accustomed to bloodshed, but they were shocked by this massacre. War in the ancient world was a brutal business, and the Romans were notoriously more brutal than most. But they generally tried to make it at least seem that they had right on their side, and the scale and blatancy of Caesar's aggression disturbed many. Cato proposed handing Caesar to the Germans as a war criminal, but instead the senate sent a commission to 'examine the state of things in Gaul'.

Caesar did not stay to welcome the commission: it was late in the campaigning season, and he had Britain to invade. The expedition was launched in haste, and went badly from the start. Caesar's ships could not find a proper anchorage and suffered from the weather. The soldiers had inadequate supplies, and their attempts to help themselves to the British harvest were foiled by the light British war chariots which could move infantry to different points in a skirmish faster than the Romans could react. With the weather deteriorating, Caesar retired to Gaul.

He tried again in 54 BC with five legions and 800 ships, landing near Sandwich on the south coast. In his haste to get to grips with the enemy, Caesar again failed to secure his fleet's anchorage, and his ships were again mauled by inclement weather, which handicapped the whole campaign from the outset. The Britons fought for most of the summer, but in the autumn their leader Cassivellaunus surrendered, perhaps knowing that the gesture was meaningless since the Romans had to return to Gaul in any case (though his surrender later gave the emperor Claudius justification for his invasion of the island in AD 43). In the short term, Caesar's British escapade achieved little apart from giving the Gauls the idea that the Romans could be forced out of a country if conditions were made sufficiently adverse.

In 52 BC a revolt began with the Eburones (near modern Liège), and went on to engulf the entire country. It was put down with considerable brutality, and one of the ringleaders was flogged to death. This mistreatment of a fellow-chieftain aroused the Gallic leaders, and they were further inspired by news that Crassus had been defeated and killed while attempting to invade the Persian empire.

The Gauls captured Cenabum (modern Orléans) and massacred its Roman inhabitants. In their battle for survival the Gauls put aside their tribal rivalry and united under the charismatic leadership of Vercingetorix of the Arverni. This revolt caught Caesar by surprise. He had retired to his province to be nearer to Rome, and the rebellion was between himself and his armies – one under the command of his capable subordinate Titus Labienus, and a smaller force commanded by Quintus Cicero, the brother of the orator and ex-consul.

Caesar put together a scratch force and set out through the last snows of winter to where the Boii, one of the last tribes still allied to Rome, were under attack. Caesar equalled Vercingetorix in energy and skill, and his army, supplemented by

9 *Coin celebrating Caesar's victory in Gaul. A captured Gaul sits at the base of a 'trophy' – a monument to victory erected on the battlefield by mounting the arms of the defeated enemy on a tree stump with a spear as the crossbar.*

German cavalry, was far superior. Caesar recaptured Cenabum, and forced Vercingetorix to fall back. The Gallic leader adopted a scorched earth strategy, attacking Caesar's supply lines and destroying all forage before Caesar's army could reach it.

Vercingetorix's allies agreed to destroy all cities in Caesar's path except Avaricum. Despite Vercingetorix's pleas that this was undermining his entire strategy, they could not bring themselves to turn one of the most beautiful cities in Gaul into a smoking wreck. After a brisk siege, Caesar turned it into a smoking wreck for them and replenished his supplies in the process.

Caesar now turned on Gergovia (in modern Roche Blanche), capital of the Arverni, and there received one of the few defeats of his career. He was unable to take the city, and was forced into a humiliating withdrawal. Even the news that Labienus had taken Lutetia (Paris) was not enough to prevent the few tribes that had stayed neutral from joining the rebellion. Vercingetorix tried to get the Gauls in Caesar's province to join the rebellion, but Caesar had given command there to a kinsman, Lucius Caesar, and since the province was still chastened from an earlier failed revolt, it did not rise again.

The Romans now advanced to secure the valley of the river Saône, and Vercingetorix moved to intercept them. A furious battle resulted, in which Caesar's German mercenary cavalry turned the tide. Vercingetorix withdrew to the fortress town of Alesia (Alise-Ste-Reine), there to await reinforcements.

Caesar followed and built a circuit of walls completely encompassing the town. These fortifications also faced outward (plate 5), as Caesar expected soon to be besieged himself when the Gallic hordes came to Vercingetorix's rescue.

This extraordinary double siege of 52 BC was one of the turning points of European history. Had the Gauls broken Caesar's circumvallation, Caesar would have lost his army and probably his life. Even if he had survived, he would have been so weakened politically that his enemies in the senate could have destroyed him. And a united Gaul would have cast off the Roman yoke as the Germans under Arminius did a generation later.

Caesar admits the fight was a close one. His commentaries give an impression of the desperation of the struggle.

The Gauls attacked at midnight…with a great shout to inform the besieged of their approach they began to throw bundles of wood to fill the trenches and drove the Romans from the ramparts with arrows, slingshots, hand-thrown stones and every other means of assault.

Meanwhile, hearing the tumult, Vercingetorix sounded the trumpets and led his men out of town. The Romans moved into their battle stations, and kept the Gauls at bay with slingshots, stakes and stones which had been piled up on the ramparts, while the artillery rained missiles down on them. It was too dark to see, and both sides took heavy casualties…. While the Gauls were some distance from the entrenchments, the javelins they rained down gave them some advantage, but as they closed in they were impaled on the stakes, tumbled into spear-filled pits or killed by the artillery.

Caesar *De Bello Gallico* 7.81–82

Eventually, discouraged by their failure to break the Roman lines, and running out of supplies, the relieving force dispersed, leaving the defenders of Alesia to Caesar's mercy. Vercingetorix was sent to Rome for eventual display in a triumph, and most of the remaining warriors were sold into slavery. The non-combatants had already perished, for when food ran low the Gauls had driven them from the town. Caesar refused to allow them out, and they perished through hunger and exposure in the space between the two armies. They were among the estimated two million Gauls killed or enslaved during the conquest of their country (plate 6).

The Gallic War showed the darker side of Caesar's character. Though his military genius was proven beyond doubt, the conquest of Gaul caused huge human suffering for which he seems to have felt not the slightest remorse. The purpose of the war was dubious to say the least – it was for the enrichment and political advantage of Julius Caesar, with the security of Rome very much a secondary consideration. Caesar's amoral outlook was far from unique among Roman generals, but the resources and ability which he applied to the business of conquest and massacre made him uniquely deadly. It would be wrong to judge him by the standards of the modern era, but it is telling that even Caesar's contemporaries found this war disturbing.

The Civil War

Gaul was pacified, and Caesar was determined that it would remain so. Consequently he imposed only the mildest of peace settlements, leaving power largely in the hands of tribal chiefs and levying few new taxes.

Caesar moved to Cisalpine Gaul to be nearer Rome. His agent in the city, Cornelius Balbus, had informed Caesar that matters were getting out of control. Caesar's daughter Julia had died, weakening Caesar's link with Pompey, who was now the dominant figure in Rome. (Pompey was theoretically governor of Spain, but remained in Rome and governed indirectly through men called 'legates', an innovation later adopted by the Julio-Claudian emperors.) The death of Crassus, along with the destruction of most of his army by the Parthians at the battle of Carrhae in 53 BC, had combined with the tumultous tribuneship of Clodius (pp. 32–35) to cause such unease in Rome that the senate took the unusual step of making Pompey sole consul in 52 BC. This was the start of Pompey's rapprochement with the senate, something which boded ill for Caesar.

Caesar's long absence from Rome had left him dangerously short of allies. Even those senators he had sponsored to office were untrustworthy. His command would expire in 49 BC, and Caesar knew that he would not last long as a private citizen in Rome. Cato was already planning his prosecution. Caesar's influence was strongest in the college of tribunes, and this body passed a law allowing him to stand *in absentia* for the consulship of 48 BC. Pompey did not interfere, which indicates that he was trying to remain neutral in the struggle between his old ally and his new friends.

The consuls of 49 BC were a Claudius of the Marcellan branch of the family, and the patrician Aemilius Paullus. Caesar used his massive financial resources to purchase the loyalty of Paullus and the influential tribune Curio, but he could do little against the implacable hostility of the Claudian. Marcellus Claudius proposed that since Caesar had accomplished his mission in Gaul, he should lay down his command immediately and return to Rome. Curio vetoed this, whereupon the senate ordered Caesar and Pompey each to contribute a legion for a proposed war against the Parthians.

Pompey had lent Caesar a legion for the war in Gaul, and he now asked for this back, so Caesar ended up contributing both legions. To no one's surprise, these soldiers were not sent to the East, but held in reserve in Italy. Caesar offered to lay down his command if Pompey would do the same, but the senate refused to consider the proposal.

Instead Metellus Scipio, Pompey's new father-in-law, proposed that Caesar should disband his army, or be considered a public enemy. The tribunes Mark Antony and Cassius interposed their veto, but Caesar's enemies were determined to crush him and were no longer deterred by mere legalities. They passed the *senatus consultum ultimum* – the same resolution which had sanctioned the lynching of the tribune Saturninus in the year of Caesar's birth. With the state effectively under martial law, the tribunes opposing the senate had to flee for their lives.

The battle lines were drawn. The senate had effectively declared war against him, and Caesar had his own *casus belli*. He declared that he was acting to protect the rights of the tribunes – a potent claim, for the tribunes were the traditional protectors of the Roman people against the power of the aristocracy.

It is unlikely that Caesar intended matters to go this far. For all that he had ridden roughshod over his fellow consul in 59 BC, Caesar had never believed that the oligarchs would ignore the constitution which was the very basis of their own power. However, the senate was genuinely terrified of Caesar – a man with eight battle-hardened legions at his back who had shown little respect for constitutional niceties. In previous decades, Sulla, Marcus Aemilius Lepidus (father of the triumvir) and Catiline had all marched on Rome and seized power. Now in their desperation to stop Caesar, the senate effectively gave him no choice but to do the same.

War was almost, but not quite, inevitable. Caesar was a proconsul who had a major disagreement with the senate, but he had not been proven guilty of any wrongdoing. If he left his province with his army, however, he would become a rebel in arms.

Caesar himself remarked as much, that winter morning when his advance guard reached the river Rubicon at the southern limit of his province. 'We can still draw back. But once we cross that little bridge there, we will have to fight it to the finish.' Caesar was a man who had built his career by taking risk after risk. Each had paid off, and he was not the man now to pass up the greatest gamble of his career. '*Alea iacta est.*' 'The die is cast,' he exclaimed, and took his legions across the river to war with Rome.

That war began rather well for Caesar. In part the senate had struck early to cement the fickle allegiance of Pompey while they had it. Pompey had once boasted, 'If I stamp my foot, Italy will rise.' In the event Italy remained conspicuously dormant, while northern Italy welcomed Caesar, possibly prompted by the veterans who were grateful for Caesar's land legislation which had settled them there.

The senate declared that all who were not with them were against them. Caesar responded by claiming that everyone not against him was for him, thus gaining by default the allegiance of the neutrals in what was now a naked power struggle. Caesar's advance became a triumphal progress which easily brushed aside the slight resistance of Domitius Ahenobarbus at Corfinium. Pompey had raised some legions, but knew his raw levy was no match for Caesar. He retreated to Greece, leaving the port of Brundisium (Brindisi) even as Caesar's legions closed in.

Caesar took Rome, urging those senators who remained to share with him the task of government. ('With you, if I may, senators, without you if I must!') There was no purge in the tradition of Marius and Sulla, but there was also no doubt that Rome was under military occupation. Caesar took control of the treasury, grimly informing the young Caecilius Metellus who refused to surrender the keys to Caesar's furious soldiers, 'Believe me, at this moment it is considerably harder for me to keep you alive than it is to kill you.'

Domitius, freed by Caesar after the fall of Corfinium, proceeded to Massalia (modern Marseilles) to block Caesar's move against Pompey's *imperium* in Spain. Domitius was again pushed aside – more brutally this time – and Caesar took the war to Pompey's legates Petreius and Sextus Afranius Burrus, whose resistance was equally ineffective, not least because their legionaries were prepared to fight for Rome, but saw little point in killing fellow soldiers over a political disagreement among senators.

Caesar was made dictator by Lepidus, a senatorial ally, but this first dictatorship was only so as to organize elections for the consulship, which – to no one's surprise – Caesar won. Nevertheless, Caesar could claim that all was being done according to the law, though this would have impressed few of those with Pompey in Greece. Leaving Mark Antony in charge of Italy, Caesar set off for his showdown with Pompey.

Caesar's speed and decisiveness in seeking a final confrontation were typical, but there were disadvantages to landing in hostile territory seven months before the harvest, especially since Caesar's opponent was a master of logistics.

Because Pompey controlled the sea Caesar could get no supplies. His army was on the edge of starvation and had to make bread from roots. Deserters brought examples of this bread to Pompey thinking that he would be pleased by such a sight, but on the contrary, Pompey exclaimed, 'We are fighting wild animals here!'

Appian *Civil Wars* 2.61

Caesar tried to force Pompey to a decisive battle, but Pompey was in no hurry. He had the option of returning to Italy and retaking Rome, or starving Caesar's men into mutiny. But his hand was forced by the arrival of Metellus Scipio, bringing fresh troops for the Republican cause. These reinforcements decided Pompey's senatorial allies that Caesar could now be broken for once and for all, and they pushed for the decisive battle that Caesar also desired.

Pompey was new to generalship by committee. Nor was he particularly good at set battles (his last had been against the rebel Sertorius in Spain, and it had gone badly). Pompey had the greatest skill of a general – he could defeat his enemies without needing to gamble on a pitched battle – but on this occasion he was not allowed to use that skill. On 9 August 48 BC (properly 6 June – the Roman calendar was in a state of confusion at this time) the two sides met at Pharsalus in southern Thessaly to decide the destiny of the Roman Empire.

Caesar describes the battle with the satisfaction of a technician regarding a job well done. Pompey had ordered his men to stand to receive Caesar's first charge, rather than counter-charging as was the custom. Caesar comments that this was bad for morale, and anyway his men were equal to the occasion.

Our men ran forward, throwing spears at the ready, but observed that the Pompeians were staying where they were. Being battle-hardened veterans, they [our men] spontaneously slowed so that they would not be winded when they had run the extra distance to the enemy lines. After a brief pause they renewed their charge....

Caesar *Civil War* 3.93

The battle was a close one, for Caesar's men were considerably outnumbered. But Pompey was shaken by early setbacks, and probably knew that Caesar outmatched him as a battlefield commander as comprehensively as Caesar's veterans outmatched Pompey's recruits.

Seeing his cavalry repulsed and the forces in which he had most confidence thrown into panic, he [Pompey] lost confidence in the rest, left the battlefield and rode off to his camp...there he took himself to the general's tent, waiting for the issue to be decided, but in no optimistic frame of mind.

Caesar *Civil War* 3.93

In contrast Caesar was everywhere, urging his men forward until the Pompeian line was broken, driving them on when they might have paused to loot the wealth of the enemy camp, pushing them to complete the victory as night fell. All the while, he urged his soldiers to remember that their opponents were Romans, and to spare whomsoever they could.

After their total defeat, the senators were pleasantly surprised to find Caesar magnanimous to those who surrendered. But the hard core of Caesar's enemies refused to abandon the struggle. Metellus Scipio went to Africa with Cato, Pompey's sons went to Spain to try to raise a revolt, and Pompey himself went to Egypt, the last power of the Mediterranean world not in thrall to Rome.

The Egyptian leaders promptly and correctly divined that where Pompey went, Caesar would follow, and they wanted nothing to do with the struggle. Pompey was assassinated before he had even set foot in Egypt, and his head was handed to Caesar who arrived soon afterwards on 2 October 48 BC. The Roman presence caused trepidation and unrest in Alexandria, which was exacerbated by the arrival of Cleopatra, daughter of the late king, who had been excluded from power by her brother

Ptolemy XIII. Cleopatra and Caesar rapidly formed a sexual and political partnership which involved Caesar in a short but unpleasant war with Ptolemy and his supporters.

Caesar was unprepared for this unexpected campaign, but his veteran troops were more than a match for the Egyptians, though the Great Library of Alexandria, a wonder of the ancient world, was destroyed in the struggle. After his victory, Caesar installed Cleopatra as monarch – a move which caused some unease in Rome, for Cleopatra gave birth to a son of Caesar. This child traced his paternal family through the Julian line, and his maternal lineage through generations of Ptolemies to a Macedonian general of Alexander the Great, and so had a lineage greater and more royal than any in Rome.

Pharnaces, the king of Pontus, had exploited Rome's troubles to conquer a good part of Asia Minor, Caesar's next destination. Pharnaces lasted exactly five days after the arrival of Caesar, who summarized the campaign with the famous words '*veni, vidi, vici,*' 'I came, I saw, I conquered.' He also remarked that Pompey had been fortunate to make his reputation against such feeble opposition.

For the past eleven years Caesar had been at war. He was now fifty-two years old, and master of the known world. With his immense power came immense responsibility – the civil war had created administrative chaos which would need all of his famous energy to sort out. It was time to return to Rome.

Absolute Power

Caesar frequently remarked that to govern one required only soldiers and money. On the financial front, civil war had destroyed Caesar's fortune, so he had to rebuild it at a time when levels of debt were causing public unrest. Caesar could not declare a remission of debt without alienating large sections of the upper classes, who were mainly creditors. Instead he confiscated and auctioned off the property of his enemies. Some of Caesar's supporters, like Mark Antony, put in huge bids assuming that they would never have to pay. But Caesar was displeased with Antony's inept stewardship of Italy during the civil war, and forced his dissolute subordinate to settle in full.

Only Servilia, Caesar's paramour, received a large discount on her purchases. Cicero, no less acerbic for having been on the losing side at Pharsalus, remarked that Servilia's discount was greater than it seemed, for a third (tertia) had been knocked off. This referred to a rumour that Caesar had also seduced Servilia's daughter Tertia.

On the military front, the tenth legion, Caesar's most loyal soldiers, were mutinously demanding to be discharged and paid their promised bounty. Caesar addressed them, calling them *quirites* ('citizens') rather than 'companions' as before. He offered to discharge them immediately and pay their bounty once he and the loyal part of the army returned from Africa, where Cato and Metellus Scipio still held out. Shamed and horrified, the soldiers begged to be taken back into service, which Caesar graciously permitted.

Metellus Scipio was no mean opponent, and Caesar had many raw recruits in his new army. Unable to campaign with his usual flair, Caesar settled for slow and deliberate progress until he brought Metellus to battle at Thapsus in April of 46 BC. On this occasion Caesar's men, rather than Caesar himself, took the initiative and threw themselves at the enemy, forcing their commander to engage in battle sooner than he had wished.

It is possible that Caesar wanted time to recover from what Plutarch refers to as his 'usual sickness', by which he meant epilepsy. Caesar had always suffered from this, but as he grew older (he was now fifty-four years old) his demanding lifestyle took an increasing toll of his health.

With Metellus defeated, Caesar advanced on Cato, who commanded the garrison at Utica, a coastal city near Carthage. Loathing Caesar as he did, Cato would never surrender, yet his cause was utterly lost. True to his stoic principles, Cato ate a last meal with his friends and then killed himself, causing Caesar to exclaim, 'I resent your death – just as you resented my having the opportunity to spare you!'

Among the defenders of Utica who were not spared was a kinsman, Lucius Caesar. This young man had taken extreme measures to prove his loyalty to the Pompeians, killing Caesar's slaves and freedmen in Rome at the start of the civil war, and even butchering the animals which Caesar had put aside for public entertainments during his proposed consulship. Now Lucius was killed, perhaps without Julius Caesar's direct orders or even foreknowledge. This execution of a kinsman began the trend by which political necessity caused the house of Caesar to devour itself slowly from within.

Caesar went on to campaign against the sons of Pompey in Spain. With him came a sickly young relative called Octavius (known today as Octavian) whom Caesar had marked for special favour. As might be expected of their ancestry, the Pompey boys resisted bravely, but were soon overwhelmed. The elder son of Pompey was killed and the younger, though forced to flee, gallantly campaigned for his father's doomed cause for many more years.

Caesar returned to Rome 'honoured and feared as no man had ever been before', says Appian. He celebrated a triumph for his victories, and this caused some disquiet. It seemed that in part Caesar was celebrating the conquest of his fellow citizens.

This was not a victory over enemy generals or barbarian kings. What was being celebrated was the complete destruction of the line of the mightiest in Rome. They had met with disaster, yet Caesar was making a triumph of the calamity which had befallen his homeland; taking pride in actions which were inexcusable before gods and men except in that they were expedient.

Plutarch *Caesar 56*

Caesar was now undisputed master of Rome, and no one knew what he would do next, quite possibly not even Caesar himself. His extraordinary power had somehow to be fitted into the constitutional framework. Caesar was made dictator for the next ten years, presumably an attempt by the senate to deter him from seeking a monarchy. It also gave Caesar constitutional powers which he would probably have taken anyway, such as the right to nominate candidates for elections. When one consul died a few hours before his term of office ended, Caesar gave the remainder of the consulship to a crony. 'A strange consulship indeed, in which no one ate or slept,' remarked Cicero acidly.

A new forum was built near the Forum Romanum, and there a temple was erected, both to honour a promise Caesar had made before the battle of Pharsalus, and to remind the Romans of his family's divine origins. (The temple was dedicated to Venus Genetrix – that is, Venus the mother – whom the Julians claimed as the founder of their clan. Its remains still stand in Caesar's forum today.)

Caesar needed to be seen as almost more than human, for his position in Rome was so far outside the established order that his exceptional position and privileges could only be excused if he himself were viewed as totally exceptional. The senate was aware of this, and Cassius Dio says 'extravagant honours were proposed, some as exaggerated flattery, some as ridicule.... Others, and these were in the largest group, voted the honours to make him as hated and envied as possible.'

It was decreed that he should run affairs from a throne of ivory and gold, that when he presided over sacrifices he should always do so dressed in triumphal clothing. Every year Rome would celebrate the days that he had won his victories, every five years the priests and Vestal Virgins would offer prayers for his safety. As soon as the magistrates had been sworn into office, they should take a further oath never to oppose any of Caesar's decrees...temples were dedicated to him as if he were a god, and one was dedicated to him together with the goddess Clementia.

Appian *Civil Wars* 2.106

One senator, in a snide reference to Caesar's renowned libido, proposed a decree that Caesar should be allowed access to any woman he desired 'for the purpose of fathering children'. There were repeated attempts to have done with pretence and to call Caesar the monarch he was in all but name. This would have been a public relations disaster and (in public at least) Caesar strongly opposed the idea.

He accused the faction of Marullus [a hostile tribune] of cleverly trying to smear him with the allegation of monarchy. He added that they deserved death, but he would be content with their being deprived of office and removed from the senate. In this way Caesar confirmed the idea that he secretly wanted to be called king, and that he knew in advance of attempts to promote the idea. He also showed the completeness of his tyranny, for by ancient tradition the tribunes were sacred and inviolable, yet Caesar had acted even before the tribune had laid down his office.

Appian *Civil Wars* 2.108

There is a certain irony in that just as Pompey was a great general without the ability to win pitched battles, Caesar attained supreme power but was ultimately a failure at politics. His coup had been forced on him because he was unable to carry the senate and faced political and possibly personal extinction. Nor was it coincidence that matters reached that point just as Caesar lost the political friendship of Crassus and support of Pompey. Now, though Caesar remained popular with the people, the senate portrayed him as a power-seeking tyrant.

Caesar reformed the calendar, bringing it back in line with the solar year, and passed effective legislation to deal with the debt problem. Yet senators remembered only that when they went to confer yet more honours on Caesar, he did not rise to greet them, but remained seated, as a monarch would. (Realizing his faux pas, Caesar explained that he had suffered a violent stomach upset, and getting to his feet might have precipitated a yet more embarrassing incident.)

Senators were also displeased that Caesar enlarged the senate from 600 to 900, packing it with his supporters. Wits made jokes about baggy-trousered Gauls wandering about Rome asking to be directed to their places in the senate house. And if he could make Gauls into senators, Caesar could certainly raise to the patriciate the family of his favourite relative, Octavian, and this he did.

There was more embarrassment for Caesar when Cleopatra appeared – with Caesar's infant son in tow. Ostensibly Cleopatra wanted to negotiate a treaty between Rome and Egypt, but in fact she sought to renew their relationship on a more personal level. Fortunately an ancient statute forbade monarchs from setting foot in Rome, so Caesar was able to accommodate this problem in a villa beyond the Tiber.

Caesar allegedly had commented that Sulla had been a political illiterate for laying down his dictatorship. He did the opposite and declared himself dictator for life in February 44 BC. Coins bearing his image (the first showing a living Roman) were immediately stamped bearing the legend *dictator perpetuus*.

This move made Caesar a marked man, yet he seemed not to care. He disbanded his Spanish bodyguard to make himself more accessible. When warned that his henchmen might seize power from him, he replied that he did not worry about sleek characters like Mark Antony, but 'lean

10 *Caesar wearing a laurel wreath (a head covering he was fond of since it obscured the hair loss which he felt so acutely). The legend* Caesar Dic. Perpetuus *was a self-designated title meaning 'dictator for life', though 'dictator' did not carry the strongly negative implications it does today.*

and hungry' men such as Cassius and Brutus. Surely not Brutus though, whom Caesar had spared after Pharsalus, and whom rumour said he had himself fathered with Servilia? (Either rumour was mistaken, or Caesar was precocious indeed, for Brutus was born when Caesar was fifteen.)

Yet his ancestry also concerned Brutus. A Brutus whom his clan claimed as an ancestor had expelled King Tarquin and freed Rome. Now statues of this Brutus were daubed with slogans asking 'Brutus, are you sleeping?', 'Your descendants disgrace you' and 'Where are you now that we need you?' Brutus signalled his availability to any would-be conspirators by divorcing his Claudian wife and marrying Porcia, the daughter of Cato and widow of Caesar's old adversary Bibulus.

Cassius was one of the few men to have fought with distinction in Crassus' Parthian debacle, yet Caesar had no place for him in the new campaign against Parthia. Another conspirator was Trebonius who served in Gaul with Caesar, but was alienated by his old commander's dictatorial ways. By March, dozens of senators had been recruited into the plot.

Did Caesar know? He sent his heir, Octavian, to Greece – allegedly to continue his education, but also moving him out of harm's way. At a dinner, there was discussion of the best way to die, and Caesar chose to go 'suddenly, as if struck by lightning'.

Caesar had great personal bravery. The victor of dozens of battles would not cower before a pack of senators. One suspects he knew much was amiss, but he would soon be out of Rome on campaign and until then, well, fortune had not betrayed him yet.

On the Ides of March (15 March) 44 BC, the senate met. Antony, who accompanied Caesar to the meeting, was detained outside in conversation by Trebonius. This was a necessary precaution, for Antony was a powerful man and skilled fighter. Caesar took his place, with a group of conspirators standing behind him. One seized Caesar's toga and pulled it down to expose his neck, and another struck with his dagger.

Caesar turned, grabbed the knife and held it tightly. 'Damn you, Casca, what are you doing?' he demanded, while at the same moment Casca cried to his brother 'Help me!' So it began, and those not in the secret watched in confusion and horror not daring to help, to run away or even to say a word. Those who had prepared themselves for the murder drew their daggers and surrounded Caesar on all sides. Wherever he turned there were daggers striking at his face and eyes, he was driven backwards and forwards like a wild animal. Everyone was tangled together for each conspirator had sworn to take part in this sacrificial slaughter. Caesar defended himself, darting left and right and calling for help. But when he saw that even Brutus had his dagger drawn, he pulled his toga over his head and collapsed. Either by chance, or because the conspirators pushed him there, he fell against the pedestal of a statue of Pompey; drenching it with his blood so it seemed as though Pompey himself was presiding over his revenge.... It is said that Caesar received twenty-three wounds in all, and many of the conspirators injured each other as they all struggled to stab just the one man.

Plutarch *Caesar* 66

The tradition that Caesar said '*Et tu Brute?*' ('You as well, Brutus?') is apparently invention. Suetonius reports that 'some writers' say Caesar said, 'You also, my child?' as Brutus stabbed him, but other than Dio, who generally follows the same line as Suetonius, there is no record of this.

Caesar had already claimed his place as one of the most remarkable men in history. Had he not been so good a general, there is every chance that Pompey might have defeated him, as he so nearly did in any case. And if Caesar had failed as had Catiline, could the Republic have weathered its crisis and survived? Without Caesar there would have been no Augustus, and the imperial principate (had there been one) would have taken a very different shape.

11 *Caesar's assassination on the Ides of March is celebrated on this coin by a freedman's cap and two daggers. Brutus is depicted on the obverse, an unprecedented honour to living Romans until Caesar came to power. The word* Imp[erator] *here means 'successful general' rather than 'emperor'.*

Once he was dictator, Caesar remarked that no sane man would assassinate him, knowing the chaos that would follow. He was right about the chaos, but once again he had underestimated the short-sighted vindictiveness of the oligarchs, and the depth of their hatred for him.

The Family of Julius Caesar

Julius Caesar left two sons, one natural, one adopted. The son whom he had fathered was Caesarion, his child by Cleopatra. His adopted child was Octavian, later known as Augustus, whom he made his heir. Caesar also had a daughter from his first marriage whom he married to Pompey.

By all accounts, this Julia possessed her father's charm and intelligence. She and Pompey were devoted to one another, for all that Pompey was twenty-three years her senior. Julia died an indirect victim of the political unrest in Rome. In late 55 BC Pompey was in the thick of a riot in the forum, and his toga became liberally splattered with blood. He gave it to a slave to take home, and Julia, seeing the blood-stained toga, leapt to the conclusion that her husband was dead. She was pregnant at the time and the shock was such that she went into premature labour and miscarried. Her constitution was badly weakened and she died in 54 BC after another pregnancy in which the premature child – Caesar's grandchild – followed her to the grave within days.

Julius Caesar had two sisters. The elder married twice, each time into a patrician family, and had at least one son from each marriage. These nephews made little impact on history; but the same cannot be said of Caesar's niece by his younger sister. This niece was called Atia, and she married an Octavius. She later claimed that her child, Caesar's grand-nephew Octavian, was not fathered by Octavius, but by the god Apollo. Apollo was later to be the favoured deity of Atia's son who became Augustus, Caesar's heir.

Since it was the Roman habit to call daughters by the feminine form of their patronymic, there were other Julias in Rome from other branches of the Julian house. The most important of these was the daughter of Lucius Caesar, the consul of 90 BC. This Julia married into the Antonine clan, and one of her children was Mark Antony, Julius Caesar's second-in-command.

Mark Antony's uncle, Julia's brother, was called Lucius after his father. Though he had served with Julius Caesar in Gaul, and accompanied him on his march into Italy, this Lucius Caesar took little part in the fighting. When Julius Caesar followed Pompey to Greece, Mark Antony was left in charge of Italy, and he made uncle Lucius governor of Rome for a brief period.

Yet another of the Julian clan was Sextus Caesar, a distant relative (the grandson of Julius Caesar's uncle). He served with Julius Caesar during the Spanish campaign of the civil war, and was later killed in Syria by soldiers who revolted against Julius Caesar to support the Republican cause. He is worth mentioning as he is yet another of the Julian clan who perished in the civil war which brought his famous relative to power.

12 *Caesarion, the ill-fated son of Julius Caesar and Cleopatra. Though not born of a legitimate marriage, his descent from Caesar and the Ptolemies of Egypt made Caesarion enough of a rival for Octavian to have him put to death at the earliest opportunity.*

CHAPTER 4

FROM OCTAVIAN TO AUGUSTUS: CAESAR'S DEADLY LEGACY

I wish that I did not have to take matters into my own hands as much as I did.
I mean, I would have preferred that the city did not need me to do as I did....
But fate arranged matters so that you needed me, despite my youth, and put me
to the test. I was totally successful, more through good luck than ability.
(Augustus addresses the senate) Cassius Dio *History* 53.5

Mark Antony was later to remark in disgust: 'You, boy, owe everything to a name.' Certainly, without being adopted as the son of Caesar, Octavian could never have become undisputed ruler of Rome. His father's family...

...by chance or choice remained simple equestrians until the entry into the senate of the Gaius Octavius who became famous as the father of Augustus [Octavian]. His [Octavian's] grandfather possessed a reasonable fortune, and lived happily to a great age in the town where he had been a magistrate [Velitrae]. These details do not come from the memoirs of Augustus himself – he merely records that he was from an old and wealthy equestrian family and that his father was the first of the line to enter the senate. Mark Antony put the libel on record that Augustus' great-grandfather was a mere freed slave, a ropemaker from somewhere around Thurii, and the grandfather had been a money-changer. And that is all the information I have managed to scrape together about Augustus' antecedents.
Suetonius *Augustus* 2

Atia, Octavian's mother, was from nearby Aricia. Some alleged that Atia was descended from a baker in that town, which Suetonius indignantly denies, claiming that Atia's paternal family boasted 'many senators' in its line. Atia's mother was Julius Caesar's sister, which made Octavian one of Caesar's closest male relatives.

Octavian, the man who was to become Rome's first emperor, was born just before dawn on 23 September in the Palatine district, the richest and most respectable part of Rome. The year was 63 BC, when Cicero was consul, and Caesar's political career was endangered by Catiline's conspiracy. However, it seems that Octavian was brought up in his family's home town of Velitrae, and Suetonius says that the local people insisted he had been born there as well. As a boy Octavian was nicknamed 'the Thuriian' – not a reference to his ropemaking ancestor, but probably after a slave revolt near Thurii which his father crushed soon after Octavian was born. (It was the habit of Romans to take as an extra name the place where they had won a great victory, and often to pass this name to their sons. A minor campaign against undistinguished opposition might have caused the son to be nicknamed as a good-humoured jest.)

Octavian's father was praetor in Rome in 61 BC, and he probably died in 59 BC. Thereafter, Octavian was probably taken into the tutelage of his grandmother and when she died he returned to his mother and Marcus Philippus, her new husband. Despite his hectic political and military affairs, great-uncle Julius Caesar took a keen interest in Octavian's education, seeing great promise in the youth's good looks and intelligence, notwithstanding his sickly constitution.

At the age of sixteen Octavian received the *toga virilis* in the rite of passage which made a Roman boy into a man. At the same time he was raised to the college of pontiffs to fill a vacancy created when Lucius Domitius died in Caesar's victory at Pharsalus. Octavian was eager to accompany Caesar on his expeditions against the remnants of the republican opposition, but his mother kept him back from the African campaign of 47 BC, fearing the effect of the harsh environment on Octavian's fragile health. Caesar took Octavian's willingness as the deed, and awarded him military honours for the campaign. He also allowed Octavian to accompany him on horseback at his triumph, an honour usually reserved for the *triumphator's* male children.

Octavian was ill again when Caesar went on his Spanish campaign, but he joined his great-uncle as soon as he was well enough to travel, though he had to survive being shipwrecked on the journey. When the campaign ended, Caesar returned to Rome in 45 BC as dictator, and Octavian asked to become his Master of Horse (the dictator's second-in-command). Caesar had raised the Octavian family to patrician rank, and betrothed Octavian to the daughter of the noble Servilius Isauricus, but he was not prepared to bring his protégé so swiftly to the front line of Roman politics. Instead he sent him to Apollonia in Illyricum, allegedly to continue his education. Caesar knew that Octavian would become his son and heir if he died, and Apollonia was both far from Rome and conveniently near several trustworthy legions.

The wisdom of these arrangements became clear after Caesar's assassination in March 44 BC. When the news reached him, Octavian must have known how high his adoption had raised the stakes. As an Octavius, he might withdraw into obscurity – as Julius Caesar, son of Julius Caesar, he had to succeed or die. But at least in Appollonia he was outside the hothouse of Roman politics. He could consult with his friends Maecenas and Agrippa, sound the sentiments of the soldiery and look for allies in Rome.

Rome itself was gripped by rumour and uncertainty. Caesar himself had predicted that his murder would bring chaos, while the assassins hoped that liberty and the rule of the senate would be restored. Many senators such as Cicero hailed the murder 'a joyous banquet' and hastened to give the assassins their allegiance, but the common people took their 'liberation' with an ominous lack of enthusiasm.

Power, both legal and actual, remained with Caesar's henchmen. Caesar's unofficial second-in-command, Mark Antony, was now sole consul, as Caesar had been his co-consul when he died. The Master of Horse whom Caesar had chosen instead of Octavian was Marcus

13 *Mark Antony. This coin shows the future triumvir's genial good nature and a certain plumpness caused by his love of luxurious living. But Antony could also be a bloody and vindictive killer when war or politics demanded it.*

Aemilius Lepidus, who commanded a substantial military force. Tensions ran high between Caesar's supporters and his murderers until Cicero brokered a compromise by which the murderers were pardoned, but Caesar would be properly buried and the terms of his will respected.

Caesar's will left his estates beyond the Tiber to the Roman people, and bequeathed each Roman 300 sesterces. This generous bequest created more animosity towards Caesar's murderers, and Antony inflamed popular sentiment still further at the funeral where he displayed Caesar's perforated toga and delivered the speech which Shakespeare begins with 'Friends, Romans, countrymen'. The crowd changed from mourners to a rioting mob, and Brutus and Cassius were forced to flee from Rome.

For all his shrewd use of Caesar's legacy, Antony was not Caesar's heir. But he was consul in Rome while that heir was currently in the Balkans. Antony intended to be firmly in power by the time Octavian arrived to claim his inheritance.

Antony brought the impetuous young Cornelius Dolabella to his side by making him co-consul, and secured the allegiance of Lepidus by making him Pontifex Maximus in Caesar's place. Other senators were reassured when Antony abolished the office of dictator, and allowed those conspirators who had held public office to depart to their provincial commands unhindered. Antony took control of Caesar's papers, and put his supporters in key positions by claiming Caesar's papers showed this had always been his intention. (These appointees were known ironically as 'Charonites' after the boatman who had already ferried their master over the river Styx.)

Thus, by the time Octavian arrived in Rome at the end of April 44 BC, Antony had helped himself to much of Caesar's inheritance, both literally and figuratively. With unexpected diplomatic skill he had pacified the senate, kept peace between Republicans and Caesarians, and appeased Caesar's veteran soldiers. He also had Caesar's wealth and was in no hurry to relinquish it, either to the heir who was entitled to it, or to the common people who had been promised it.

Octavian made his position clear from the start. He did not style himself as 'Octavianus' (the Latin convention which showed the family he had been adopted from, and which is the origin of the name by which he is called today), but simply called himself 'Julius Caesar' after his adoptive father, the source of his political strength.

His relatives urged him to renounce his adoption and inheritance from Caesar, but he thought it would be dishonourable if he did so and left Caesar unavenged. Accordingly he crossed to Brundisium, though not without first checking if the murderers [of Caesar] intended also an ambush for him there. People flocked to him in great crowds, some because he was Caesar's son, others from their friendship with Caesar, others being Caesar's freedmen and slaves. Many soldiers came with them as well.

Appian *Civil Wars* 3.11

Octavian's stepfather and mother, Marcus Philippus and Atia, were among those relatives unhappy with Caesar's inheritance. They became even more worried when Antony not only completely ignored Octavian's arrival in Rome, but also allowed the passing of a senatorial decree guaranteeing immunity for Caesar's murderers. However, parental opposition vanished when they saw that the young man was determined to take up Caesar's inheritance and avenge his murder.

Octavian first presented himself to the city praetor (also an Antonius) and formally accepted his adoption. He then went to Mark Antony, who pointedly kept him waiting some time for his audience – an audience in which he made it plain that Octavian would wait even longer for his inheritance. When Octavian insisted, the senate announced an inquiry into the public finances. This carried Antony's implied threat that much of Caesar's money might be confiscated as illegal gains unless Octavian at least partly withdrew his claims.

In response Octavian sold land once owned by Caesar, and used this money, and his own funds, to pay Caesar's promised legacy to the people. This was costly (Octavian had to borrow money from Marcus Philippus) but hugely popular, for the gift was seen to come not just from Caesar, but also from his adopted son.

In the summer of 44 BC Octavian staged Caesar's funeral games. While these games were taking place (not coincidentally, Octavian had chosen for the games the month to be named July in Caesar's honour), a comet bright enough to be seen in daylight appeared in the sky. The

Romans generally regarded comets as a baleful omen, but Octavian deftly turned this one to his advantage by claiming it was not a comet, but a new star which represented Julius Caesar taking his place among the gods. Later this idea was developed further, and in 42 BC Julius Caesar was officially deified, making Octavian *divi filius* – the son of a god.

Octavian's increasing popularity attracted the attention of Cicero. From the beginning Octavian had courted Cicero's friendship, but until his opposition to Antony hardened into intense mutual dislike, Cicero was lukewarm about working with Caesar's heir. Now he wrote:

Young Caesar has incredible natural qualities. I just hope that once he gets rank and influence we will be able to keep him in line as easily as we have until now. That's a tougher proposition, but I'm not yet desperate. The boy is convinced (and I may have done some of the convincing) that he is the man who will save us.

    Cicero *Letters to his Friends* 1.3

Between Caesar's would-be successors, relations were growing increasingly fraught. Antony still refused to hand over any money, claiming that the young man had no idea of Antony's difficulties as the executor of Caesar's will. When Octavian decided to start his political career by standing for the tribunate (for which he was doubly unsuitable as a candidate, being neither a plebeian nor at the correct stage of the *cursus honorum*), Antony made sure the measure came to nothing and warned Octavian to stop currying favour with the people or be thrown into prison. Whenever possible, Antony contrasted his own aristocratic lineage with the relative obscurity of Octavian's natural parents – a line of attack which brought Cicero to Octavian's defence.

14 *Cameo showing Octavian (by then Augustus) holding a staff on which the eagle of Jupiter and Rome sits perched on a thunderbolt. Augustus is wearing a victor's wreath and an expression of grim determination.*

He [Antony] accuses Caesar of filthy acts. No doubt he remembers these from his own immoral conduct. But this young man is a very model of purity and good conduct – there's no better example of traditional respect and honour to be found in any young man today. He mocks the son of Julius Caesar with his lack of nobility, even though his natural father would have been consul had he lived. His mother was from Aricia. So? We are not talking about Tralles or Ephesus [in Asia Minor]!

Cicero *Philippics* 3.6.15

His consular year over, Antony took Gaul as his proconsular command for five years. He had been due to go to Macedonia, and he still retained command of the legions earmarked for that province. Decimus Brutus, whom Antony intended to replace in Gaul, was a firm anti-Caesarian and, as Brutus refused to budge from his command, the legions were needed to displace him. To Antony's vast irritation, these legions showed that they distinctly preferred Octavian to himself.

But in leaving Rome, Antony left Cicero and Octavian a free hand. The senate, urged on by Cicero, turned against Antony and declared him a public enemy. The consuls of 43 BC, Hirtius and Pansa, together with Octavian (who had been given the extraordinary rank of propraetor), were sent to the aid of Decimus Brutus, whom Antony was besieging in Mutina in Cisalpine Gaul.

In two hard-fought battles Antony was convincingly defeated and forced to flee to Transalpine Gaul. Both consuls died – Hirtius in battle, and Pansa later from his wounds. Pansa's doctor was later asked some searching questions about this convenient death which left Octavian with command of two consular armies, but the allegation that Octavian had Pansa killed was, and is, unproven. With Antony apparently disposed of, the senate gave Caesar's assassins, Brutus and Cassius, proconsular commands in Macedonia and Syria. Sextus Pompey, the son of Pompey the Great, was put in charge of the Roman fleet. Decimus Brutus was offered a triumph and Octavian was instructed to hand over to him command of the consular armies. Octavian was given no place in the new order, perhaps because the senate believed that his usefulness was at an end. '*Laudandum adolescentem, ornandum, tollendum*', Cicero had commented – 'The lad is to be raised, praised and erased.'

Octavian promptly demonstrated the danger of alienating the commander of eight loyal legions. He refused to co-operate with Decimus Brutus and instead demanded the consulship. The senate vacillated and, encouraged by fresh legions which had arrived from Africa, offered a praetorship instead. Allegedly, one of the centurions sent by Octavian to negotiate slapped the sword at his side and warned, 'If you won't make him consul, this will!'

The legions from Africa promptly went over to the son of their former commander, who was now camped just outside Rome. In a hasty election, Octavian and Quintus Pedius, an obscure relative, were made consuls. Although Octavian was not yet twenty years old, there were precedents for such premature honours, including the consulship given to the thirty-five-year-old Pompey the Great in 71 BC, in rather similar circumstances. Anyway, the senate had discovered that it needed a charismatic commander for its armies, for from Transalpine Gaul came the bitterly disappointing news that Marcus Aemilius Lepidus had joined forces with the defeated Mark Antony, and that the pair were marching on Rome.

It seemed that a battle to decide the fate of the Republic would take place somewhere in north Italy. But Octavian had learned not to trust the senate once he had defeated its enemies. Instead of fighting, he negotiated. Near Mutina, the armies of Lepidus, Antony and Octavian drew up in plain view of an islet in the river Lavinus. Lepidus went to the island first, and waved a cloak to show that he had searched it, and no ambuscade lay in wait. Then Octavian and Antony joined him, and under the eyes of their soldiers they debated the fate of Rome and its Empire.

It was agreed that each of the three would hold consular power for five years and decide between them who was to hold magistracies in Rome. Antony would command most of Gaul, Octavian would command Rome's territory in Africa, and Lepidus those in Spain and part of southern Gaul. Collectively the three would wage war against the assassins of Caesar who now controlled the east of the Empire. Antony, Octavian and Lepidus styled themselves the triumvirate, after the alliance between Pompey, Crassus and Caesar. Unlike Caesar, these new triumvirs were to be merciless.

A list was made of those men who must be put to death, more than two hundred of them in all. But the name which caused the most violent argument was that of Cicero. Antony would negotiate no further unless Cicero was the first of those whom they put to death, and while Lepidus sided with Antony, Caesar [Octavian] held out against them both. For two days, Caesar struggled to save Cicero, but on the third he surrendered him up. Each made the following concessions – Caesar was to abandon Cicero, Lepidus was to give up his own brother, Paullus, and Antony Lucius Caesar, his uncle on his mother's side. So far had fury and vindictiveness driven them from humanity, or rather they showed that humanity is more savage than any wild beast when power is added to human emotion.

Plutarch *Cicero* 45–46

Again Octavian returned to Rome. He had come once as a private citizen, once to be elected as consul, and now as one of the three most powerful men in the known world. He was not yet twenty-one years old.

The Triumvirs

Let no one shelter anyone whose name is appended to this edict. They are not to be concealed, sent to safety or allowed to bribe their way free. Anyone caught helping, saving or conniving with them is to be added to the list of the proscribed without excuse or pardon. Anyone who kills the proscribed and produces their heads shall be rewarded as follows. For a free man 25,000 Attic drachmas for each head, for a slave his freedom plus 10,000 Attic drachmas, and his master's right of citizenship. The same rewards shall be given to informers. That they should remain forever unknown the names of those who receive these rewards will not be written in the records.

Appian *Civil Wars* 4.2.8–11

With these chilling words the triumvirs, Octavian, Mark Antony and Lepidus, began their reign. Unlike the triumvirate of Pompey, Crassus and Caesar, theirs was a legal entity, created by an assembly of the plebs on 27 November 43 BC. The triumvirs proscribed over 2,000 people, most of whom had little connection with politics, but were wealthy enough to be victims of what modern historians believe was a cynical way of raising funds to pay for the coming campaign against Brutus and Cassius in the East.

Lucius Caesar survived the proscriptions. He sensibly fled to his sister, who told the soldiers who followed, 'If you want him, you will have to step over the corpse of the mother who gave birth to Antony.' But there was no refuge for Cicero. The head and hand which forever damned Antony as a drunken wastrel were displayed on spikes in the forum by the vindictive triumvir. Others took refuge with Sextus Pompey, who had taken control of Sicily, and repulsed all attempts to dislodge him.

In the East, Julius Caesar's killers had not been idle. Cassius was a formidable soldier. He had campaigned with distinction against the Parthians, and in Asia Minor he easily disposed of Dolabella, Antony's consular colleague of 44 BC. Now he joined Brutus in Macedonia with the intention of taking control of Greece.

Octavian's ill-health delayed him in following Antony and the army to confront Brutus and Cassius in Greece. He was present when the armies met at Philippi in the autumn of 42 BC, but his health was still impaired. Octavian faced Brutus while Antony took on the formidable Cassius and won his side of the battle. Believing that all was lost, Cassius committed suicide. In fact Brutus had pushed Octavian's men back into their camp, and for a while it was rumoured that Octavian himself had been slain. Furthermore, Brutus' fleet had fallen upon the ships of the triumvirs and destroyed their supplies.

With the battle still undecided, the two sides re-engaged and this time victory went unambiguously to the triumvirs. The son of Cato died in this battle, standing his ground to the last, and Brutus killed himself. In the aftermath of battle, perhaps because his part had gone so badly, Octavian was particularly hard towards the conquered.

He showed no mercy to his beaten enemies. He sent the head of Brutus to Rome, there to be thrown at the feet of a statue of Caesar, and he insulted his distinguished captives. When one of these humbly asked for at least a decent burial, he was coldly told to 'discuss that with the crows'.... This behaviour so disgusted the other prisoners that when they were being led off in chains – including Marcus Favonius, the well-known follower of Cato – they saluted Mark Antony as their conqueror, but cursed Caesar to his face with the most obscene epithets.

Suetonius *Augustus* 13

Lepidus had stayed behind to govern Italy and the West. The victors of Philippi felt strong enough to reduce his powers, though they later gave him command in Africa. Octavian took the rest of the western Empire, though Gaul remained for a short period under a governor who supported Antony. Antony himself took the East which Brutus and Cassius had once held.

Since his command included Italy, Octavian had the job of finding land for tens of thousands of newly disbanded legionaries. He did so with little compunction for the small landholders he dispossessed, or for the cities whose municipal lands he seized. Yet still he failed to satisfy the soldiers, who felt that they deserved better. Octavian became deeply unpopular. Crowds in the theatre cheered statues of the sea god Neptune as a proxy for Sextus Pompey and his fleet. Though Pompey threatened Rome's corn supply and drove up the price of grain, the people blamed Octavian for this, and admired Pompey for his indomitable resistance to the triumvirs.

Antony's wife, Fulvia, was a woman of terrifyingly strong character who was ambitious both for herself and her husband. Capitalizing on popular discontent, she and her brother-in-law Lucius Antonius (Antony's brother and the consul of 41 BC) led a revolt. They briefly occupied Rome before Octavian's generals, including the highly competent Marcus Vipsanius Agrippa, drove them to the fortress town of Perusia (modern Perugia) and took the town after a brutal siege through the winter of 41/40 BC.

Fulvia died, exhausted by the privations of the siege, and Octavian was careful to spare Mark Antony's brother. No one else received the same consideration.

After the city had fallen, Augustus [Octavian] revenged himself on whole crowds of prisoners. Everyone who offered excuses for their presence among the rebels, or who begged for mercy, received the same answer – 'You must die.' Some historians report that he chose 300 prisoners, all senators or knights, and offered them as human sacrifices at the altar of the divine Julius on the Ides of March.

Suetonius *Augustus* 15

**THE JULIAN FAMILY
OF AUGUSTUS**

Gaius Julius Caesar m. Aurelia
(ancestor)

GAIUS JULIUS CAESAR
(dictator)

Julia m. Marcus Atius Balbus

Atia m. Gaius Octavius

The marriage of Augustus to Livia
Drusilla (not shown here) was
childless. However, it significantly
affected the dynasty as Augustus'
adoption of her son Tiberius
introduced the Claudians into the
imperial family, though the lines were
only combined by the marriage of
Tiberius' nephew Germanicus to the
daughter of Julia the Elder and
Agrippa (Agrippina).

Octavia **AUGUSTUS** m. Scribonia

Julia the Elder m. Agrippa

*The family members to the left are siblings of the
primary figure, and the name following the m. denotes
the marriage partner from whom the child of the next
generation was born. Rulers in caps.*

Antony now arrived with his fleet, and being denied the harbour at Brundisium landed in southern Italy, assuming that Octavian was now hostile.
After some hasty diplomacy the two triumvirs patched up their alliance
so effectively that the just-widowed Antony married Octavian's sister
Octavia. This burst of détente included Sextus
Pompey. Antony and Octavian made peace with
him at Misenum in 39 BC and allowed the safe
return of the exiles who had fled to Pompey
for shelter. These refugees included
Claudius Nero, who had led a brief rebellion in Campania, Livia Drusilla, his
wife, and his son Tiberius Claudius –
the future emperor of Rome.

Octavian had repudiated his fiancée
Clodia when her mother Fulvia led the

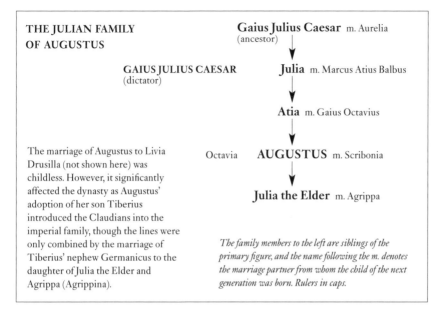

15 *Octavia, sister of Octavian, was first married to
Claudius Marcellus, and later to Mark Antony. Octavia's
son by Marcellus was to have been Augustus' heir had he not
died prematurely.*

revolt against him, and married Scribonia, a relative of Sextus Pompey. He divorced her soon afterwards when the peace with Pompey predictably broke down (Octavian had treacherously seized Sardinia from Pompey's control), doing so the very day that Scribonia gave birth to Octavian's daughter, Julia. In exchange for overlooking Claudius Nero's seditious conduct, Octavian compelled him to divorce Livia and took the nineteen-year-old girl for himself as his new wife.

Sextus Pompey became a constant threat. After losing yet another fleet, Octavian vowed vehemently, 'I'll win this war, no matter what Neptune does!' But first Octavian had to deal with Lepidus, who had come to Sicily in massive force to support Octavian against Pompey. With Octavian embarrassed by defeat and with few soldiers of his own, Lepidus felt strong enough to demand a more prominent position within the alliance. Though sickly, Octavian was physically brave. He went to Lepidus' camp and appealed as the son of Caesar to Lepidus' soldiers. He took a flesh wound from an intemperately hurled javelin, but carried the day. Abandoned by his soldiers, Lepidus was forced to beg for his life, which, to the surprise of many who knew young Octavian, he was granted. Finally, in 36 BC, Agrippa defeated Pompey at Naulochus off the coast of Sicily, making Octavian undisputed master of the West. The reckoning with Antony could not now be long delayed.

Like Octavian, Antony must have known how fragile their alliance was. To a certain extent, peace endured only because each was uncertain of winning a decisive victory. Under Octavian government was centralized and focused as never before. After decades of near anarchy, coordinated, efficient governance was more welcome in Italy than liberty, and Octavian's stock rose with the strength and prosperity of the lands under his control. Agrippa, made aedile for 33 BC, restored the dilapidated water supply infrastructure and the sewers of Rome as well as building and restoring a number of temples.

Antony on the other hand opted not for slow consolidation, but for a grand gamble of which Julius Caesar would have approved. Antony intended to conquer Parthia and proclaim himself the new Alexander the Great. His new power, authority and wealth would be sufficient to defeat Octavian, if Octavian was not sensible enough to surrender first.

Antony allied himself closely with Cleopatra, the queen of Egypt – so

closely that Cleopatra was soon to bear Antony younger siblings to Caesarion, the child of Julius Caesar. Octavian's propaganda made much of
this. Cicero's earlier portrayal of Antony as a weak-willed debauchee was
exploited to claim that Antony was bewitched by his Egyptian queen,
and would betray Rome for her as readily as he betrayed his wife Octavia.
In Italy, Octavia resolutely looked after Antony's interests, an image of
Julian fidelity which Romans contrasted with Antony's waywardness.

Antony's Parthian campaign was a disaster, albeit mitigated by the
fact that the Romans had become more adept at fighting Parthians since
Crassus' time, and Antony proved a strong general. Consequently, much
of the army came out of Parthia intact, although with little to show for
their efforts. The major impact of the campaign was on Antony's credibility. Nor did it help that Octavian had conducted a successful war in
Illyricum while Antony was losing in Parthia. As a final propaganda coup,
Octavian illegally seized Antony's will which he had deposited with the
Vestal Virgins in Rome. Antony's request to be buried in Alexandria, and
the inheritance left to his children by Cleopatra, alienated many of his
supporters. In 32 BC Octavian declared war – not against Antony, his
fellow Roman, but against Cleopatra, the 'decadent queen' who had
allegedly seduced his loyalty.

It mattered not that Cleopatra was in reality a hard-working, conscientious monarch who desperately tried to remain on good terms with
Rome. Octavian wanted his war against Antony to appear as Roman
virtue against Egyptian vice. Also, despite his motto of *festina lente* ('make
haste slowly'), time was against Octavian. Antony was recovering his military strength after the Parthian setback, and the legal term of the
triumvirate had expired on the last day of December 33 BC.
Thereafter Octavian's rule was based on little more
than his personal authority, and it was only a matter
of time before that was questioned.

16 *Coin of Cleopatra. Note that the quality of Eastern mints at
this time was equal or superior to those in Rome, and also note that
Cleopatra was trying to look both unromantic and queenly in an
attempt to limit the political damage caused to her image by her
liaisons with Egypt's Roman masters.*

To lead the war against Cleopatra (and Antony), Octavian made himself consul for 31 BC, and required all in the western Empire to swear loyalty to him personally. (This may have evolved into the oath of allegiance given to all future emperors on their accession.) Antony and Cleopatra moved their army to Greece, and Octavian followed. Almost the only significant action of the war was a naval battle off the peninsula of Actium in 31 BC. Perhaps Antony put his faith in Octavian's poor record at sea against Sextus Pompey. Or in a fight against Caesar's heir, Antony might have trusted the fleet, with its strong Egyptian complement, more than the loyalty of his soldiers. Even before the battle, he had sails loaded onto his ships – the action of a man contemplating a sea voyage, rather than a general who wanted to fight unencumbered. This suggests that Antony intended to break through Octavian's lines. How the entire fleet and the army were to be salvaged is unknown, for it is probable that the plan broke down. The two fleets seemed evenly matched at the first clash, but as the battle intensified, Cleopatra's ships crowded on sail and broke through the Roman lines. The rest of Antony's fleet were too closely engaged to do the same, which left Antony to choose between following Cleopatra or staying with his men. He chose to follow Cleopatra, leaving the remainder of his fleet and the victory to Octavian.

Even with their leader gone, his men continued to fight bravely, and when they knew the battle was lost, they were determined to fight to the death. Caesar tried to conquer with words those whom he could have killed with the sword. He kept shouting at them that Antony had fled, and asking whom they were fighting against and who they were fighting for.

Velleius Paterculus *History* 2.85.3

After Antony's disastrous manoeuvre had lost him his fleet and army, sanctuary in Egypt could only be transitory. Octavian followed at his leisure, using his southward progress to consolidate the provinces of the eastern Mediterranean seaboard through which he passed. On Octavian's arrival in Egypt, Antony committed suicide to avoid capture. Cleopatra fell into Octavian's hands, but though Octavian promised mercy, the best the queen could hope for was a humiliating march in chains before Octavian's triumphal chariot, and probably death soon afterwards. She chose to kill herself and die as queen of Egypt.

Now that he had supreme power, Octavian was more merciful than previously. Many of Antony's retinue who begged for pardon received it. Even Antony's sons by Cleopatra were taken into the household of Octavia. But there was no mercy for Caesarion, the child of Julius Caesar. As Octavian commented, 'One can have too many Caesars'. It was a sentiment shared by later emperors, with lethal effects for their dynasty.

The Augustan Peace

As for Caesar's return to Italy and to Rome, well, this would be impossible to describe adequately, even in the scope of a formal history. The procession which greeted him, the enthusiasm of the welcome from men of all ages, class and social standing, the magnificence of the triumphs and spectacles which he staged, are all beyond the compass of this limited document.

Velleius Paterculus *History* 89

Octavian had attained power equal to that of his adoptive father, Julius Caesar. Now he needed to avoid Caesar's fate. By 29 BC some immediate issues had been taken care of. The last rivals to Octavian's power were hunted down and killed (for example Antyllus, the son of Antony and Fulvia). Egypt became a Roman province, but under the personal supervision of Octavian himself. Many of Antony's arrangements for the East were allowed to stand, though the huge bequests of Antony to his children were cancelled. On the Euphrates, both Roman and Parthian were careful not to disturb the fragile *de facto* peace. The historian Cassius Dio recognized that Rome was now at a turning point. His history has a fictitious debate between Agrippa and Octavian's other most intimate associate, Maecenas. Agrippa argued for the full restoration of the Republic, but Octavian sided with Maecenas and chose autocracy.

However, he did not try to implement all of his advisor's suggestions overnight, because he knew that he would fail if he tried to change the social structure too rapidly. Instead he introduced some reforms at once, and others later. Yet others he left to his successors.

Cassius Dio *History* 52.41

To symbolize the re-establishment of order, Octavian had the doors of the temple of Janus closed. This only happened when Rome was at peace – and during the Republic they had almost invariably stood open.

A massive demobilization programme cut the legions from sixty to twenty-eight. The veterans were paid off by the wealth of Egypt, of which enough remained afterwards to set the economy on a sound footing, and allow some relief for debtors. An amnesty was proclaimed, and some of the unjust laws of the triumvirate were repealed. Colonies were established in Italy and the provinces – both as housing for disbanded soldiers and as bastions of support for the new order. The consuls carried out the first census for decades, and the more egregious appointments of the triumvirs were weeded from the senate, reducing it from 1,000 to 800 members.

As normality returned, Octavian's position appeared increasingly abnormal. He governed through his huge personal authority and by holding one of the consulships every year.

In January 27 BC Octavian announced that he was renouncing all his powers and offices, though he would finish his year as consul. (In fact he was to hold continuous consulships until 23 BC.) The senate would not accept Octavian's return to private life, and 'forced' him to accept control of Spain, Gaul and Syria which he reluctantly agreed to administer through legates, as Pompey had ruled Spain while he was governor in 52 BC.

Undoubtedly Octavian had carefully gauged what powers he could safely give up, but the contrast with Julius Caesar is striking. Caesar boldly proclaimed his dominance of the state; Octavian tried to blend into its constitutional background. Where Caesar became dictator for life, Octavian came to be known as 'first citizen', or *princeps*, a title held partly through his personal authority, and partly as a reflection of the traditional title of *princeps senatus* ('foremost senator'). The senate wanted to call him Romulus as the re-founder of Rome, but Octavian chose a name for one who is respected and revered – Augustus. This name distanced him from Octavian the bloodthirsty triumvir, and from Caesar the closet monarchist. As is conventional, Augustus he will be called henceforth in this text.

Augustus proclaimed the Republic restored, and went on a prolonged trip to Gaul and Spain. The classically minded recalled Solon's self-imposed exile from Athens after he had settled the city's laws. Those with different mindsets noted that Augustus left Livia in Rome, but took his mistress *du jour* with him. Caesar's heir famously shared his adoptive father's libidinous tendencies. When he had once reproached Antony for his affair with Cleopatra, Antony shot back,

Are you faithful to Livia Drusilla? My congratulations if, by the time this letter arrives, you have not bedded Tertulla, Terentilla, Rufilla or Salvia Titisenia – or the lot of them. Does it matter so much where, or with whom, you have it off?

Suetonius *Augustus* 69

Macrobius adds this story:

A quip made by a man from one of the provinces is well known. He closely resembled the emperor and…the likeness attracted much attention. Augustus sent for the man and on seeing him enquired, 'Tell me, young man, was your mother ever in Rome?' 'No,' replied the youth, who could not resist adding, 'but my father often was.'

Macrobius *Saturnalia* 2.4.20

Augustus returned to Rome in 24 BC and realized, as Caesar had before him, that absence from the capital could be politically damaging. Augustus clashed with the aristocracy when Licinius Crassus (a descendant of the triumvir) defeated a Macedonian tribe and personally killed its leader, thus earning the *spolia opima* – an honour achieved only twice before in Roman history. Augustus jealously blocked the award, which created much bad feeling in the senate. An aedile called Egnatius Rufus had used his remarkably successful organization of a fire brigade to make a bid for the consulship, which was so disruptive that the

17 *Coin of Augustus. Although he was eager to distance himself from the more dictatorial aspects of his adopted father's reputation, the name of Caesar was still too politically powerful for Augustus to abandon altogether.*

consul of the day had him executed for treason. This was a stark warning that the 'liberties' of the late Republic would no longer be tolerated. Another who took republican liberties was the governor of Macedonia, who invaded Thrace without authorization and was brought to trial for his conduct.

In 22 BC a conspiracy was discovered which was led by Fannius Caepio and included Varro Murena, a man who had been elected to the consulship with Augustus. The conspiracy may have originated during the previous year when Augustus fell so gravely ill that his very survival was in doubt. He gave the senate documents accounting for his handling of affairs and handed his signet ring to Agrippa. This caused speculation as to whether Augustus intended Agrippa as his heir, or the charismatic Claudius Marcellus – the son of the consul who had opposed Caesar twenty years previously, and of Octavia, Augustus' sister.

In the end, Augustus recovered and Agrippa went to the East, his position strengthened by an *imperium* giving him authority over senatorial and imperial officials there. Agrippa remained in the East, Spain and the Balkans until 13 BC – an arrangement reminiscent of Caesar's keeping his heir out of harm's way lest anything befall him in Rome. Agrippa's putative rival Marcellus died during the autumn of 23 BC, probably through illness. The Romans lived in a world without antibiotics where an attack of appendicitis, or even an infected cut, was often fatal. It was not only Julio-Claudians who died young or unexpectedly, though deaths in the imperial family inevitably aroused rumour and dark speculation among the Roman public, where some whispered that Livia had poisoned Marcellus to promote her son Tiberius as a potential heir.

18 Marcus Vipsanius Agrippa, a formidable admiral and administrator. As Augustus' loyal subordinate, Agrippa married his daughter Julia, thus adding his bloodline to that of later Julio-Claudians, including the emperor Gaius Caligula.

Augustus now renounced the consulship, where his tenure of office was creating a shortage of ex-consuls available to administer the provinces. In return the senate awarded him *maius imperium (proconsulare)*, meaning that the authority of Augustus overrode that of any other pro-consul, and this authority did not lapse when Augustus was within Rome, as did that of other proconsuls.

Augustus also took the *tribunicia potestas* – the powers of a tribune. As tribunes the Gracchus brothers had radically changed the state, and Clodius had desired that power avidly enough to abandon his patrician status and Claudian name. It allowed Augustus to call meetings of the senate, veto legislation and, as had been done on rare occasions, actually arrest sitting magistrates. This 'second settlement' of 23 BC allowed Augustus to control Rome through the *tribunicia potestas*, and the provinces and their armies through the *maius imperium*. This was to be the constitutional basis of imperial rule for the centuries which followed.

Yet for all that power had been effectively transferred from the people and senate of Rome to Augustus Caesar, peace and good governance had brought him genuine popularity – in fact Augustus had actively to reject attempts to give himself more authority. When plague struck Italy,

The people of Rome decided that this disaster had afflicted them for no other reason than because Augustus was not consul at that time. Therefore they decided he should be made dictator. To compel the senators to pass a law to this effect the people shut them up in the senate house and threatened to burn the building and them inside it. Then they took the twenty-four fasces [the symbols of a dictator] to Augustus and begged him not only to become dictator, but also to take charge of the corn supply, as Pompey had once done. Augustus reluctantly agreed to supervise the corn supply, but refused to allow himself to be named as dictator. He even tore his own clothes when he discovered that neither calm reason nor pleading would change the popular desire for his appointment. He was well aware that the power and honours he already possessed made him more powerful than any dictator Rome had ever had, and he was understandably unwilling to provoke hatred and jealousy by taking the name as well.

Cassius Dio *History* 54.2

Augustus did not have a master plan for taking over the Republic. Each tentative step was designed to make himself more secure and his power less blatant. Certainly Augustus did not proclaim that he intended his imperial settlement to be permanent, both because this would outrage the senate and because Augustus himself was feeling his way towards the final shape of his principate. Unfortunately for Rome, circumstance and necessity nudged Augustus towards a settlement riven with internal contradictions, which needed a politician of his own genius to manage – as the difficulties of his successors made plain.

Augustus seldom flaunted his powers. His laws were generally passed by others, and he found his moral authority more useful than force. Augustus' forum near the Forum Romanum in the city centre has a narrow, awkward shape, testifying more eloquently to his memory than anything more expansive and elegant; for Augustus respected the rights of those in adjoining properties, and would not eject any who would not sell. One wall of this forum is obtrusively high and severe: unaesthetic, but a useful firebreak in the centre of a highly combustible city.

Lepidus died in 12 BC. Despite his betrayal of Octavian in Sicily and a later plot by his son, Augustus had allowed Lepidus to remain a senator and keep the post of Pontifex Maximus, an office which Augustus now took for himself. Another casualty of 12 BC was Agrippa, whose death forced another adjustment of Augustus' dynastic plans.

Agrippa had been fighting Celtic raiders in Macedonia and rebels on the Danubian frontier in Pannonia. After his death, Tiberius, Augustus' stepson and an experienced general in his own right, was the obvious replacement. In 15 BC Tiberius campaigned north of the Alps, where the provinces of Noricum and Raetia were soon to be created, and later further east in Pannonia.

Rome's frontier now reached the Danube, and there Augustus felt the growth of the Empire should stop – or at least pause. Peace was breaking out elsewhere as well. After a series of revolts in 24, 22, 19 and 16 BC, Romanization was slowly taking hold in Spain, enabling Augustus to reduce the garrison from three legions to one.

19 *The Forum Romanum at the time of Augustus.* A *Tabularium;* B *Temple of Concord;* C *Temple of Saturn;* D *Basilica Julia;* E *rostra;* F *Temple of Castor and Pollux;* G *Temple of the Deified Julius Caesar;* H *Temple of Vesta;* I *Regia,* J *Basilica Aemilia;* K *Curia Julia;* L *Forum of Julius Caesar;* M *Temple of Venus Genetrix;* N *Forum of Augustus;* P *Temple of Mars Ultor.*

On the other side of the Empire, Augustus made Galatia in Asia Minor into a province after the client king Amyntas died in 25 BC. The uneasy peace with Parthia remained unbroken, and in 20 BC the Parthians returned the standards which they had captured from Crassus, a diplomatic victory which Augustus celebrated in his propaganda. Tiberius exploited Parthian quiescence to install a pro-Roman client king in nearby Armenia.

Apart from some minor forays, such as an attempt to exert Roman control over southern Egypt, Augustus was mostly engaged in tidying up the massive but disorderly growth of the Empire at the end of the Republic. The exception was Germany, where the Romans seem to have decided to advance from the Rhine to the Elbe, and possibly further in that direction thereafter.

Back in Rome, a further pruning of the senate reduced its numbers to 600. In 18 BC, despite his numerous mistresses and affairs, it appears that Augustus became infected with morality. He professed himself shocked by the scandalous behaviour of the upper classes and that so few of the nobility were marrying, and even fewer were having children. The poet

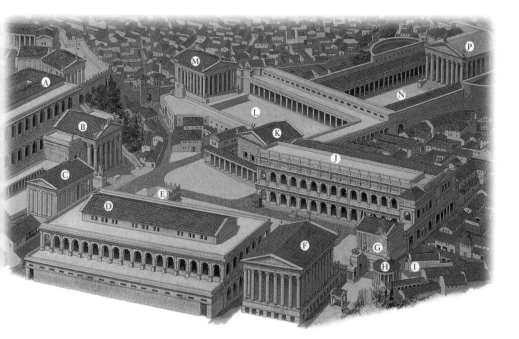

Ovid, whose *Ars Amatoria* ('The art of love') was a witty handbook to sexual immorality in Rome, fell from favour and was exiled to the shores of the Black Sea in AD 8. Augustus passed a series of laws on marriage (the *leges Julia*) which contained some severe and startling provisions, many of which were to rebound on future generations of his own family.

In the second chapter of the *lex Julia* concerning adultery, either an adoptive or a natural father is permitted to kill with his own hands an adulterer caught in the act with his daughter in his own house or in that of his son-in-law, no matter what his rank may be.

A husband who does not at once dismiss his wife whom he has discovered committing adultery can be prosecuted as a pimp.

Women convicted of adultery shall be punished with the loss of half of their dowry and a third of their goods, and by relegation to an island. The adulterer shall be deprived of half of his property, and shall also be punished by relegation to an island, provided the parties are exiled to different islands.

The Opinions of Paul in *The Digest of Justinian* 2.26 passim

Taxes were increased for unmarried Romans and for childless married Romans while financial rewards were given to families with children. All but senators were permitted to marry freedwomen, and their children were granted legitimate status.

In other legislation, Augustus tried to ban excessive spending on banquets, wedding parties and other forms of conspicuous consumption. Julius Caesar had tried this too and, as his adopted son was to discover, morality is extremely difficult to legislate into existence. However, laws such as these (known as sumptuary laws) had another purpose. Romans gained much of their political potency through followers called clients, and displays of wealth were a way of attracting clients. By banning such displays, Augustus weakened potential rivals.

For all that they disliked and tried to evade the strictures of his sumptuary and marriage laws, the people of Rome saw Augustus as acting not just as a politician, but in the role they themselves had given him, that of *pater patriae*, the father of his country. As such, whatever his personal views on adultery and immorality, the guardian of Rome had to act in her interests.

There was nothing that a man might desire from the gods, and nothing that wishes or good fortune could bring about that Augustus…did not give to the Republic, the people of Rome and the world. After twenty years of civil wars, there was finally respite from the frenzy of battle. Wars abroad were muted, the laws again valid and the courts strong. The senate had dignity, and the power of the magistrates was again as before. (Apart from the addition of two extra praetors to the existing eight.) The ancient Republic was restored, agriculture returned to the fields, piety to religion, and humanity freed from fear. The property of each citizen was protected by law – the old laws were adapted and new ones passed for the general good….

    Velleius Paterculus *History* 2.89

Such praise was intended to do more than inflate the imperial ego. The above laudation states in no uncertain terms what was expected of their first citizen by the Roman people. Popular opinion obliged Augustus to be a patron of the arts, to sponsor building projects and to encourage popular morality. Unfortunately, Augustus' offspring had the same sexual appetite as both Julius Caesar and Augustus himself – and the next generation of Julians were among the first victims of his legislation.

Daughters and Heirs

That her immediate family were so distinguished mattered not at all to his [Augustus'] daughter Julia. Everything she did was polluted by extravagance and lust, and there was nothing so disgraceful that she did not do it, or have it done to her. She was accustomed to judge the greatness of her fortune by the latitude it allowed her for wrongdoing, and she set no limits on the latitude she allowed herself.

    Velleius Paterculus *History* 2.100

If Augustus, an incorrigible womanizer, fell short of the standards which he set for others, he at least could claim political expediency – what better way to dispel rumours that he had been Julius Caesar's catamite? Furthermore, Romans had the double standard common in the ancient world, where fidelity was desirable in husbands but compulsory for wives. In fact Suetonius compliments Augustus on the 'decent normality' of his sex life!

In other aspects of his personal life, Augustus was a model of restraint. Suetonius tells us that some of Augustus' furniture was on display in his own time and 'many items would now hardly be considered fit for use even by a private citizen'. Augustus lived in a house taken from the orator Hortensius (another victim of the proscriptions) on the Palatine hill. Part of this house still stands today, confirming Suetonius' assertion that it was a relatively modest building.

Despite their lofty rank, Augustus' sisters, his wife Livia and his daughter Julia were supposed to set a domestic example to the nation by their proficiency with loom and sewing needle. When not dressed for special occasions, Augustus wore clothing made by the women of his household, his one concession to vanity being built-up shoes which concealed his modest height.

Unfortunately it was hard for Julia to conform with this image of docile domestic submissiveness. Macrobius, writing several centuries after the event, tells that Julia once turned up at a dinner party in a scandalously revealing dress. Augustus was offended but held his peace. But the next day his daughter appeared in the dress of a demure Roman lady, and he exclaimed, 'But this dress is so much more suitable for the daughter of Augustus!' Julia told him, 'Today I am dressed for my father's eyes. Last night I was dressed for my husband's.'

In part, Julia may have been reacting against a childhood in which she had been strictly supervised and rigorously educated. A register was kept of what she did and said. Anything, whether in public or private, which was unsuitable for entry into that record was forbidden.

20 *Julia, daughter of Augustus. Like any daughter of the Roman aristocracy, Julia was supposed to be modest, preoccupied with domestic affairs and busily breeding the next generation. That he had a vivacious, adventurous daughter of considerable intelligence was a great disappointment to the emperor.*

Her friends were carefully scrutinized and their visits recorded. When the young Lucius Vinicius, whose breeding and conduct were above reproach, visited Julia at the seaside resort of Baiae he received a stinging rebuke from the emperor for his ill-mannered conduct in doing so. Julia was a true heir to the Julian tradition of waywardness, and this heavy-handed approach merely incited wilder acts of rebellion.

Her first husband was her cousin, Marcellus. This match is interesting because it marks a move from the exogamy which often characterized matches in the Julian family. One such marriage had paired an earlier Julia with Marius and catapulted the Julians to the forefront of Roman politics. But in the imperial era marriages outside the imperial family created rivals at a time when Augustus was starting to plan for a smooth transfer of power to the next generation.

Julia's marriage lasted two years, from 25 BC until Marcellus died in 23 BC, leaving Julia a widow at sixteen years old. Augustus was still reluctant to marry Julia to a potential rival, so his most trusted general, Marcus Vipsanius Agrippa, became Julia's next husband despite being twenty-five years her senior. A family connection of sorts already existed, for Agrippa was married to a sister of Julia's late husband, whom he put aside for this new marriage.

Julia bore Agrippa three sons – Gaius, Lucius and Agrippa Postumus – and two daughters, Julia (known as Julia the Younger) and Agrippina. Such was the importance of the Julian name that the older daughter was called Julia rather than both girls being called Vipsania as convention would have it. The names of the first two sons, Gaius and Lucius, were both traditional Julian family names.

Before long rumours of Julia's numerous infidelities were flying around Rome. A close friend asked her how, despite this, she had contrived to bear children who unmistakably resembled Agrippa. Julia replied, 'I never let passengers board ship until the cargo is in the hold.'

Given her father's moral crusade in the capital, Julia wisely decided to accompany her husband to Asia Minor, where she almost drowned crossing the river Scamander, bringing her husband's wrath down upon the nearby town of Ilium, which he deemed to have paid insufficient regard to her safety. When Agrippa died in 12 BC Augustus cast about for a third match for his daughter, eventually settling on his own stepson

Tiberius. Tiberius was enjoying marital bliss with Agrippa's daughter by a previous marriage, a lady called Vipsania. He was deeply unenthusiastic about divorcing his love to marry his father-in-law's widow, especially (Suetonius reports) since Tiberius had already once rebuffed Julia's amorous advances while she was still Agrippa's wife. But Augustus was a less benevolent despot to his own family than to the Empire as a whole. The loveless marriage which he compelled lasted only until 6 BC. The couple had a son who died in infancy.

Augustus suddenly became aware of his daughter's licentiousness, perhaps because Livia sought to shift the blame for the failure of the marriage from Tiberius. In accordance with Augustus' new laws, Julia was exiled to the island of Pandateria off the Campanian coast, and there forced into a monastic existence with few luxuries or visitors. Phoebe, one of Julia's handmaidens, committed suicide when her part in the affair came out, and Augustus remarked feelingly, 'I wish I were Phoebe's father!' Not everyone agreed. Augustus' ex-wife Scribonia ostentatiously went to join her daughter, and perhaps Augustus was glad to see her go. ('She nags me', he once confided to a friend who asked why he and Scribonia had divorced.)

So savage was Julia's punishment that some (including the writer Pliny) speculated that Julia had been involved in a conspiracy. Certainly there was rivalry between Tiberius and Julia's children Gaius and Lucius. Augustus doted upon his grandchildren to the extent that Tiberius withdrew to Rhodes, feeling overshadowed in Rome, where Augustus had adopted the two children as his own, thus giving one grandson and his presumptive heir the name of his famous forebear – Gaius Julius Caesar. In 1 BC Gaius was dispatched to Asia Minor for his first military command.

21 *Augustus – whose head appears on the obverse of this coin – describes himself as the son of a god (Julius Caesar), and Gaius and Lucius Caesar as his own sons, the leaders of youth and consuls designate. Gaius and Lucius hold shields and spears, between which are religious instruments indicating their priesthoods.*

Caesar is preparing to fill a gap in his conquests
Orient, you'll be ours!
Rejoice, buried Crassus [father and son], now Parthia will pay.
Rejoice, you standards in foreign hands
Now an avenger is alive who sends a general in the bloom of youth
A boy with a man's task
You who fear, don't count the birthdays of gods –
The Caesars mature before their time.

> Ovid *Ars Amatoria* 177 ff.

On his sixty-fourth birthday Augustus wrote to Gaius, his 'dear little donkey': 'I pray to the gods that whatever time is left to me I may pass with you, safe and well, with the country flourishing, while you are acting as a man and preparing to succeed to my position.' The following year, in 2 BC, Augustus held his thirteenth and last consulship, an office which he had not held since 23 BC. This was to pave the way for Gaius, who was designated consul for AD 1, and to introduce his other grandson, Lucius, into public life. But Augustus' plans for his heirs fell victim to ill fortune. Lucius died from a sudden illness while *en route* to Massalia in Spain. Gaius, on campaign in Asia Minor, was severely wounded during a siege. He never fully recovered, and died in AD 4 while returning to Italy.

Augustus had now outlived four possible successors – something that would have seemed highly improbable thirty years previously during the dangerous days of the triumvirate. Now, Marcellus, Agrippa, Gaius and Lucius had died leaving only Julia's youngest son, Agrippa Postumus, as a potential heir from the Julian line. Sadly, Postumus was considered too vicious and erratic to pick up the reins of Empire from his ageing grandfather.

Postumus had a character unfit for high command. He spent so much time at his hobby of fishing that he called himself Neptune. He was subject to violent fits of anger, cursing Livia, his stepmother, and blaming Augustus for depriving him of the inheritance of his father [Agrippa]. Since he was evidently incorrigible, he was disinherited and his money added to that of the army treasury. Agrippa [Postumus] himself was sent to Planasia, an island near Corsica.

> Cassius Dio *History* 55.32

Livia may have been responsible for Augustus' low opinion of his youngest grandson. Rumour alleged that Livia had a hand in the deaths of Tiberius' other rivals, but if Lucius and Gaius were poisoned, blood poisoning from Gaius' wound is a strong probability, while we have absolutely no idea what caused the death of Lucius. While poisoning was extremely rare in Roman political life (the last major case was in 154 BC when two ex-consuls were allegedly poisoned by their wives), interest in poison was growing among the Roman upper classes, and the shadow of the poisoner hung over the remaining Julio-Claudians until the entire family was extinct.

Augustus now turned to the Claudians in his search for a successor. Tiberius returned from Rhodes after a seven-year absence and was adopted as Augustus' son. As an extra guarantee, Tiberius was required to adopt his nephew Germanicus. Germanicus was a true Julio-Claudian, the grandson of Livia and Claudius Nero on his father's side; and on his mother's the grandson of Octavia, Augustus' sister. It is ironic that the remaining Julio-Claudian emperors were all close relatives of Germanicus, for the mother of Germanicus was Antonia, child of Octavia and Octavian's arch rival, Mark Antony. Later Roman historians were quick to associate the debaucheries of the later Julio-Claudian emperors with the bloodline of the pleasure-loving triumvir, and ostentatiously noted that the tyrannical emperor Nero was Antony's great-great-grandson.

Augustus transferred his wayward daughter to slightly less severe conditions in Rhegium on the Italian mainland. Julia the Younger, his granddaughter, was married to Aemilius Paullus, and the couple called their first child Lepida in defiant memory of the ex-triumvir of the same family.

22 *If not the power behind the throne, few doubted that Livia Drusilla quietly exercised considerable influence over Augustus. While ambitious for her son Tiberius, rumours that she resorted to the wholesale poisoning of his rivals are improbable and unproven.*

Thus, by AD 6 the succession was resolved. Power would pass to the uninspired but solidly reliable Tiberius, and after him to the combined line of the Claudians, the Julians and Mark Antony, as embodied in the young Germanicus. For an institution which did not officially exist, the principate now had a remarkably well-charted future.

The Final Years

As the ruler of the Roman world entered the final decade of his life, he could look with satisfaction at a job well done. When he had begun his rule as the triumvir Octavian, the economy had been shattered and society brutalized by repeated civil wars and proscriptions. The provinces had groaned from merciless exploitation by governors desperate to squeeze every penny from their subjects for the vastly expensive political battles in Rome.

Now, after more than three decades of imperial rule, Rome and her Empire were stable and prosperous. Augustus' anomalous constitutional position was cloaked in a shroud of republican legality. For every fervent republican there were many who remembered the greed, selfishness and vast incompetence of the senate during its final years in power, and contrasted this with the stability and good governance Augustus had brought. The mainstay of the Julio-Claudians was that their rule was genuinely popular.

Even Julia, the black sheep of the family, aroused public sympathy.

The people pressed Augustus strongly, urging him to recall his daughter from exile, but he replied that fire would sooner mix with water than she would be allowed back. Immediately people started lighting torches and throwing them into the Tiber. At the time the emperor seemed unaffected, but it was at the insistent urging of the public that Julia was finally allowed to return to the mainland.

Cassius Dio *History* 55.13

Sadly, it appeared that the younger Julia took after her mother, and when her adulterous affairs came to light, Augustus despairingly exiled her too. Julia the Younger was sent to live out her days on the island of

Trimerum off the Apulian coast. She bore a child which was killed by exposure on Augustus' orders, and she remained on the island until her death over two decades later. With Agrippa Postumus already exiled at Planasia for his violent conduct, the imperial family was demonstrably less happy than the Empire it ruled.

This was in part because Augustus ruled his Empire more tolerantly than he ruled his family. He patiently endured lampoons of his character and interruptions to his speeches in the senate. When a close associate was put on trial – for poisoning – Augustus asked to be left entirely out of the matter, saying, 'If I speak in his defence, I may seem to be protecting a wrongdoer, yet if I remain silent, I may tacitly condemn an innocent man.' When the prefect of Egypt, Cornelius Gallus, offended Augustus, the emperor recalled him to Rome and refused to see him. The senate promptly condemned Gallus for treason, causing Augustus to request the privilege of not having to be nice to everyone he did not want killed.

Augustus was relaxed and outgoing with his friends. His dinner parties were not particularly grand, but the emperor made an effort to make guests feel welcome and appreciated. Maecenas came in for friendly teasing about his 'myrrh-distilling ringlets' and slightly decadent lifestyle. Though Maecenas knew all the secrets of Octavian's bloody past, friendship triumphed over expediency. The man who knew too much kept his life and Augustus' trust, and in return he also kept his silence.

Augustus wryly admitted that he was not the equal of Julius Caesar, who had been an accomplished speaker and writer. Someone who asked about the progress of Augustus' epic on the Greek hero Ajax was told that the protagonist 'has fallen on his sponge', meaning that the work had been wiped away. Nevertheless, literature was the better for Augustus, who patronized, and encouraged the patronage of, other writers. The poetry of Virgil and Horace are one reason the Latin of Augustus' day is called 'golden Latin' by philologists, who contrast it with the 'silver Latin' of subsequent decades. Livy produced his epic history of Rome, and art and sculpture blossomed. Augustus launched a massive building programme which included the Pantheon, a temple which still stands intact in Rome today. On the front there is an inscription by Agrippa who was in charge of construction. It was with justification that Augustus later boasted, 'I found Rome a city of brick, and left it a city of marble.'

As his people expected of him, Augustus expanded the frontiers of the Empire. History had given the Romans long memories of invaders sweeping down on Rome through the Alpine passes, so Augustus pushed this frontier northward and eastward. Much of what is now southeastern Switzerland was brought under Roman control. The trophy of Augustus at La Turbie lists forty-six tribes subdued in the process.

For his drive to the Danube, Augustus had two capable generals in the sons of Livia. Both Tiberius and Drusus campaigned extensively in the lands which were later to become the provinces of Moesia and Pannonia. For Tiberius this military experience gave him vital credibility with the army when he became emperor. From 12 BC to 2 BC, the Romans also concentrated much of their military effort on expansion into Germany.

> Who fears the hordes produced from Germany's rough loins,
> Let the northern Scythians or the Parthians rearm
> Let the wild tribes of Spain rally once more to war.
> We can sleep if Caesar is safe from harm.
>   Horace *Odes* 4.5

Even so, Horace might have had a few sleepless nights at the news that the governor of Germany in AD 9, Quintilius Varus, and the men of the seventeenth, eighteenth and nineteenth legions had been slaughtered in battle. Varus was a distant relative of Augustus by marriage who had governed competently enough in the important province of Syria. Now entrusted with the newly conquered provinces of Germany, Varus and his fellow Romans were unaware of the seditious plans of a former officer, a young German of the Cherusci tribe called Arminius.

Arminius lured the Romans into the Teutoburg forest where the legionaries were hampered by trees and swamp. A confederation of German tribes fell on the Romans near modern Kalkriese, and almost the whole Roman army of the Rhine was lost.

Though Rome was completely exposed, with only the Alps between the city and the army of Arminius, Augustus did not panic. He ordered a hasty levy of able-bodied citizens and sent the elite fifth Alaudae Legion ('the Larks') north, before dispatching the First Germanica and the sixteenth legion to complete the repair of the Roman lines. According to

Suetonius, even months later Augustus would bang his head against the wall and exclaim, 'Quintilius Varus, give me back my legions!'

The campaigning season of AD 10 opened with Augustus assuaging Rome's wounded pride by unleashing a vengeful Tiberius across the Rhine. Tiberius continued his campaign against the Germans until the increasing feebleness of the emperor necessitated his recall to Rome. Augustus was deeply affected by the German setback, and reportedly warned Tiberius against any further expansion of the Empire.

In AD 13 Augustus had reached the ripe old age of seventy-five. At the urging of the senate, he undertook to govern the Empire for another ten years, but in fact he shared this burden with Tiberius. Since AD 4 Tiberius had possessed the *tribunicia potestas*, which, added to his other powers, made him almost co-emperor with Augustus.

In AD 14 Tiberius set off for Pannonia on the Danube frontier. Augustus accompanied him for part of the journey, for the aged emperor had been fond of travel when he was younger. (Before 23 BC he had seldom spent a complete year in Rome.)

Returning, Augustus dallied at Capri, where he was troubled by diarrhoea – probably a symptom of a graver malaise. Still unwell, he stopped in the town of Nola and, recognizing the gravity of his symptoms, ordered Tiberius to be recalled. Other members of his family rushed to his bedside from Rome, to find Augustus preparing for death with remarkable equanimity. He ordered his jaw to be propped up, as it kept dropping open, and his hair to be properly brushed. He worried that rumours of his condition were upsetting the people, and constantly asked if there were any reports of disturbances.

He joked with his friends that he was like an actor finishing a long spell on the stage. 'Well,' he enquired, 'did I play my part in this comedy well?' and he left them with the stock line of a departing actor, 'If I have pleased you, then signify/Your appreciation with a warm goodbye.'

His final words were to Livia, whom he kissed and admonished, 'Goodbye Livia – never forget whose wife you have been.' At about 3 pm on 19 August AD 14, a month before his seventy-sixth birthday, Augustus passed away – dying, as it happened, in the same room where his father Octavius had died before him.

Senators competed to propose posthumous honours for Augustus. Among the motions proposed were the following: that his funeral procession should pass through the Triumphal Gate, preceded by the image of victory from the senate house, and that his funeral dirge should be sung by boys and girls of Rome's noble houses. On the day he was cremated, iron rings were to be worn instead of gold. His ashes should be collected by members of the leading priestly colleges.

Suetonius *Augustus* 100

Two of the measures proposed remain today – the month of his death was renamed August, and the time between his birth and death was (according to Suetonius) officially recorded as 'the Augustan Age', a term still used by historians for the period between the battle of Actium and the principate of Tiberius. In those few decades the entire character of Rome and her Empire was subtly yet wholly changed.

He had seduced the army with gifts, the common people with a constant supply of cheap food, and everyone by the siren song of peace. Step by step he increased his powers, taking over those of the senate, the magistrates and the laws. The aristocracy received wealth and position in proportion to their readiness to accept servitude, and they preferred the existing security to the dangers and uncertainties of the past....

The young men had been born after Actium, the older generation during the civil wars – how many remained who remembered the Republic? The state had been transformed, and the old Roman character was gone forever. Equality among the citizens was completely abandoned, all waited for the imperial command.

Tacitus *Annals* 1–5 passim

Senators and *Princeps*

Augustus' skill as a politician was such that he appears to have shared power equitably with the Roman elite. He made it seem as though his extraordinary position in the state was not assumed by force but accepted reluctantly at the urging of the senate. So complete was this illusion that the great German historian Theodor Mommsen referred to Augustus' principate as a 'dyarchy' in which emperor and senate shared the rule of the Empire between them. The reality was that Augustus dominated the senate as did no other Julio-Claudian emperor, but he did so tactfully because he understood that no *princeps* ('first citizen') could long survive alienation from the aristocracy. Caesar had demonstrated this, and Gaius Caligula and Nero were later to prove it yet again.

If Augustus was to respect the senate, the senate had again to become a respectable body. Both Caesar and the triumvirs had packed the senate with their supporters, some of highly dubious provenance. In his role as censor, Augustus ejected some two hundred of these, some directly, and others more discreetly by raising the financial level for senatorial qualification, and then giving financial help only to those he regarded as worthy to remain.

At the same time, the civil wars had decimated the Roman elite, and this allowed Augustus to replenish their ranks with his own supporters. Some plebeian families were elevated to patrician status, and deserving equestrians were elevated to the rank of senator. Membership of the senate was regularized through a series of junior posts leading up to the quaestorship, which gave access to the senate proper. For those who remained within the ranks of the equestrians, the expansion of the Empire meant that many positions held by aristocratic amateurs in the Republic came to be held by career equestrians in the imperial service.

Senators were given extra duties and privileges. They were not permitted to marry freedwomen, but they were entitled to the front row of seats at the theatre. Non-attendance of senate meetings became punishable by fines, and by AD 8 the senate had the power to try and condemn those accused of certain crimes. Though decrees of the senate were not yet *ipso facto* legally binding, Augustus either consulted the senate before he acted, or occasionally would issue decrees effective 'until the senate has had time to deliberate this matter'.

Within the senate, the ancient privilege of free speech was still exercised on occasion. While Augustus was reforming the senate, he required the senators to nominate each other for membership, the better to remove unpopular members. When one Antistius Labeo nominated Lepidus (whom Augustus still did not permit to live in Rome), the emperor asked, 'Doesn't someone better deserve this?' Labeo replied, 'You wanted my opinion – you've got it.' Yet, comments Suetonius, 'He never punished people for speaking their mind at times like this, even if they spoke insolently.'

His speeches to the senate were often interrupted by comments such as 'I don't get that!', 'I'd say that was wrong if I could'. On several occasions he became so frustrated by recriminations which ruined the quality of the debate that he stormed out of the house followed by shouts from senators who claimed that they had the right to speak their minds about matters of national importance.

Suetonius *Augustus* 54

Perhaps dealing with the senate as a body became an increasing trial for Augustus, for in later life he attended its meetings ever less frequently, making his opinions known through informal meetings with a group of trusted senior senators who became known as the *consilium principis*.

It helped that Roman aristocrats felt that Augustus genuinely cared about them. He conscientiously greeted them and enquired about their health and families when they met. (Like many elite Romans Augustus had a slave to remind him of these details – except that his had such a bad memory that the exasperated emperor once offered to give him letters of introduction and send him to the forum to meet the people he was supposed to remind Augustus about.) The emperor took a morbid interest in wills and bequests to himself – presumably because these represented the one occasion when he was certain that the nobility were expressing their opinion without fear or flattery. But he also took insulting lampoons and reports of criticism in his stride, remarking to Tiberius when the latter became particularly incensed, 'I don't mind them speaking evil – we should just be grateful if we can prevent them doing it.'

He would often attend birthdays, betrothals and other family celebrations and was a solicitous host and undemanding guest. (Though on one occasion when the person giving the dinner had been somewhat offhand and the fare particularly meagre, he murmured politely to his host on leaving, 'I had no idea I was such a good friend of yours.')

As Octavian, the future ruler of Rome had been thrust into the political arena without that nexus of political allies and connections which every elite Roman built up over his political life – one reason why he had been forced to rely so heavily on demagoguery and naked force during the early years. Augustus chose to ally his Julian house closely with the Claudians. He was not only engaged to a Clodia in his youth, and later married Livia and adopted Tiberius, but he made his families' peace with the Marcellan Claudians who had so bitterly opposed Caesar. A Marcellus married one of his sisters and their child married Julia, Augustus' daughter.

The Aemilians, another powerful family which included the ex-triumvir Lepidus, were bound to the Julio-Claudian alliance through marriages, with the younger Julia marrying an Aemilian, and Augustus' ill-fated heir Lucius Caesar betrothed to an Aemilia Lepida. Another Julia – Augustus' great-granddaughter – was married to an Aemilius Paullus. Octavian's great rival Antony was also represented in the imperial family by the children of Antonia, daughter of Octavia and Antony. A shortage of marriageable offspring, combined with Augustus' reluctance to create too many rivals to his immediate family, precluded marriages to other great houses of Rome, though Augustus tried to co-opt the Valerians and Calpurnian Pisos into the imperial project by making them close advisors and colleagues in office. The following quotation shows how Augustus drew the ruling elite into his power.

Sallust, a Cocceius and a Dellius, and his whole inner circle he recruited from opposing parties, his own mercy gave him a Domitius, a Messala, an Asinius, a Cicero and all the flower of the Republic...this mercifulness brought him safety and security and made him popular and beloved even though the necks of the Romans had not been humbled when he laid his hand upon them.
    Seneca *On Mercy* 1.10

In short, Augustus either totally destroyed his enemies or made them his friends, leaving no focal point in the aristocracy about which his enemies could gather. He managed the senate with charm, diplomacy and easy political skill – all abilities which, as clearly as the next Roman, he knew to be lacking in the character of Tiberius, his eventual successor.

1 A bust of Julius Caesar from the Vatican museum. Certainly one of Rome's greatest generals, Caesar was also an outstanding orator and writer. Had Caesar combined these talents with the political genius of his successor Augustus, Rome might have been spared his assassination and a further round of civil wars.

2 (*left*) Bust of Cicero. Cicero joined the senate in the civil war against Caesar, and rejoiced at the latter's assassination, but he wrote to a friend that Caesar was a great orator and had an engaging character. He later allied himself with Caesar's adopted son, Octavian.

3 (*above right*) Pompey was senior to Caesar for most of his career, and even when he became Caesar's son-in-law he was the dominant partner in the relationship. In part it was his envy of Caesar's increased reputation and wealth after his conquests in Gaul that made Pompey turn against him.

4 (*left*) The Roman senate house as it appears today. This building had a tempestuous career and was destroyed or damaged several times. In the year of Caesar's birth a rebel tribune was stoned to death with its roof tiles, and the repaired building was burned down during the funeral of Caesar's contemporary, Clodius.

5 (*above*) A reconstruction of the Roman siege lines at Alesia, modern France. In a famous double siege in September 52 BC the Gauls besieged Caesar, who was in turn besieging Alesia. The Gauls came very close to breaking Caesar's lines. Had they done so, the future of Europe would have been dramatically altered.

6 (*right*) A Gallic warrior, having just killed his wife to save her from slavery, holds her body with one arm even as he defiantly faces his Roman enemies and plunges a sword into his own chest. This Roman depiction of the noble barbarian is reflected also in the writings of historians such as Tacitus. (The sword must be a captured Roman *gladius*, as Gallic swords were generally longer and often blunt-tipped.)

7 (*right*) A bronze bust of Augustus (formerly Octavian) excavated at Meroe and now in the British Museum. Augustus was an adroit propagandist, who ensured that his image was widely distributed on coins, statues and busts so that he was instantly recognizable throughout the Empire.

8 (*below*) A bust believed to be of Lepidus, who was thrust to power through being commander of the only army near to Rome at the time of Caesar's assassination. Though he initially sided with the senate, he later betrayed their cause and formed an alliance with Mark Antony.

9 (*right*) Basalt bust of the young Mark Antony. This bust is unusual in being a slightly idealized depiction. Antony's coins show that by the time he met Cleopatra, good living had rounded his face and added an extra chin.

10 (*above*) Early imperial cameo showing a reclining figure, believed to be Augustus seated beside Victory. The shield prominently displayed is probably a reference to the shield in Virgil's epic poem the *Aeneid* describing Augustus' victories, and the design in the foreground is a reminder of Augustus' capture of Egypt.

11 (*right*) Augustus as a general. This larger-than-life statue was found at Livia's villa at Prima Porta, just outside Rome. The decorations on Augustus' breastplate symbolize the various successes of his career. The cupid at his right leg has the dual role of showing the Julian connection with Venus, and providing extra scaffolding for the weight of the statue.

MVNIF. PI. IX. P. M.
AN. XVIII

12, 13 The Ara Pacis or 'Altar of Peace'. The detail of a frieze on the south side (*above*) depicts members of the Julio-Claudian family in procession. Note the spiked caps of the priests who precede them. This altar, the largest in Rome, was consecrated by Augustus in 9 BC, built entirely of marble, and was part of a complex of buildings on the Campus Martius which included an obelix sundial and the tomb of Augustus itself. The monument was set on a podium and approached by steps. It was almost entirely disassembled during the Middle Ages; the various parts were retrieved from about Rome and the monument reconstructed in the late 1930s.

14 (*above*) A statue of Augustus from when the emperor was almost certainly older than he appears in this image. The sculptor depicts a serene Augustus in a civilian toga, with his head covered. The covering of the head suggests that Augustus was about to sacrifice, which he could do in his capacity of Pontifex Maximus, or as *paterfamilias* of the Julio-Claudian clan.

15 (*right*) Livia and the young Tiberius. The baring of the shoulder is a statuary convention rather than an indication of how Livia (who liked to be thought of as a chaste *materfamilias*) would have appeared in public. As Tiberius' mother, Livia wielded considerable influence over the emperor during the early years of his rule, though this came to be bitterly resented by Tiberius later.

16 (*below*) Wall paintings from the House of Livia. Now in the Rome's National Museum, this wall decoration shows a pleasing garden scene, a retreat from what a later writer called the attempt of wall painters to 'cram mountains into bedrooms'. Paintings such as this decorated the living rooms of most aristocratic families.

From Forum to Palace: The Transfer of Power

The relationship of the Julio-Claudian emperors with the state was pro-foundly affected by the fact that Augustus lived to a ripe old age. From his victory at Actium in 31 BC until his death in AD 14 Augustus slowly gathered power to himself. Diehard republicans were mollified by the fact that these powers were temporary, at least in theory. Even the two constitutional pillars of the principate, the *maius imperium* and the *tribunicia potestas*, needed to be renewed every ten years or so. However, Augustus did not intend to give them up and there was no pressure from senate or people to do so while he used his authority with such restraint and competence. By the end of his reign the institutions of Rome were habituated to autocratic rule, and this became the settled order of things.

As dictator, Julius Caesar's role had been well defined in constitutional terms. A dictator was a supreme commander of the state, appointed to bring a temporary crisis to a swift end. The dictatorship was by definition a short-term post, so a 'dictator for life' was a contradiction in terms, a blatant seizure of regal power which the senate would not tolerate.

Since he wanted to live, Augustus adopted a more subtle approach. He did not put himself at the head of the government. Instead, as he claimed to have done, he handed many of the tasks of government back to the senate and people of Rome. But as he himself points out, he retained his precedence in rank and prestige. He used this, together with his great wealth and greater political skill, to construct a parallel administration which slowly drained the power from the old institutions of the Republic.

For example, democracy seemed restored, in that elections resumed once more. And as Augustus intervened at least twice to prevent bribery, it appears that the results were by no means a foregone conclusion. But the hidden power of the principate ensured that no candidate hostile to Augustus took office, and the popularity of the emperor meant that a hostile candidate would have been defeated in a fair vote anyway. Furthermore, political office in Rome, even the consulship, had always been merely a springboard to power. Republican Romans used their year in office to promote allies, create alliances, and to give offices and contracts to their supporters, building up a reserve of favours owed which could be exchanged for further favours in later years.

Now many of the appointments which republican politicians had used to reward supporters were held by equestrian supporters of Augustus, and the scope of elected officials to deal in contracts and favours was greatly limited. Thus the nexus of power created by holding office was somewhat attenuated. The consuls kept their dignity, but their position became steadily more ceremonial. It became traditional for consuls to resign after six months to allow a replacement (*suffect*) consul to take office, and a consul who held office for only half a year had half the opportunities to increase his influence.

After the consulship, a Roman usually went on to govern a province or command an army, which in the Republic was the key to wealth from extortion or booty. Augustus appointed his own generals, and made it plain to provincial governors that any transgressions would be punished. Provincials found appealing to Caesar much more effective than an appeal to the republican senate had been. Republican senators had all either been or had hoped to be in the position of these robber governors, and naturally took their side. Augustus judged cases on their merits. Nor did he allow the prosecution and condemnation of governors purely for selfish political ends, as republican equestrians had once done when they, instead of the senate, judged trials for extortion. Some governors still abused their powers, and scandals did not stop overnight, but overall the system was stricter and fairer for being under the emperor's control.

Taxation was spread more evenly among the provincials after a series of censuses (including the famous one in Judaea in AD 6 which saw Joseph go to register himself in Bethlehem), and though the infamous private tax companies of the *publicani* continued to gather the taxes, they did so under the control of officials appointed by the emperor. Among Romans in the provinces, it became customary to leave a bequest to the emperor in their wills, a custom which led to an ever-increasing amount of land and property in imperial hands. This was managed by an imperial procurator, which gave Augustus a further presence in the provinces.

To bring the provinces yet more firmly under his personal control, Augustus – who resisted attempts to make himself a god in Rome – was happy to be deified outside Italy, especially in those Eastern provinces where the ruler was customarily worshipped as a god. Indeed, the famous *Res Gestae* comes from just such a temple to Augustus.

Some provinces were governed directly by Augustus himself, and had not proconsuls but *legati* in command. That these imperial legates governed provinces with legionary garrisons was no coincidence. Augustus knew full well that Caesar had seized power as a provincial governor with a loyal army. As the son of Caesar, Augustus had an automatic claim to the loyalty of the troops, but as his principate went on, he relied less on his status as Caesar's son, and looked for more concrete ways to gain the loyalty of a new generation of soldiers. This was the main motive in the establishment of the military treasury which took over the payment of the bounty paid to each soldier on his discharge. In the Republic and the triumvirate, it was the responsibility of the general to see that his soldiers were given a decent stipend when they stood down. Now the state took that responsibility, and Augustus' propaganda made it plain that 'the state' meant the emperor, not the senate.

Nevertheless, it would be a mistake to look at the shift in power from senate to emperor in purely legal and constitutional terms. In Rome, law and the constitution had always been little more than guidelines for the exercise of personal influence and authority. Rome operated on the exchange of favours and influence in a manner which would be regarded as deeply corrupt in a modern society.

In consequence, the atrium of every Roman of any influence was thronged every morning by those seeking favours. At this morning *salutatio*, the Roman patron would find jobs, resolve disputes and give gifts or favourable references to his clients. Augustus was, of course, the supreme *patrone* and it is this power which has caused a recent biography to refer to him as 'the Godfather of Europe'.

If Augustus wanted an appointment for someone, or a law to be passed, it was seldom necessary for him to act officially. A word to a 'friend' at a dinner party or wedding was enough to set the wheels in motion. Everyone knew that Augustus was conscientious in repaying such favours, and no one wanted him as an enemy. It was this, much more than any constitutional change, that gave Augustus supreme power. Throughout the history of the Republic, the elite kept each other in check. What one patron refused, another might grant. If one was unfairly accused by one elite Roman, an ordinary citizen could appeal to a member of an opposing faction for help. And the elite did help, because they needed the electoral support, and would lose *auctoritas* – personal authority – if they appeared afraid of preventing the abuses of power by another.

Under Augustus, none of these checks and balances applied. Augustus was more than a 'super patron' of the old republican type. If ever his dominance of the social machinery of Rome failed him, the emperor personally commanded the loyalty of the legions. The brutal truth was that despite its republican façade, the principate was essentially a military dictatorship.

CHAPTER 5

TIBERIUS: EMPEROR BY DEFAULT

He had that old arrogance which is bred into the bones of the Claudians.
He tried to repress signs of his cruel temper, but every now and then
they broke out. From earliest infancy he had been reared in an imperial
household. Triumphs and consulships were granted him while he was
still a youngster. But even in the years which, under the pretence of
needing privacy, he spent on Rhodes, his thoughts were wrathful,
hypocritical and full of secret sensuality.
Tacitus *Annals* 1.4

The final testament to the political genius of Augustus is that the succession passed smoothly to Tiberius, his designated heir. It was far from certain that this would be so. For although Augustus' long reign had accustomed the Romans to the rule of a single, pre-eminent citizen, this did not mean that control of the Republic could be passed on like a family heirloom. Some hoped that the death of Augustus would end the despotism of the Caesars, while others among the Roman elite considered that if Rome must be ruled by a single individual, they themselves had every much as good a claim to pre-eminence as the Caesars, for the principle of dynastic succession was far from established.

Against this, Livia, Tiberius and Augustus – mother, son and adoptive father – had each worked in their own way to make sure that Tiberius assumed power with a minimum of opposition. Augustus had publicly made Tiberius his successor and had already shifted much of the burden of government to his shoulders. He had also given Tiberius the powers to match, so that on his death Tiberius was already the most powerful man in the Empire. Furthermore, as Augustus' adopted son, Tiberius became the *paterfamilias* ('father of the family') of the house of Caesar. This gave him control of Augustus' fortune, but more importantly, Tiberius inherited the loyalty of Augustus' numerous debtors and clients – and there were few, even among the Roman elite, who did not fall into one of these categories.

Livia had been with Augustus throughout his last days. She surrounded the house with guards, and issued bulletins intended to give the impression that Augustus was recovering. This gained Tiberius time to come to Augustus' bedside, and afterwards to make sure of the loyalty of others who came to pay their respects.

The disloyal might have turned to Agrippa Postumus, natural grandson and adopted son of Augustus. But as soon as Augustus breathed his last, a body of picked soldiers attacked and slew the young exile, who, though alone and unarmed, reputedly put up a desperate fight and was only killed with difficulty. When the centurion who did the deed reported to Tiberius that his orders had been carried out, the discomfited Tiberius replied that he had given no such order. Fevered speculation was calmed by the announcement of a public inquiry into the matter (which was first postponed and then quietly forgotten).

Tiberius did not explain the matter to the senate in any other way, but pretended that his father [Augustus] had left standing orders that those in charge of the prisoner should slay him as soon as they heard of his own death. Undoubtedly Augustus had often complained about the young man's character, and through these complaints had gained the acquiescence of the senate in his banishment. But Augustus was never so callous as to butcher his own kin, and he was not the man to condemn his grandson to death just so that his stepson might feel more secure. More probably Tiberius and Livia, through suspicion, and a stepmother's jealous enmity, hastened to destroy the young man whom they feared and hated.

Tacitus *Annals* 1.6

Thus, almost from the beginning of his history, Tacitus' animus against Tiberius is plain beneath the thinnest veneer of impartiality. In fact, the daughter and granddaughter of Augustus could eloquently testify to Augustus' callousness towards his kin, as could the shade of Caesarion, Augustus' stepbrother by adoption whom Augustus executed when he captured Egypt. Augustus had been merciless in winning the civil war which followed the assassination of Julius Caesar, and one might assume that he would be just as merciless, even with his own family, in ensuring that no such war followed his own death. Whatever faults his stepson possessed, Augustus knew that loyalty and durability were not lacking, and that the Empire would be safe in Tiberius' hands. Yet he had plainly yearned for someone with more flair and charisma.

I know that it is commonly believed that when Tiberius left the
room…Augustus was overheard by his chamberlains to say: 'The poor Roman people, to be ground by those slow-crunching jaws!' I also know that some writers say that Augustus so openly and unreservedly disapproved of Tiberius' austere manners that he sometimes broke off his looser and more carefree conversation when Tiberius came in. Nevertheless, his wife's persuasion caused his grudging adoption, or there may have been a yet more selfish motive, that with such a successor he himself [Augustus] might one day be missed all the more. But in the end I cannot be persuaded that an emperor of the utmost prudence and foresight acted so inconsiderately, especially in a matter of such importance. I believe that after weighing the faults and the virtues of Tiberius, he decided that the virtues were greater. In fact, he swore before the people that he was adopting Tiberius for the good of the state, and in various letters he refers to him as a thoroughly competent general and the sole defence of the Roman people.
    Suetonius *Tiberius* 21

Suetonius did not need to say that in the absence of a Julian emperor, a Claudian was most likely to be accepted by the senate and people of Rome; and Tiberius was a Claudian through and through.

Livia, his mother, was a Claudian from both sides of her family, for all that she bore the name of Livius Drusus, the family into which her formerly Claudian father had been adopted. Livia had married another Claudian, Tiberius Claudius Nero, of the Neronian branch that had distinguished itself in the war against Hannibal more than two centuries before.

Tiberius was born on 16 November 42 BC, in an exclusive residential area at the foot of the Palatine hill in Rome. His future stepfather, then called Octavian, had just joined with Mark Antony and Lepidus to form the triumvirate, and Tiberius' father was a praetor in Rome. Tiberius pater supported Mark Antony and therefore he also supported Antony's wife and brother when they attempted a military coup against Octavian in 41 BC. When this failed, he fled to Sicily and Sextus Pompey, taking his wife and infant son with him. When peace was restored, he returned to Rome, perhaps already a sick man. He obediently divorced Livia when Octavian ordered him to and died soon afterwards.

Tiberius was only three years old, and consequently all his memories would have been those of an imperial prince, with Augustus as his step-father. Like most young aristocrats, he learned Greek and became fluent in that language. He developed a taste for literature, and was so knowledgeable in mythology that he gave his tutors extemporaneous quizzes on the subject. Among several attempts at Greek poetry, he wrote an *Elegy on the Death of Lucius Caesar* which has not survived, perhaps because Tiberius' writing style was laboured, extravagant and pedantic, though he was considered a good extempore speaker.

He was a sturdy young man, taller than average. As a teenager he was grievously afflicted with pimples, but his health was generally sound. Suetonius tells us that he walked with a rigid gait, and that his left hand was strong enough for him to drive his thumb right through a fresh apple. Though he spoke seldom, his speech was vigorous and to the point, often accompanied by emphatic gestures.

We are given the impression of an intelligent, yet rather withdrawn young man who was overshadowed by a household of dominant personalities, and keenly aware of his lack of Julian charisma and mercurial talent. Perhaps as a reaction to this, Tiberius grew his hair long at the back, emphasizing his Claudian origins by adopting a hairstyle peculiar to his family.

23 Bust of Tiberius. After domination of the state by two Julians, it was the turn of a Claudian. It would be another generation before the lines of the two families combined to produce a truly Julio-Claudian emperor in Gaius Caligula.

Tiberius followed the tradition of aristocratic youths of the Roman Republic and joined the army while a teenager. In 25 BC, in his seventeenth year, he began his uniformly successful military career by fighting against rebels in Cantabria in Spain. In that year his stepsister Julia married another Claudius, Claudius Marcellus, whom Augustus adopted as a son (Marcellus died two years later from illness). Tiberius became a quaestor, and successfully prosecuted the aristocrat Fannius Caepio for conspiring against Augustus. His steadiness and aptitude for hard work made him a natural choice for Augustus to take on a tour of the Eastern provinces. In 20 BC following diplomatic negotiations, Tiberius took back from the Parthians the standards which Crassus had lost at the battle of Carrhae in 53 BC. Augustus also delegated to Tiberius the task of settling the Armenian succession, which he did efficiently and without fuss.

These diplomatic actions needed to be given to a subordinate who could credibly shoulder the blame if things went wrong, but who could not object if Augustus took the credit, as he did (*Res Gestae* 27, though Tiberius receives an honourable mention).

On returning to Rome, both Tiberius and his brother Drusus were married. Tiberius wed Vipsania, daughter of Augustus' second-in-command Agrippa, and his younger brother married Antonia, daughter of Octavia (Augustus' sister) and the ex-triumvir Mark Antony.

As with all Julio-Claudians, Tiberius enjoyed accelerated progress through the *cursus honorum*. Augustus took him and Drusus to Gaul, where over the next four years Tiberius first governed as propraetor, and then led a campaign against wild Alpine tribesmen. In the course of his campaign against the Rhaetian and Vindelician tribes Tiberius took to the waters of Lake Constance to oppose an enemy fleet in one of the very few naval battles ever to take place in Switzerland. In recognition of his efforts he was made consul in 13 BC. His colleague was Quintilius Varus, the man who, as we have seen, later lost three legions in the Teutoburg forest.

Tiberius' future seemed reasonably clear. He was established as a conscientious administrator, diplomat and general, evidently suited to high command within the imperial system. He can hardly have expected to command the system itself, since Agrippa was Augustus' probable successor, and after him, his children by Julia. Yet after Agrippa's death in 12 BC Augustus chose Tiberius as the new husband of the twice-widowed Julia. Tiberius was compelled to divorce Vipsania and become Augustus' son-in-law as well as his stepson.

Tiberius took this very badly. He was in love with Vipsania, and he knew, as did everyone else, that Julia had wanted to start an adulterous affair with him while she was still married to Agrippa. Tiberius deeply regretted his divorce. Once when he accidentally later caught sight of Vipsania, he followed her with tears in his eyes and such misery written all over his face that steps were taken to prevent the two ever coming into contact again.

Suetonius *Tiberius* 7

Tiberius had little chance of domesticity with Julia – Rome's armies were on the move again, with the sons of Livia at their head. Drusus led a push to the river Elbe in Germany, and Tiberius undertook the dour struggle in the Balkans against the Illyrian and Thracian tribes.

Drusus defeated first the Frisians and then the Cherusci in 11 BC, bringing much of northwestern Germany under Roman control. Another successful campaign against the Chatti added middle Germany

24 *Members of the imperial family thought to be (from left to right) Agrippa, one of Julia's children, Julia and Tiberius, in a frieze on the Ara Pacis. This massive 'Altar of Peace' was a magnificent combination of art and propaganda which depicted the ideals of the Augustan age and glorified the imperial family.*

to Rome's conquests, and in a final drive, Drusus reached the Elbe in 9 BC, taking the Roman eagles as far into Germany as they would ever get. But Drusus broke his leg when his horse fell and landed on him. His forces were already pulling back towards the Rhine, but they hastened that withdrawal when the broken leg became infected.

When word reached him that Drusus was ill, Tiberius hurried north to find his brother on his deathbed. Afterwards Tiberius accompanied the bier to Rome, walking in front of it for the whole way. Both Augustus and Tiberius delivered funeral eulogies for Drusus and laid his ashes to rest in the family mausoleum.

With Drusus gone, Tiberius took up his task in Germany, and did so all the more gladly since his marriage to Julia had degenerated into mutual loathing. The son Julia had given Tiberius had died in infancy and now Julia wrote to her father Augustus with bitter complaints and accusations, and began to spread rumours denigrating Tiberius among her many associates in Rome. This must have been doubly galling for Tiberius, since he could hardly insult Augustus by divorcing his daughter, yet he must also have been aware of Julia's numerous adulterous affairs.

Among his legionaries Claudius Tiberius Nero became known as Biberius Caldius Mero ('boozer flushed with strong wine'). Yet despite his domestic distractions, he was a commander of skill and discretion who governed the newly conquered people with moderation. Back from Germany he became consul for the second time in 7 BC, and thereafter he received the tribunician power, one of the main constitutional powers of the principate and the basis of Augustus' own rule.

25 Coin of Drusus. The legend on the coin establishes Drusus as the brother of Tiberius, son of the divine Augustus. Drusus was the father of Germanicus Caesar, whose children had a central role in the history of the family thereafter.

Exile and Return

Tiberius was now the second citizen of the Empire after Augustus. With Augustus he held the tribunician power, he was a respected general who had celebrated a triumph and received an ovation, he was a politician who had been quaestor, praetor and consul – a formidable record for a man still in his mid-thirties. In 6 BC he received yet further responsibilities and honours – the *maius imperium* and a command in the East. Yet suddenly Tiberius announced that he was tired of public office and wanted a break. He was going on indefinite leave of absence.

This decision was as inexplicable to Tiberius' contemporaries as to later historians. Augustus complained publicly in the senate of desertion by his most trusted subordinate, while Livia bombarded her son with entreaties to change his mind. With true Claudian stubbornness, Tiberius not only refused to listen, but actually went on hunger strike for four days until he was grudgingly allowed to leave.

He might have been motivated by his intense dislike of Julia, and frustration at being unable to charge her with adultery or divorce her for any other reason. Perhaps he decided not to bore his compatriots by remaining too long in the public eye, indeed he might even enhance his reputation by a spell away from Rome, to where he would triumphantly return when his services were desperately required. Others say that he had waited until his two adopted sons and Augustus' grandchildren, Gaius and Lucius, were of age and he now voluntarily stepped down from his position as second citizen of the Empire in order to leave the political sphere for them without a rival. Indeed, this is the reason which Tiberius himself afterwards gave.
Suetonius *Tiberius* 10

There may have been some deeper motive which is now forever lost; or there may have been no single reason – none of the motives which Suetonius gives are mutually exclusive. Tiberius was young, he had no doubts of his own worth, and presumably even fewer doubts that once his leave was done, he would resume his former position in the imperial hierarchy.

Consequently, he made a hurried departure from Ostia, leaving Drusus, his son by Vipsania, in the care of female relatives. While his ship was off Campania, word reached him that Augustus was unwell. Tiberius delayed, waiting for further news; but when that news revealed that he was believed to be waiting in the wings for the best moment to seize power, he ordered his ship to set out immediately for Rhodes.

On Rhodes, once his *imperium* had expired, Tiberius did away with most of the accoutrements of his rank and appeared to enjoy his holiday. He attended debates in the local gymnasium and even took part in one. (He was roundly abused by one of the other participants, who was afterwards hauled off to jail as a reminder that Tiberius' tolerance had limits.) In an incident that reveals much about his character, Tiberius expressed a wish to visit the sick on the island. His instructions were misunderstood, and the sick were hauled from their sickbeds and placed in the forum for him to inspect. The shocked and mortified Tiberius went to each of the invalids and personally apologized for the inconvenience.

Then came the news that someone (probably Livia) had summoned the courage to tell Augustus what his daughter had been up to. Augustus was stunned to discover his daughter's penchant for drunken fornication, in one instance allegedly on the speaker's rostrum of the forum. An Appius Claudius and a Sempronius Gracchus were involved, the bearers of names revered in the Roman Republic. Iullus Antonius, the son of Mark Antony, committed suicide rather than face Augustus in his cold fury.

Tiberius was informed that Julia had been exiled to the island of Pandateria, and, incidentally, that he had been divorced. With his own conduct vindicated, Tiberius wrote to Augustus attempting to heal the rift between father and daughter. With his marriage to Julia over, Tiberius seems to have felt little antagonism towards his ex-wife, whom he allowed to keep all the gifts he had given in the early years of their marriage. Revealingly, Tiberius told Augustus that he was now ready to return to Rome. His timing was unfortunate, for Augustus was still furious. He wrote back that Tiberius had chosen to go into exile, and he, Augustus, would decide when he could return.

Gaius and Lucius were now of age, which meant that Augustus needed Tiberius less, and the emperor had evidently been personally wounded when Tiberius left Rome in the first place. The mentor of Gaius was now Marcus Lollius, whom Tiberius had once succeeded as governor of Gaul and upon whose incompetence Tiberius had made scathing comments. When Gaius travelled east on his first military command, Tiberius visited him at the island of Samos. Lollius made the occasion as difficult as possible, and cultivated an atmosphere of hostility towards Tiberius. At a later dinner party someone mentioned 'the exile', as Tiberius was now known. A young man leapt up and told Gaius he needed only to say the word and the head of Tiberius would be presented to him. Gaius politely declined.

Informers brought tales of seditious behaviour by Tiberius, who was regularly visited by dignitaries travelling to and from the Eastern provinces. Despite his anger, Augustus seems to have trusted Tiberius' loyalty and simply referred the reports to him for comment. Tiberius knew his enemies in Rome would continue to blacken his name and asked that some trusted person be sent to keep watch on him. Augustus was not prepared to double the number of trusted subordinates wasting time on Rhodes, and declined the request.

Nevertheless, Tiberius abandoned his exercises on horseback, and took to wearing an unmartial Greek cloak. He redoubled his petitions to be recalled from exile, causing Augustus to joke about his 'youthful zeal' (Tiberius was now forty-two). Augustus consulted Gaius, perhaps to see how his heir would deal with the matter. Gaius had recently fallen out with Lollius and replied that he would welcome Tiberius back in Rome so long as he took no part in politics, thus explicitly warning Tiberius not to challenge his position as Augustus' designated successor.

Nor did Tiberius do so. He had spent seven years on Rhodes, and now spent another two living quietly in Rome. Gaius Caesar went east to establish a military reputation, but instead took a wound which cost him his life. His death, in AD 4, shifted the political landscape in Rome. Lucius, the younger brother of Gaius, had died two years before, so Augustus was again without heir. The only candidates were Agrippa, the moody and unpredictable son of Julia, Germanicus, the nineteen-year-old nephew of Tiberius, and Tiberius himself. Agrippa was evidently unsuitable, and Germanicus young and untried, so Augustus bowed to the inevitable and adopted Tiberius into the line of the Caesars – with the implication that he had more or less reached the bottom of the barrel.

However reached, the decision was vindicated, for the next decade saw the Empire prosper. Augustus the wily political operator and

Tiberius the grimly efficient executive made a splendid team. Their partnership was tested by adversity, for the years AD 6–9 saw a military emergency which threatened the Empire.

The problems started in Illyricum. Tiberius had campaigned successfully before in this Balkan province, but the area had not been totally subjugated. When he heard of a major revolt, Tiberius hastened from his winter quarters in Germany. He was accompanied by a young quaestor called Velleius Paterculus, who later wrote a history in which he praised Tiberius' care for the men under his command.

If any of us fell ill, his health and welfare was looked after as though this was the main preoccupation of [Tiberius] Caesar, quite apart from his other heavy responsibilities. There was a horse-drawn vehicle for those who had need of it, and even his own litter was available. I, among others, have enjoyed its use….
Velleius Paterculus *History* 114.4

Velleius also mentions a heroic action by Valerius Messala, a friend of Augustus, and a general of a noble house which was soon to enjoy even closer links with the Julio-Claudians. Another general who was given the opportunity to distinguish himself was Marcus Lepidus – a sign that the families of the triumvirs were becoming ever more closely linked with the Julio-Claudians.

This war was concluded early in AD 9 and Tiberius returned home in triumph. He had just five days to rest before the news arrived that Quintilius Varus, his consular colleague of 13 BC, had been killed in Germany, and with him the bulk of the garrison on the Rhine. Augustus was distraught – he who was so proud of regaining the eagles lost by Crassus at Carrhae had himself lost three more. The Empire's troubleshooter-in-chief was immediately sent north.

With hastily levied legions shored up with veterans from the Pannonian campaigns, Tiberius led punitive expeditions over the Rhine for the next three years in succession. For the first of these campaigns, he was ably assisted by Germanicus, his nephew.

One of the terms of Tiberius' adoption by Augustus was that Tiberius should adopt Germanicus as his heir. As might be expected of one second in the imperial succession, Germanicus had an accelerated career. In

26 *Detail of the* Gemma Augustea, *a cameo dating from about 10 BC commemorating Tiberius' successful campaigns in Raetia and Pannonia. From left, the figure of Victory looks on approvingly as Tiberius, in triumphal dress, steps from his chariot to greet the enthroned goddess Roma and deified Augustus. The young Roman officer is probably Germanicus.*

AD 12 he served in Rome as consul. When Germanicus returned to the Rhine, Tiberius handed command over to him and left the frontier. Augustus was in obvious decline and Tiberius wanted to be at his side. He was never to leave Italy again.

Emperor

Tiberius used his tribunician power to convene a meeting of the senate, and there he officially broke the news of Augustus' death. After reading a few words of a prepared speech, he groaned that grief had taken his voice, and the task of reading the rest of the speech was given to his son Drusus, to whom Tiberius handed the scroll. A freedman then read Augustus' will.

Suetonius *Tiberius* 23

Rome's new emperor gave the strong impression that he did not want the job. With his usual cynicism, Tacitus suggests that this was a ruse by which Tiberius intended to flush out opposition to his rule. But, unlike Julius Caesar who had relished the cut and thrust of political life (at least while the cut and thrust had remained metaphorical), and Augustus who not only enjoyed politics but was also good at it, Tiberius was always deeply ill at ease in the snake pit of factions, rivalries and ambition which made up Roman political life – although his distaste for politics did not stop him from mastering the game, and compensating with ruthlessness what he lacked in charm.

Tiberius strongly warned the populace against repeating the unrest which had marked the death of Julius Caesar, and helped with legislation to make Augustus a god, as Julius Caesar had been before him. On Livia's behalf, Tiberius turned down many of the honours proposed for her, and asserted that he intended to be equally circumspect about his own titles.

Though he was already emperor in fact, Tiberius was so slow to accept the name that one senator complained, 'Some people are slow in doing what they have promised; you are slow to promise what you have already done.' Eventually Tiberius, who had been trying to shift a part of the responsibility for decision-making back to the senate, agreed to serve 'at least until I grow so old that you might be kind enough to allow me rest'. This was a good point – at fifty-six years of age, Tiberius had come late to the career of emperor.

This first meeting of the senate showed first of all that Tiberius lacked his predecessor's skill at handling that fractious body, and secondly that many senators did not accept Tiberius as Augustus' successor, and indeed saw no reason why Augustus should have a successor at all. Tension between *imperator* and senate was a defining feature of the Julio-Claudian dynasty, and this meeting signalled that the relative truce under Augustus was nearing its end.

Nor was only the senate restless. When word of the change of regime reached the garrisons along the Rhine and Danube, they rose in mutiny. The main grievances were the length of service and severe punishments and extortion by the centurions. In the rioting and disorder which followed, some centurions were killed and civilian villas looted.

Tiberius sent his son Drusus to the mutineers on the Danube, and posted with him Aelius Sejanus, a promising young officer. Drusus put down the mutiny and executed the ringleaders, while Germanicus, the designated successor of Tiberius, did the same on the Rhine. Fortunately for Germanicus, much of the army remained loyal, and he won others back with some well-timed concessions. The remainder he shamed back to the standards by pointedly sending his wife Agrippina to safety with their young child Gaius (the future emperor Gaius Caligula).

Tiberius was criticized for remaining in Rome throughout this dangerous uprising, since his reputation with the army meant that he personally could have quickly restored order. But Tiberius may have considered that these mutinies were suspiciously well-timed and coordinated. If they had been instigated by senatorial enemies, then Tiberius would not leave the fountainhead of the problem in Rome to deal with its symptoms on the frontier. To warn the senators that he was not to be trifled with, Tiberius sent soldiers to kill the aristocratic Sempronius Gracchus on the island where he had been exiled for his affair with Tiberius' ex-wife Julia.

The legions of the Rhine were distracted from their grievances by going into action. Rome had not finished with Arminius, leader of the Cherusci and architect of the ambush which had killed Varus and the men of three legions. Germanicus pushed deep into Rome's lost lands and found the site of the massacre. Modern archaeologists have recently done the same, and found bones weathered by years in the open which had then been reverently entombed by the soldiers of Germanicus. Germanicus captured Arminius' wife and son, but was unable either to capture Arminius himself, or to defeat him convincingly in battle.

In Rome it was whispered that Germanicus' increasing popularity with the troops was causing Tiberius unease, and rumours of plots and treason swirled about the capital. One of the Marcellans, Granius Marcellus, was accused of knocking the head off a statue of Augustus and substituting Marcellus' own. It was also claimed that he had talked insultingly of both the late and the present emperor. When the question of treason was put to the senate, Tiberius allowed the accused to go free rather than allow his evident fury to influence the vote. Perhaps he, like Augustus, was mindful of the fate of Julius Caesar, for he avoided any overt demonstration that his power was so much greater than any other senator's. Tiberius certainly considered himself a senator, and conducted himself accordingly.

27 *Coin of Germanicus. Note the inscription associating him with the family of Caesar, and the typically Claudian features and hairstyle. Germanicus was adored by the Roman people, who avidly followed his career.*

He so disliked flattery that he would not let senators near his litter, either for business or even to exchange greetings. Once an ex-consul came to apologize for some offence. He made as if to embrace his [the emperor's] knees as though he were a supplicant, causing Tiberius to back off so rapidly that he fell over backwards. If anyone, in either conversation or oration, addressed him too fulsomely, Tiberius would sternly interrupt and correct the offending phrase. Once, when he was addressed as 'Dominus' [Lord and master], he said that he never wished to be insulted like that again…moreover, he imperturbably ignored abuse, slander and lampoons about himself and his household, often remarking that freedom of thought and speech was the mark of a free country.

Suetonius *Tiberius* 27–29

For all his moderation, Augustus had faced several attempts on his life and rule, and Tiberius had no doubt that he would face similar challenges. There had in fact already been an abortive uprising by one of Agrippa's slaves, who pretended to be his dead master. When the man was captured he was brought before Tiberius who asked him, 'And how did you become Agrippa, then?' The slave grinned and retorted, 'The same way that you became Caesar.'

By AD 17, it was clear that Germany would remain unconquered for the foreseeable future. Tiberius remarked that for all their glory, Germanicus' victories were wholly ineffective and more than the country could afford. Of all the Julio-Claudian emperors, Tiberius was the most careful with money (the imperial budget had both an annual surplus and a huge cash reserve by the end of his reign). It was probably reluctance to waste money on futile campaigns more than jealousy of Germanicus which caused the latter's recall to Rome. On his arrival, Germanicus was awarded a lavish triumph and promptly dispatched to the east of the Empire.

To the admirers of Germanicus who protested that their hero had been given too little time in Rome, Tiberius responded that it was the fate of the imperial heir to serve in distant corners of the Empire, as his personal experience could testify. Cappadocia had only just become a Roman province, Judaea was restless, and there was friction with Parthia. Furthermore, the region had been shaken by a violent earthquake, and a member of the imperial house was required to add moral support to the substantial sums of money already sent for rebuilding.

To counterbalance the dashing young general and his glittering entourage, Tiberius appointed as governor of the important province of Syria the gruff unbending Calpurnius Piso, son of one of Julius Caesar's bitterest enemies. Piso was an aristocrat of the old school and unlikely to be swayed by Julio-Claudian charisma. Also, Piso's wife Plancina was one of Livia's closest friends. There was some tension at this time between Tiberius and Livia, who was finding that she had less influence as an emperor's mother than she had exercised as an emperor's wife. Consequently, Tiberius probably considered the temporary removal from Rome of one of his mother's allies as a further bonus.

Germanicus went east, where cities vied to outdo each other in competing for his favour. After pausing at Actium to view the scene of the battle in 31 BC between his grandfather Mark Antony and his great-uncle Augustus, Germanicus went to Athens and then to Asia Minor. On the Euphrates he had an interview with King Artabanus III of Parthia, which did much to dispel tension between the two empires.

Sadly, the famous diplomacy and charm of Germanicus left Piso untouched. Piso flatly refused an order to lead troops into Armenia, where Germanicus was deeply involved in arranging the succession of the monarchy to a pro-Roman king. Meanwhile, relations were never less than poisonous between Germanicus' wife Agrippina, the daughter of Julia, and Plancina, friend of Livia, the woman who had been instrumental in getting Julia exiled.

If Germanicus had gone east as an ambassador, Piso would have been quite right to ignore his orders, but Germanicus almost certainly had *maius imperium*, as had Tiberius and Agrippa when on similar missions. Therefore, Piso was being downright treasonable unless, as many suspected, he was under orders from Tiberius to ensure that the almost limitless power and admiration that Germanicus had received did not go to his head. Germanicus demonstrated why Tiberius may have had reservations by impetuously going to Egypt, from which all Roman senators were barred. Germanicus had received word of a famine, and on his arrival he promptly took charge, ordering the imperial grain houses opened, and the corn therein sold at a reasonable price.

In this Germanicus had acted expeditiously, but he unwisely prolonged his stay by playing the tourist among the antiquities of Egypt. It is quite possible that while on his expeditions up the Nile he contracted malaria, with devastating consequences for the Roman Empire as a whole. On his return to Syria Germanicus found that Piso had rescinded and amended many of his edicts. In a fury, he ordered Piso out of the province.

Piso left, but halted his journey at Antioch when word reached him that Germanicus was gravely ill. Not wanting to leave Syria without a commander, he sent envoys to inquire after Germanicus' health. Germanicus was not only sick, but dying, and convinced that Piso had poisoned him. He officially renounced his friendship with Piso and made his friends swear to avenge his death. He also unequivocally ordered Piso to resume his journey to Rome. Piso set off, but by the time he reached the island of Cos, Germanicus was dead. Piso received the news with grim satisfaction, his wife with outright rejoicing.

Piso returned to Syria, despite the warnings of his son that it would be far wiser to proceed to Rome as ordered. In Syria, Piso was seized by the governor whom Germanicus had left behind, and dispatched ignominiously back to Rome where public opinion was overwhelmingly against him. Rome was in an orgy of grief at the death of the Empire's favourite son, and sympathy was high for the widowed Agrippina. Tiberius did his best to calm public sentiment and arranged for the ashes of Germanicus to be interred in a quiet ceremony, during which the crowds were kept well away. Neither Tiberius, Livia nor Antonia (Germanicus' mother) made a public appearance or gave any statement about the tragedy.

Inevitably, Piso was brought to trial. The charge of poisoning proved impossible to sustain, as Tacitus explains with the relish of a hardened jurist.

The best the prosecution could allege was that at a banquet given by Germanicus, the food had been tampered with by Piso who sat higher up the table from him [and so was served earlier]. But it was ridiculous to suppose that he would have dared to do such a thing under the noses of servants he did not know, among so many possible witnesses, and before Germanicus himself. Furthermore, the defendant offered his slaves for questioning by torture, and insisted the same be meted out to the attendants who had been at the banquet.

Tacitus *Annals* 3.11

More serious was the charge that Piso had interfered with the decrees of Germanicus, suborned the loyalty of the soldiers, and attempted to seize back Syria by force when he returned to the province. Nor did it help Piso's case that the senate before whom he was tried could hear the baying of a restless mob as it destroyed any statues of Piso which it could find.

Tiberius remained studiously neutral. 'To you, his [Piso's] advocates, I urge each to help him in his peril as far as your eloquence and diligence can do. And I urge the prosecutors to similar exertions…. Let no notice be taken of my own sorrow, or the tears of Drusus. This case should be tried in the same manner as any other.' He also ordered the statues of Piso overthrown by the mob to be restored.

Since Germanicus outranked Piso with his *maius imperium*, Piso was guilty of flagrant disobedience and armed mutiny. A guilty verdict was inevitable and Piso, foreseeing this, forestalled it by suicide. Tiberius left matters at that and took no action against the rest of the family, though some of his supporters, such as Valerius Messala, urged that Tiberius should exploit the moment to purge his opponents.

That the entire affair benefited Tiberius is the one reason for crediting accusations that his influence lay behind the death of Germanicus. His only credible rival was gone, and the way was clear for the succession of his son Drusus. Furthermore, Livilla, the wife of Drusus (and ex-wife of Augustus' intended heir Gaius) had just given birth to twins, much to the emperor's delight.

The rest of Rome was less excited about the succession reverting to the direct Claudian line, for Drusus was both violent and dissipated, though a good soldier and politician. Drusus and his supposed rival Germanicus had got on well together and, after the death of Germanicus, Drusus took particular care of his cousin's sons. However, a new rivalry was growing between Drusus and Aelius Sejanus, the man who had risen to become Tiberius' *de facto* second-in-command.

The Rise of Sejanus

He [Sejanus] had a body which could endure hardship, and a daring spirit. He protected himself while he attacked others, he was as servile as he was imperious. He pretended humility towards the world, but his heart lusted for supremacy. To attain this, he could be lavish and splendid, but more often he was energetic and watchful – something just as damaging to the state when it is done for the hypocritical purpose of obtaining supreme power.

Tacitus *Annals* 4.1

In AD 20 Tiberius had been in power for six years. He had governed with moderation, and Rome had prospered both economically and in its foreign wars. (Indeed, that very year, Drusus celebrated an ovation for victories over the German king Maroboduus.) Tiberius kept good governors in power longer than the traditional year (in one case for a record twenty-five years), but supervised them closely. Once he ordered a governor to reverse a steep rise in taxes, saying, 'I want my sheep shorn, not skinned.' The peace and prosperity brought by the Caesars' rule was their underlying strength. The previous century of civil unrest, proscription and warfare had been so traumatic and ruinous that the common people of the state were prepared to support even a dictator, so long as he remained benevolent.

The senate were less content. The aristocratic families had long memories and many saw the Julio-Claudians as a faction which unfairly monopolized power. They bitterly resented Tiberius as the vehicle by which Augustus had passed on power to the next generation, especially since, after three generations, this monopoly was becoming entrenched.

There were tensions too within the Julio-Claudian faction. Livia was a lonely and increasingly isolated figure, estranged from her son and loathed by the Julians – currently represented by Agrippina, the daughter of the exiled Julia. Yet even in Agrippina's children the blood of the Caesars mingled with that of the Claudians, since Germanicus had himself been a grandson of Livia. It is probable that about Agrippina a secret alliance began to form between reactionary senators, ambitious Julians and enemies of Sejanus.

Tiberius was too good a politician to be unaware of this, and he increasingly gave his trust to Sejanus, an outsider wholly dependent on Tiberius for his political survival. Sejanus was not a Roman, but an Etruscan, and not a senator, but an equestrian – that order of the Roman upper class just below the rank of senator. Like his father before him, he was commander of the Praetorian Guard, the elite squad of soldiers formed by Augustus principally to protect the imperial house. Now, with its units combined into a single barracks near the Viminal hill, the Praetorian Guard had become the most significant military force in Rome, a fact which gave its commander no little political significance.

Like another Etruscan before him, Maecenas, Sejanus was a polished sophisticate on whom the emperor relied for information of rumours and plots in the capital. Sejanus had another weapon in his arsenal: professional informers known as 'delators'. Delators had originally been freelance agents employed by the treasury to locate tax defaulters, but under Tiberius their role included reporting those guilty of *maiestas* – a statute which was basically the charge of bringing the Roman Empire into disrepute. Because this charge was so all-encompassing, it was a handy weapon for use against senators suspected of treason.

A poet who had written a widely admired elegy to Germanicus was discovered to have prepared another for Drusus when the imperial heir became ill. Drusus recovered, and the poet was charged before the senate and executed. This was done without the knowledge of Tiberius, who afterwards ordained that those whom the senate condemned should not be executed before he had been given time to review the sentence. By killing the unfortunate poet, the senate seems to have been trying to discredit the imperial administration by the meticulous and small-minded application of its edicts in the most unreasonable way – a form of industrial protest known in modern Britain as 'working to rule'. As the historian G. P. Baker has written, 'Tradition has done less than justice to the senate. Much of what later ages supposed to be servility was sarcasm.'

Tiberius had an ambivalent relationship with the senate. He publicly deferred to it, standing when the consuls approached, and giving way to their retinue in the street. He wanted a strong and independent senate, yet whenever it acted as such, his nervousness and discomfort were evident. Many senators took the easy route and plied Tiberius with all the flattery he could stomach.

So corrupted and debased was that age by sycophancy that not just the leading citizens (who were forced to save their grandeur by servility) but every ex-consul, most of the former praetors and a host of lesser senators eagerly competed to propose preposterous and shameful motions. Tradition says that

Tiberius often used to leave the senate house saying to himself in Greek, 'How ready these men are to be slaves.' Evidently he too, despite his dislike of public freedom, was disgusted at the abject abasement of his creatures.

Tacitus *Annals* 3.65

In AD 20 Sallustius Crispus died. Sallustius had been an unwavering supporter of the regime, a hard man who was trusted with delicate and unsavoury missions – he was for example deeply involved in the killing of Agrippa Postumus. In AD 21 Drusus was elevated to the tribunician power, explicitly marking him as Tiberius' successor. Drusus was bitterly resentful of Sejanus, and often complained of him to Tiberius. He once took his fists to the Etruscan, possibly because he suspected the growing intimacy between Sejanus and his own wife Livilla. His suspicions were justified. It is highly probable that Livilla had a secret affair with Sejanus. Livilla took her aunt's doctor Eudemus into her confidence and used him as a go-between for her assignations. Despite her precautions, Livilla must have been terrified of suffering the fate of the Julias, Augustus' adulterous daughter and granddaughter. She was also ambitious for her sons. Eventually, perhaps persuaded by Sejanus, she decided to dispose of Drusus by poison. Another physician, a eunuch called Lygdus, supplied a potion which Livilla allegedly administered to Drusus personally.

The illness and subsequent death of his heir and only child hit Tiberius hard, though in the best Roman tradition he tried not to show it. He attended the senate regularly through Drusus' illness and even in the period between Drusus' death and funeral. When an embassy from Ilium (on the site of ancient Troy) arrived much later bearing condolences for the death of the emperor's son, Tiberius commented with wintry humour on their delay by offering his condolences to them for the death of their fellow citizen Hector, over a thousand years before.

Tiberius immersed himself in work, and with his usual hard impartiality decided that the children of Germanicus (once his designated successor) were more suitable heirs than his own grandchildren. Accordingly, two of Germanicus' offspring, Nero and another Drusus, were marked for the succession. The feud between Sejanus and Agrippina was rapidly coming to dominate political life in Rome. This decision, favouring the children of Agrippina, inflamed matters further. Sejanus had gathered the scattered units of the Praetorian Guard into a single bar-racks at the edge of Rome, making himself master of the city's military power, but he received a further setback when Tiberius refused to allow him to marry Livilla.

Agrippina was getting the worst of the campaign. She was allied with several senators who opposed Tiberius and were increasingly blatant about showing it. This allowed Sejanus to pick them off with treason charges. These trials, few in the early years, became more numerous, directly reflecting the heightened political tension. A Claudia Pulchra, of the once-senior house of the Claudian clan, was accused of adultery and exiled. As Claudia was a close friend of Agrippina, this signalled that the widow of Germanicus could not protect her own.

In a fury, Agrippina went to Tiberius whom she found sacrificing to an image of Augustus. How could he, she demanded, worship the man yet persecute his descendants? The spirit of Augustus had not passed into the statue, but into herself, his granddaughter. Tiberius responded by taking her hand and quoting to her a Greek verse, 'Have I done wrong to you, my daughter, because you do not rule?'

Relations between the two continued to deteriorate. Agrippina asked for permission to remarry, which Tiberius refused. Thereafter, whenever she was summoned to an imperial meal, Agrippina refused to eat, making it plain that she feared poison. Livia now joined in by releasing letters of Augustus, selecting those which showed Augustus' opinions of Tiberius in the least flattering light. It was too much for Tiberius. He was now sixty-seven years old, and had received little appreciation for a lifetime of service to the state. His kinsfolk loathed him, the senate was treacher-ous, and even his own mother had turned on him.

Though he occasionally needed and followed his mother's advice, he strongly disliked people thinking that he was doing so. He was bitterly offended when [in AD 14] the senate proposed adding 'son of Livia' to his honorifics [which, given the senate's talent for sarcasm, may have been why they did it]…. He often warned Livia to remember that she was a woman and that she should not interfere with the governance of the state.

Suetonius *Tiberius* 50

Almost the whole of Tiberius' reign had so far been spent in Rome. He had so often prepared to leave Rome on business only to cancel at the last moment that he was nicknamed 'Callipedes', after a comedian whose stage trick was to appear to be running at full speed without moving an inch. When Tiberius did leave, in AD 26, it was to dedicate a temple in Campania. Passing by the island of Capri, he was struck by its beauty and tranquillity.

It is unlikely that Tiberius originally intended his stay in Capri to be more than a brief respite from his family and the hosts of petitioners and hangers-on who dogged his footsteps everywhere in Rome. But gradually it dawned on him that there were advantages in administration from a distance, with the senate operating more autonomously, and Sejanus keeping an eye on subversive elements who might take advantage of his absence. Chief among the latter were Agrippina and her son Nero (not the future emperor by that name), whom Tiberius made no secret about keeping under surveillance. His faith in Sejanus was all the greater since a dining room built into a natural grotto collapsed while Tiberius was dining there. Sejanus protected the emperor by shielding him with his own body from the falling rocks.

28 Tiberius' villa on Capri. The luxury and isolation of this island retreat inspired rumours that Tiberius had withdrawn there to lead a life of debauchery. Pique at the reluctance of their emperor to live among them may have made many in Rome eager to believe such scandal.

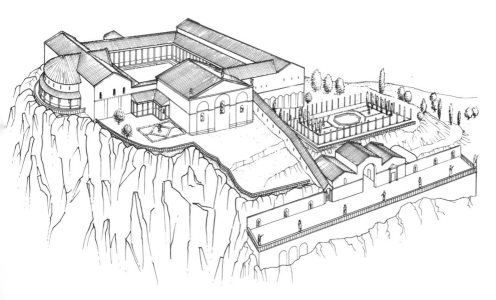

As Sejanus was clearly a creature of Tiberius, it was certainly in his interest to protect his master, with whom his fortunes were so closely linked. Sejanus was aware of his vulnerability, and was actively trying to construct a power base independent of the emperor, allying himself with the faction opposed to Agrippina and her sons. A further casualty of this power struggle was one Sabinus, a former friend of Germanicus. He was accused – with how much justification it is now impossible to tell – of canvassing support against Tiberius, and duly executed.

Another death which occurred at this time was that of the younger Julia, after twenty years of exile on the island of Trimerum. In her final years Julia had received considerable support from Livia, possibly from a combination of guilt at her part in Julia's downfall, and to annoy her son, who still despised both Julia and her daughter Agrippina.

In fact Livia was now the main protector of Agrippina and her children against the increasingly bold attacks of Sejanus and his faction. It was probably she who persuaded Tiberius to allow Agrippina's daughter (also called Agrippina) to marry, and even personally to give the girl to her new husband, Gnaeus Domitius, of the ancient family of the Domitii Ahenobarbi (the 'Domitiuses of the Bronze Beards'). Domitius was the son of the consul of AD 16 and his wife Antonia, and thus the grandson of Mark Antony and Octavia, the sister of Augustus.

Livia was eighty-six in September AD 29, and in the last months of her life. Tiberius' ambivalent feelings towards her were plain from his actions. First he intended to visit her during her last illness, then, when he waited too long, he ordered the funeral delayed until his arrival. He did not come before physical decay made a burial imperative, and afterwards, when the senate proposed building an arch in Livia's honour, Tiberius said he would pay for it from his own pocket. But he never did pay, and the arch was not built. Possibly he was stung by the insultingly small amount of money Livia

29 *Coin showing Livia. By the end of her life Livia was an isolated figure, estranged from the son through whom she had hoped to influence the governance of Rome. She was not the last Julio-Claudian mother to experience such a reversal in fortune.*

left to him. Like Augustus, Tiberius took a keen interest in legacies, regarding them as commentary on his rule by those with nothing to gain or lose by expressing their opinions.

As long as the Augusta [Livia] lived, there was shelter from oppressive despotism, for Tiberius could not break his lifelong habit of filial obedience, and even Sejanus did not dare to stand against a parent's authority. Now, however, the fury of the pair was unmuzzled. In a letter to an appalled and silent senate...Tiberius censured his daughter-in-law's insolent tongue and defiant spirit.

Tacitus *Annals* 5.3

Agrippina was found guilty of immoral behaviour and exiled to Pandateria, the same island that had once housed her mother, condemned on a similar charge. There, at the mercy of Sejanus, she was flogged with such vigour that she lost an eye. Nero, her eldest son, was also exiled, while Drusus was closely watched in Rome. The youngest boy, Gaius, was under less suspicion, for he had spent the previous few years in the care of Livia herself, and he was now transferred to the household of his grandmother Antonia. It was suspected that Nero had planned to flee to the Rhine army which his father had once commanded. Lentulus Gaetulicus, commander of that army, was questioned about this. He replied that he had never done anything to harm Tiberius, but if his life was in danger, well, that could change. The barely concealed threat in this robust response gave Tiberius pause. He had enough on his hands without another mutiny on the Rhine.

With Agrippina gone, and her children imprisoned or under suspicion, the ranks of the Julio-Claudians were thinning fast. Apart from the aged Antonia, there remained two grandchildren of Tiberius from the marriage of his son Drusus and Livilla, and a nephew called Tiberius Claudius Drusus Germanicus. Tiberius also had various nieces, one of whom, Drusilla, he married to Cassius Longinus, a descendant of the assassin of Caesar. But neither the nieces nor their husbands could rule. Both grandchildren were very young, and Tiberius Claudius suffered from palsy and was believed to be weak minded. For the aspiring Sejanus, the obstacles to supreme power seemed fewer every year.

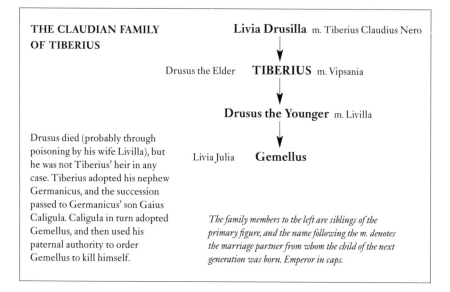

**THE CLAUDIAN FAMILY
OF TIBERIUS**

Drusus the Elder

Drusus died (probably through poisoning by his wife Livilla), but he was not Tiberius' heir in any case. Tiberius adopted his nephew Germanicus, and the succession passed to Germanicus' son Gaius Caligula. Caligula in turn adopted Gemellus, and then used his paternal authority to order Gemellus to kill himself.

Livia Drusilla m. Tiberius Claudius Nero

TIBERIUS m. Vipsania

Drusus the Younger m. Livilla

Livia Julia **Gemellus**

The family members to the left are siblings of the primary figure, and the name following the m. denotes the marriage partner from whom the child of the next generation was born. Emperor in caps.

The Fall of Sejanus

Drusus had escaped the fate of his mother and older brother by his more circumspect behaviour and what he believed to be a friendship with Sejanus. Drusus was married to a Lepida of the Aemilian house, a descendant of the triumvir who had ruled with Octavian. Probably threats or promises from Sejanus caused Lepida to lay charges of treason against her husband. She was readily believed, and Drusus was imprisoned in a cell on the Palatine hill below the imperial palace.

Sejanus seemed unstoppable. The man whom Tiberius called 'the partner in all my labours' finally obtained permission to wed Livilla and in AD 31 was consul alongside Tiberius. But young Gaius Caligula, the youngest son of Germanicus, remained an obstacle, and his grandmother Antonia was a formidable protector. It is quite probable that Antonia wrote to Tiberius warning of Sejanus' schemes. (The historian Josephus says this letter was carried by Caenis, a young maidservant who became the mistress of the emperor Vespasian three decades later.)

At almost the same time Nero committed suicide, apparently because Sejanus had convinced him that his death sentence was imminent. These two events led Tiberius to regard his favourite with suspicion, possibly even alarm. Gaius Caligula was summoned to Capri for his own protection. He was given the *toga virilis*, which marked him as a grown man, in a deliberately modest ceremony since Tiberius felt that the excessive honours given to his older brothers had gone to their heads.

With Gaius Caligula secure in Capri, and all other rivals disposed of, Tiberius no longer needed Sejanus, whose great power and greater ambition were becoming dangerous. For many years Sejanus had been a lightning rod conducting hostility against the regime towards himself. He was hated and feared, and his destruction would be correspondingly popular. Despite his reputation as a ponderous, straightforward soldier who disliked the game of politics, Tiberius was a skilful and ruthless player.

Command of the Praetorian Guard was secretly given to one Sutorius Macro, without Sejanus knowing that he had been deposed. When summoned before the senate, Sejanus came willingly, expecting to be given the *tribunicia potestas*, the power which would make him almost equal to the emperor. Instead, the consul read out a bitter denunciation from Tiberius, and suddenly Sejanus, who had started that day as the second man in the Empire, found himself a friendless prisoner. He was confined to a dungeon while the joyfully rioting populace overthrew his statues. The stunned senate reconvened and unhesitatingly condemned the usurper to death, and with him all his kin. This last measure shows how Rome had degenerated since the Republic, when, no matter how bitter the political battles, wives and young children had been safe. The blameless daughter of Sejanus suffered a tragic and horrific death:

The little girl was so oblivious as to what was going on that she kept asking what she had done wrong, and where they were dragging her off to. Whatever she had done wrong, she promised never to do it again, and couldn't she just be beaten, as other girls were? We are told that there was no precedent at that time for the execution of a virgin, so she was raped by the executioner while the rope was already around her neck. Then, just children as they were, she and her brother were strangled and their bodies thrown down the Gemonian steps.

Tacitus *Annals* 5.9

It is uncertain whether the senate overreacted, or whether Tiberius wanted no survivors of Sejanus' line to threaten his plans for the imperial succession. He may even have ordered this measure from savage vindictiveness. He was so worried about the outcome of his strike against Sejanus that he waited on the shore-facing cliffs of Capri for news, with the fleet standing by to take him to safety in Asia if necessary. If things went badly in Rome, Drusus was to be freed and put in command of the imperial forces there. (That Drusus and Agrippina were not freed in any case reflects the belief of Tiberius that Sejanus had not completely falsified the case against them.)

Tiberius used the occasion to purge the senatorial opposition. Some twenty senators were brought to trial. As always, Tiberius allowed the trial to be conducted with every appearance of impartiality. Those who felt themselves innocent pressed their claims energetically, and five were acquitted. Others, who were doomed in any case, used their freedom of speech to accuse Tiberius of a string of murders and sexual perversions. These accusations were meticulously archived in the trial transcripts, and are probably the source of a string of colourful anecdotes about Tiberius' sex life.

From all over the Empire, troupes of girls and youths, known as *spintriae*, were gathered. These were experts in unnatural practices, and excited his [Tiberius'] waning libido by performing in front of him in groups of three. Several cubicles were furnished with obscene pictures and statues, along with sex manuals from Elephantine in Egypt. These helped those who entered these rooms to get an idea of the duties they were expected to perform.... Some of his criminal obscenities are almost too vile to be believed. Imagine training little boys to follow him when he went swimming, and to get between his legs to lick and nibble him! These he called his 'minnows'....

Suetonius *Tiberius* 43

Accusations such as these are impossible to prove or disprove from a distance of two millennia, but there is no doubt that they were given considerable credence in contemporary Rome, where they contributed to Tiberius' growing unpopularity. It was also noted that Tiberius neither gave spectacular public games, nor constructed magnificent public buildings. The revenues of the accused went straight into the already bulging coffers of the imperial treasury. Although the future emperor Claudius later accused Tiberius of neglecting the Empire by his withdrawal to Capri, the available evidence indicates that despite his seventy-two years, Tiberius continued to administer and strengthen his Empire, doing so stolidly and without a trace of Julian flair and imagination. It would be remarkable if he had also found the time and energy for a fraction of the excesses attributed to him.

The family of Sejanus managed one vicious counter-punch as it went down. Apicata, the ex-wife of Sejanus, committed suicide, but not before writing to Tiberius, explaining that his son Drusus had been poisoned by Livilla, and including so much detail that the subsequent investigation appears to have verified the charge.

Tiberius took this very personally. Some modern historians have suggested that Apicata's letter was falsified as a pretext for Tiberius' purge of the followers of Sejanus. But it also makes sense to regard Tiberius' subsequent actions as those of a father engaging in the old Roman tradition of family vendetta. In a society where the person and his office were not separable, Tiberius had no compunction about using his position as emperor to pursue his feud, though today we regard this as the moment when the Julio-Claudian principate showed itself capable of despotism equal to that of any other tyranny.

Certainly, if he was a brutal but impartial ruler, as a father conducting a vendetta Tiberius was savage, unrelenting and vindictive. The delators were given free rein once more, and so diligently did Tiberius follow up their reports that the story went round of a visitor to Capri who arrived to make a social call on the emperor. Tiberius mistook him for a witness he had summoned and had him interrogated so brutally that even when the mistake was discovered, nothing could be done for the unfortunate man but put him out of his misery.

Tiberius wrote to the senate, theatrically adopting the stock role of a confused, anguished old man:

Honoured fathers, if I know what to say to you, or how to say it, or what should remain unsaid for the moment, then let all the gods and goddesses in heaven condemn me to even worse damnation than that which I already suffer daily.
  Suetonius *Tiberius* 67

In that same letter Tiberius urged the senate not to condemn Cotta – of a family long allied to the Julians – simply for calling Tiberius 'a little bundle of rags' (*Tiberiolus*). He also accepted this defence from one Terentius.

Yes, I was a friend of Sejanus. I tried hard to be, and was delighted when I succeeded…it was your son-in-law, your partner as consul, the man who acted for you in Rome – that is the man whom we all courted. It was not for us to criticize someone whom you raised so high, nor for us to criticize your motives for doing so. Heaven has arranged for you to have supreme command of affairs and for us to obey…. Plots against the state, murderous designs upon the emperor, let these be punished. But for fulfilling the obligations of friendship, the same principles must acquit me – and you also, Caesar.

Tacitus *Annals* 6.8

Livilla simply disappeared (by some reports she was starved to death). Tiberius seems to have suspected Agrippina of involvement in poisoning his son, just as she had suspected him of condoning the poisoning of Germanicus. Drusus, the son of Agrippina, was also suspected of complicity in the poisoning and was consequently starved to death in his cell below the Palatine, so hungry at the last that he tried to eat the stuffing from his mattress. When this news reached Agrippina in her exile, she starved herself to death in sympathy and protest – and perhaps also to pre-empt the same fate at Tiberius' orders.

Tiberius was now approaching his mid-seventies and like Augustus he had seen most of his potential heirs die before him. His grandson Gemellus carried the taint of being born when Livilla's intimacy with Sejanus was at its height. Claudius, his nephew, was an unprepossessing scholar (believed by many to be feeble-minded), and Gaius Caligula was both an untried youth and yet another of Agrippina's brood. One can almost imagine Tiberius shrugging his shoulders as he wrote his will, making Gemellus and Gaius Caligula his joint heirs. Perhaps he felt that they and the senate deserved each other.

Still Tiberius soldiered on. Many in the senate loathed him, but some appreciated that under his rule the Empire was peaceful and prosperous. When a fire in Rome devastated the homes of the poor, the emperor who had unhesitatingly seized whatever senatorial assets he could lay hands on just as unhesitatingly paid out a fortune in disaster relief. Yet he remained unloved. He echoed the young Pompey's statement to the ageing dictator Sulla, commenting that Macro, the new commander of the Praetorian Guard, paid more attention to the rising sun (Gaius Caligula) than to the setting sun (himself). He also commented, when he heard Gaius Caligula disparaging Sulla, dictator of Rome a hundred years previously, that as far as he could see the young man had all of Sulla's faults and none of his virtues.

In AD 37, at the age of seventy-seven, Tiberius left Capri for Campania. He reached the villa of Lucullus at Misenum, but although he denied it, he was too weak to go on. He was accompanied by Charicles, the greatest doctor of the day, and that night at dinner, on the pretence of taking Tiberius by the hand, the doctor felt the ailing emperor's pulse. Tiberius read the intention well enough, and responded by ordering another course and lingering at the table longer than was his habit. But he could not disguise the evidence of his own body and Charicles announced to Gaius Caligula that Tiberius had only days to live.

Suddenly everything became urgent. There were conferences among those already present, and dispatches to be sent to generals and armies. On 15 March it was announced that he [Tiberius] had breathed his last. Gaius Caesar [Caligula] set out to take possession of the Empire, accompanied by a rejoicing host of followers. Then suddenly came the news that Tiberius was recovering, that with strengthening sight and voice he was calling for food to revive himself. This caused universal panic. People ran in circles, everyone feigning either grief or ignorance. Meanwhile Gaius Caesar sat in stunned silence,

30 By the time this statue was made, Tiberius had secluded himself on Capri, and was seen by the citizens of Rome only through his image in statuary and coinage. The ageing emperor was aware that many were openly yearning for Gaius Caligula to succeed him.

having gone instantly from wild exhilaration to deep apprehension. Macro was undaunted. He ordered everyone out of the entrance hall, and had Tiberius smothered under a huge heap of clothes. So died Tiberius, in the seventy-eighth year of his life.

Tacitus *Annals* 6.50–51

Tiberius' Empire

And it came to pass in those days, that there went out a decree from Caesar Augustus, that all the world should be taxed…. And all went to be taxed, every one into his own city. And Joseph also went up from Galilee, out of the city of Nazareth, into Judaea, unto the city of David, which is called Bethlehem; (because he was of the house and lineage of David:) To be taxed with Mary his espoused wife, being great with child.

Gospel of St Luke, Chapter 2

Strange as it may seem to those reading the above lines today, this decree of Caesar Augustus marked a major improvement in the lives of those subject to Rome. The provincial census, instituted by Augustus in 27 BC and imposed regularly thereafter, allowed the treasury to assess the amount of tax realistically expected from each province, and to adjust the budget accordingly. This, combined with the imperial procurators who were sent to care for the emperor's personal financial affairs in each province, acted as a brake on the extortions of the public tax companies (*publicani*) which had made provincial life so miserable in the last years of the Republic.

It also helped that, in general, governors were now answerable for their conduct not to their sympathetic colleagues in the senate, but to the emperor. It is true that if matters came to trial, a governor was tried by the senate – but the senators knew that the emperor was taking a keen interest in their verdict. In this way, habits of efficient government were inculcated through half a century of close control by Augustus and Tiberius, both of whom were, in their different ways, equally merciless towards the greedy and incompetent.

None of the Julio-Claudian emperors greatly changed the system of provincial government as it had existed in the Republic, apart from inserting themselves at the top of the chain of command. The basic unit of government in the Empire was the *civitas*, a city which was autonomously governed, usually by an elected town council. Each city had its own rural hinterland for which it acted as a religious and administrative centre. The Roman Empire is best considered as a mosaic of such cities, loosely organized into provinces headed by a proconsul or an imperial legate. In the West many cities formed about colonies of discharged Roman legionaries, while cultures in the East had enjoyed a rich urban lifestyle for hundreds of years before Rome was founded.

Over all of these, for almost exactly a century, the Julio-Claudian *Pax Romana* lay almost unbroken. The intrigues of the imperial court, such as the struggle between Sejanus and Agrippina, may have gripped the senatorial class in Rome, but meant less to the huge mass of the common people than the antics of pop stars and other celebrities do today. What mattered to these people was physical security, a decent chance of justice under the law, and a market for their produce – things which became facts of life under the Julio-Claudians.

The imperial peace was not completely unbroken under Tiberius. As a general under Augustus, Tiberius had played a major part in stabilizing the northern frontier, and his nephew Germanicus had done much to repair the damage inflicted on Rome's reputation by the Varian disaster of AD 9. Nevertheless, the recall of Germanicus in AD 16 marked the end of the Roman attempt to subdue Germany by arms. Fortunately for the Romans, the Germans were not a united people. As soon as the threat of the legions was lifted, Arminius, leader of the tribes which had defeated Varus, attempted to defeat Maroboduus, a German king who had established a substantial kingdom to the east (in Bohemia). Shortly afterwards in AD 19 Arminius was assassinated, and his people fell into internal warfare.

31 *Coin proclaiming the imperial relief effort to restore Asian cities devastated by an earthquake, which may have been minted in order to pay for that restoration. The care of the emperors for their provincial subjects was one of the cornerstones of Julio-Claudian rule.*

This left Maroboduus at the head of the last organized resistance in the north, but he had problems of his own. Forced from his throne by Germanic tribes from further east, he sought shelter with his former enemies in Rome. Tiberius offered him quarters in Ravenna and free passage back over the Alps whenever he wished. After a decade or so, it became apparent both to Tiberius and to Maroboduus' disillusioned people that their king had little inclination to forsake the comforts of Ravenna for the hazards of the northern forests. He died at almost the same time as Tiberius, after eighteen years of exile, during which time the German threat to the frontiers was almost non-existent.

Some of the liveliest military activity of Tiberius' reign took place at the other side of his Empire in the north African deserts of Numidia. A Berber auxiliary soldier of the Musulamii tribe called Tacfarinas deserted and in AD 17 started a rebellion which smouldered for many years.

Tacfarinas gathered a band of bandits, ready for plunder and rape. Later, however, he organized them like soldiers in regular battalions with standards. Thenceforth, he could no longer be regarded as the chief of some undisciplined rabble, but as leader of the Musulamii people.
    Tacitus *Annals* 2.52.1

Tacfarinas was to become the mortal enemy of the legionaries of the legion III Augusta, which he initially plagued in a series of hit-and-run raids. By AD 17 Tacfarinas felt that his soldiers were numerous and disciplined enough to stand up to III Augusta in open battle. He was quickly disillusioned by Marcus Furius Camillus, descendant of a great military family of the old Republic, and thereafter reverted to guerrilla warfare. Camillus was generously praised by Tiberius, and granted a statue in Rome with a laurel wreath.

Tacfarinas was not finished, and wiped out a detachment of III Augusta near the river Pagyda before dispatching an embassy to Rome to seek a settlement. Tiberius was indignant. 'Not even Spartacus was offered terms,' he declared, 'let alone a robber like Tacfarinas now, while Rome is at the height of its power.' Instead of negotiators Tiberius sent the legion IX Hispania to keep the peace. He did, however, offer amnesty to all who deserted Tacfarinas, considerably weakening the rebel army.

Fighting with gritty determination, Tacfarinas held on until AD 24, contending against Blaesus, an uncle of Sejanus, and against his successor Cornelius Dolabella. Eventually he was cornered in a forest fort and committed suicide rather than be captured. Some of his troops were later assimilated into the Roman army as the *cohors Musulamiorum.*

A Gallic national revolt under Julius Sacrovir in AD 21–22 was crushed relatively easily, as was another in Thrace in AD 26. Fortunately, for most of the reign of Tiberius the greatest of Rome's potential enemies, the Parthians, remained quiescent. After several bruising encounters during the previous century, the two empires remained on their own sides of the Euphrates, each keeping a wary eye on the other. It helped that Phraates, the last scion of Parthia's Arsacid house, was resident in Rome until AD 35 when a delegation came to take him back to his own country. Though Phraates died soon afterwards (apparently from disease), the release of Phraates considerably upset Artabanus, the current Parthian king, and the eastern frontier became increasingly unstable. The matter was finally settled by a brisk war in which a descendant of Phraates called Tiridates was placed on the throne of Parthia. Afterwards,

Vitellius [the Roman general] thought it enough that he had displayed the arms of Rome, and he admonished Tiridates to remember his grandfather Phraates and his foster father Caesar, and all that was glorious about the pair of them. He adjured the nobles to obey their king and respect the Romans, and each maintain his loyalty and honour. This done, the legions returned to Syria.

Tacitus *Annals* 6.37

One thing which is notable about the foreign affairs of the Empire under Tiberius was the part played by the old nobility of the Republic. Names glorious since the founding of the Republic – Camillans, Valerians and Cornelians – were allowed to command Rome's armies in the field. In the campaign against Tacfarinas, Tiberius even permitted a Scipio to seek glory in the region where his ancestor had conquered Hannibal. This was evidently a deliberate policy. Tiberius, the traditionalist, saw no reason why the great aristocracies could not serve his Empire as they had the Republic. It was only a later and lesser generation of Caesars who saw the glory of these houses as a threat to their own.

Among the more interesting features of the reign of Tiberius was the lack of significant legislation. More and more often, precedent was set by imperial decree rather than by public discussion followed by a vote of the people, as was the tradition in the Republic. The senate became less of an elected body, since the huge *auctoritas* of the emperor was such that his preferred candidates tended to be the ones elected to magistracies.

While Tiberius could be ruthless on occasion, this must be seen in context. For the first fifteen years of his rule, no senators were executed at all (though some such as Libo Drusus in AD 16 and Piso in AD 20 only escaped through suicide). Of those whom the emperor had executed later, many were certainly guilty of treason. Others were victims, not so much of Tiberius as of the power struggle between Sejanus and Agrippina, and the hands of many who perished with Sejanus were far from clean.

But what the people of Rome made of Tiberius' reign was determined less by his grim efficiency and the execution of senators than by the emperor's tight-fistedness and lack of Julian flair. The Roman people were more than slightly insulted that their emperor did not choose to live among them. They readily believed that he wanted seclusion to practise sexual perversion, and by his absence avoid having to give expensive public games. The fact that those officials whom Tiberius appointed to their posts felt no need to bribe the electorate with bread and circuses did not go down well with the public either. The treasury was in good shape, and Tiberius fought few expensive foreign wars, but towards the end of his reign he still increased the much-hated sales tax which he had cut in AD 17.

Consequently, there was widespread rejoicing at his death. The Roman people were delighted when the gloomy old man (*senex et solus*, 'old and alone', he described himself) was replaced by the son of the charismatic Germanicus, and a direct descendant – through his mother – of Augustus himself. At his death, Augustus had been mourned, venerated and deified. With Tiberius the people chanted 'to the Tiber with Tiberius!', a reference to the Roman habit of throwing executed criminals into that river.

The subsequent verdict of posterity on Tiberius has been powerfully affected by the views of two historians – Tacitus and Suetonius. The panegyrics of another historian, Velleius Paterculus, have been rightly disregarded as crude flattery, and Suetonius has a deplorable fondness for lurid and unverifiable scandal, yet, despite his obvious bias, Tacitus is harder to ignore. (For example, an inscription has been unearthed in Spain which substantially supports the facts of his account of the deaths of Germanicus and Piso.) Tacitus held the common Roman belief that a man's character is fixed at birth, and he had decided that Tiberius was born cruel, lustful, jealous and vicious. On those occasions when his subject was manifestly fair, open and honest, Tacitus uncompromisingly added hypocrisy and deceit to the charge sheet.

To the last, it was the fate of the man who had served his country steadfastly and to the best of his ability to find himself unloved and his efforts unappreciated.

CHAPTER 6

GAIUS CALIGULA:
FEAR AND LOATHING AT
THE IMPERIAL COURT

Caligula loathed being described as the grandson of Agrippa because of that man's plebeian origins, and would fly into a tantrum if anyone mentioned Agrippa as an ancestor of the Caesars in speech or song. He cultivated the fantasy that his mother was child of an incestuous coupling of Augustus with his daughter Julia.
Suetonius *Gaius Caligula* 23

Gaius Caligula was the first emperor to be a Julio-Claudian, rather than a Julian (Caesar and Augustus) or a Claudian (Tiberius). Through Agrippina, daughter of Julia, the daughter of Augustus, Gaius Caligula was Augustus' great-grandson. Also, Germanicus, Gaius Caligula's father, was descended from Octavia, the sister of Augustus, who had wed Mark Antony. Yet Caligula was also very much a Claudian, since his father was the son of Drusus the Elder and nephew of the emperor Tiberius.

This was of great interest to the Roman aristocracy, who firmly believed that family traits were passed down through the bloodline. In Gaius Caligula which would predominate – Julian flair and occasional recklessness, or Claudian arrogance and general competence? In the event, the Romans saw the brutality of the worst of the Claudians combined with sadism, and a panache which was typically Julian. In short, the senate discovered a monster – with Mark Antony's taste for reckless expenditure thrown in.

However, the idea that Gaius Caligula embodied the prime characteristics of every bad apple in the Julian and Claudian family trees can partly be traced back to the mutual loathing between Gaius Caligula and the senators who ultimately wrote the history of his reign. Furthermore, many of Gaius Caligula's most undesirable characteristics may have been due not to heredity but to his upbringing, which was considerably more traumatic than most.

When Gaius Caligula was born at the end of August in AD 12, it seemed as if a golden future awaited him. His father was already the adopted son and heir of Tiberius, the emperor-in-waiting. Gaius Caligula's mother, Agrippina, was a devoted and faithful wife (something of an exception among the female descendants of Augustus), of whose nine children six survived infancy. Gaius Caligula was the youngest of three brothers. The oldest, born in about AD 6, was called Nero, as expected of the eldest son in the line of Claudian Neros. The second son, born in AD 7 or 8, was called Drusus, after his illustrious grandfather. All of Gaius Caligula's sisters were younger than he; Agrippina the Younger (future mother of the emperor Nero) was born in AD 15, and was followed by Drusilla in AD 16 and Julia Livilla in AD 17 or 18 (plate 23).

It is uncertain where Gaius Caligula was born. After meticulous research, Suetonius favours the seaside town of Antium, and this claim is probably stronger than that of Tacitus, who maintains that the child was born at Ambitarvium in Germany where his father commanded the Rhine garrison. Pliny the Elder agrees with Tacitus, quoting a bit of allegedly contemporary doggerel, 'born in the camp, of a father nurtured in arms, a clear sign, already to be emperor'. Certainly young Gaius Caligula was raised among the legions, and the youngest son of their beloved general became the legionaries' mascot. He was often dressed in a miniature soldier's outfit, so earning the nickname which infuriated him in later life – *Caligula*, or 'Little boot'.

This affection of the troops was exploited by Germanicus when the Rhine legions mutinied in AD 14.

'My wife and children, whom I would willingly put at risk if it were a question of your glory, I have to move to safety from your fury...that you might not be made more guilty by the slaughter of a great-grandson of Augustus, and the murder of a daughter-in-law of Tiberius.... Am I to call you soldiers, who have used weapons of war against your general's son?'
Germanicus to the troops in Tacitus *Annals* 1.43

Germanicus won the troops over, and led them on to campaign against the Germans with such success that he became the darling of Rome. Recalled by Tiberius in AD 16, Germanicus celebrated a triumph in which his sons, including the young Gaius Caligula, rode in his chariot with him.

From Rome, Germanicus was sent east, accompanied by his wife and children. An inscription at the Greek city of Assos suggests that Gaius Caligula addressed a speech to the city when his family passed through – a precocious achievement for a six-year-old. From Greece to Asia Minor to Egypt, Germanicus and his family were fêted and adored. One can only guess how the memory of those golden days affected Gaius Caligula in the grim times to come. At the very least, understanding how easily happiness could change to despair must have given him a haunting sense of insecurity.

On his family's return to Syria from Egypt, the long nightmare began which took up the rest of his childhood. In late September AD 19 Germanicus fell sick. He died the following month, convinced (as we have read earlier) that he had been poisoned by Piso, the governor of Syria, with whom he had quarrelled violently. It was suspected by many – and most probably by Agrippina – that Piso had been Tiberius' cat's paw in clearing the way for the succession of Tiberius' own son, Drusus.

This suspicion was strengthened when the family returned to Rome the following year. Rather than mourning his dead nephew, Tiberius seemed bent on calming the almost frantic grief of the general public. To keep public hysteria from increasing further, Germanicus was given a private rather than a state funeral, and none of the imperial family was allowed to make a public appearance. To Agrippina, convinced of Piso's guilt, the studied impartiality of Tiberius seemed either a betrayal or further proof of complicity.

32 *The father of Gaius Caligula, Germanicus was named after his own father's successful campaigns in Germany. Germanicus also campaigned in Germany, and became so popular with the Roman people that his death plunged the Empire into grief.*

33 Agrippina the Elder. Tiberius knew that Agrippina considered him responsible for her husband's death, and suspected her loyalty thereafter. This suspicion led to the death of Agrippina's two elder sons, and put Gaius Caligula's life at risk.

Perhaps to assuage these suspicions, and in any case conforming with the wishes of Augustus, Tiberius favoured the sons of Germanicus as much as his own. Yet Agrippina's evident ambition for her sons and her distrust of Tiberius drove the two apart, and the distance was enthusiastically widened by Sejanus, Tiberius' scheming and power-hungry subordinate.

As Agrippina's political position became weaker, Gaius Caligula was sent to live with Livia, the widow of Augustus, who though estranged from her son Tiberius, was very much the formidable matriarch of the clan. Livia herself may have decided to take young Gaius Caligula under her wing. She and Agrippina had feuded bitterly in the past, but the pair were probably forced into an alliance by their common loathing of Sejanus and by Tiberius' unfortunate knack of becoming alienated from the women in his life. (Not least because Tiberius was determined to keep the women of the imperial family out of politics, a topic which deeply engaged both Livia and Agrippina.) Tacitus claimed that Livia became the last defender of Agrippina, and on her death the family of Germanicus was defenceless before its enemies.

Both Agrippina and her eldest son Nero were exiled, and Drusus was so closely watched that

34 Nero and Drusus, the brothers of Caligula. These two young men, once seen as potential heirs to the imperial purple, were casualties of the dynastic struggles which eventually obliterated the entire family.

he was almost under house arrest, but Livia's protection of Gaius Caligula extended beyond the grave. She had him and his younger sister Drusilla transferred to the household of another grandmother, Antonia Augusta, the daughter of Octavia and Mark Antony. Gaius Caligula, who delivered Livia's funeral oration, was so impressed with her political nous that he nicknamed her 'Ulysses in a *stolata*' (the *stolata* was the female equivalent of a toga).

According to later reports, Gaius Caligula began an incestuous relationship with his sister Drusilla at the household of Antonia, and appalled the aged aristocrat when she caught the pair *in flagrante delicto*. If this actually occurred, it did not stop Antonia from writing to warn Tiberius of Sejanus' campaign against the family of Germanicus, raising suspicions in Tiberius' mind which the suicide of Nero seems to have confirmed. However, the fall of Sejanus brought no relief for the doomed family of Germanicus, for in the subsequent purge of Sejanus' supporters Tiberius discovered that his son had been poisoned by Livilla, Drusus' wife. Rightly or wrongly, Tiberius seems to have decided that Agrippina may have been implicated. This sealed her fate and that of her son Drusus, of whose guilt Tiberius seems to have been even more certain.

Thus at the age of nineteen, Gaius Caligula was the eldest surviving Julian male. Ever dutiful to the memory of Augustus, Tiberius brought him to Capri, both to protect him against further conspiracies in Rome and to consider him as a potential heir.

He put on the *toga virilis* and shaved off his first beard, but his coming-of-age celebrations were very subdued compared with those which had been given to his brothers. Those at the imperial court tried everything they knew to trick him into saying something against Tiberius, but invariably they failed. He showed absolutely no interest in the murder of his family, and appeared indifferent even to the wrongs he had himself endured. Instead he was so ingratiating towards both his adoptive grandfather and the entire household that it was rather aptly said of him, 'He was the best possible slave, and the worst master.'

Suetonius *Caligula* 10

It is highly improbable that Gaius Caligula was truly as indifferent to the fate of his family as he pretended, though he may even have tried to convince himself that this indifference was real. His future conduct revealed that he was in fact a very angry young man – all the more for not having a clear focus for his anger.

Of Gaius Caligula's life on Capri some sources such as Philo maintain that he lived a restrained and moderate life. Josephus, the Jewish historian, agrees, saying that Gaius Caligula applied himself conscientiously to his studies, rousing the interest of Tiberius, himself a keen classicist in his early years. Other sources such as Suetonius maintain that Tiberius encouraged his ward to watch tortures being conducted, and to join him in sexual frolics and gluttony.

Gaius Caligula's ancestor Mark Antony had sired children not only with Octavia, the sister of Augustus, but also with Cleopatra, the queen of Egypt. This Eastern connection had been maintained by Antonia, who had family connections with many Eastern monarchs, and a close friendship with the family of King Herod of Judaea. This brought to the imperial court the scapegrace Herod Agrippa (the 'Herod' in his name is inaccurate, but has become a convention with later historians). Herod Agrippa was a flamboyant man with a fondness for fast living that exceeded his income, and he was only allowed into the court of the austere Tiberius after Antonia had indulgently paid off his debts.

Given the restrictive atmosphere in which he had lived until then, it is unsurprising that young Gaius Caligula was fascinated by this free spirit, a relative of the infamous Salome who had received the head of John the Baptist on a platter. Though in his mid-forties, Herod Agrippa became a confidant of Gaius Caligula, sharing that friendship with Macro, the commander of the Praetorian Guard who had brought down Sejanus.

Gaius Caligula was now a husband. Tiberius had sanctioned his marriage in AD 33 to the daughter of the distinguished Marcus Junius Silanus, consul in AD 15 and 19. The union was brief, for the girl, Junia Claudilla, died in childbirth the following year – not an uncommon occurrence in ancient Rome, although the hostile tradition to Gaius Caligula insists on believing that anyone associated with him could only have died at his hands. Gaius Caligula found solace with Ennia Thrasylla, the wife of Macro. It seems that Macro was not particularly unhappy with this development, which he hoped would increase his influence with the young emperor-to-be.

35 Head of Gaius Caligula. Statues of Rome's third emperor are rare, because a conscious effort was made to destroy his memory in the period following his death. The relative brevity of his reign also meant that his image was not as widely propagated as the images of his predecessors.

Suetonius has given us a terse description of Gaius Caligula as he matured into a young man.

Height – tall. Complexion – pallid. Body – hairy and malformed. Neck – thin. Legs – spindly. Eyes – sunken. Temples – hollow. Forehead – wide and threatening. Scalp – almost hairless. Because he was both bald and hairy, it was death for anyone to look down at his head as he passed, or for goats to be mentioned for any reason at all. He would practise fearsome expressions in front of a mirror to make his naturally unlovely face even more horrible.

Suetonius *Gaius Caligula 50*

The evident bias of Suetonius can be balanced by the statues which have survived until the present day, the sculptors of which naturally endeavoured to make their subject as handsome as possible.

The picture is of a slender young man with the wide eyes of a Julian and the heavy brow of the Claudians. He probably inherited the family tendency for early baldness, though the statues give him a full head of hair. We observe a small mouth and a delicate chin, though if the neck was slender the statues do not show this. Far from a monstrous creature, it was a rather ordinary-looking youth who, on the death of Tiberius in AD 37, set out for Rome to claim the Empire.

A Bright Beginning

Gaius Caligula's coming to power seemed like a dream come true to the Romans, indeed, it seemed so for the entire world. The soldiers who had known him as a child, the citizens of the provinces and the people of Rome

were moved to wild delight that he was now their emperor, remembering
Germanicus as they did and moved with compassion for his family, which had
been almost wiped out by a succession of killings. Escorting the body of
Tiberius from Misenum to Rome, Gaius Caligula naturally wore mourning,
but at every altar on the way a noisy crowd greeted him with sacrifices, torches,
and called out pet names such as 'star', 'chicklet' and 'baby'.

Suetonius *Gaius Caligula* 13

The relief of the Roman people at the accession of Gaius Caligula was
matched by their antipathy to their former ruler. Some were slow to
believe the old emperor was dead, thinking this was a trick to reveal their
true sentiments. One such was Herod Agrippa, currently languishing in
jail for foolishly having earlier given voice to his longing that Tiberius
would die and be replaced by Gaius Caligula. He was only convinced
that his wish had finally come true when Gaius Caligula remarked to the
city prefect that he would consider it a favour if Agrippa was found more
comfortable quarters.

At this point, a polite request was all that Gaius Caligula could make.
Because the office of emperor did not legally exist, there had been no way
for Tiberius to formally appoint his successor. Instead he had made
Gaius Caligula his joint heir alongside his grandson Gemellus. Thus, the
accession of Gaius Caligula to power marked another step in the Julio-
Claudian takeover of the Roman world. Julius Caesar had taken Rome by
armed force, but his rule was so little recognized that Octavian effectively had to do it all again. The accession of Tiberius, the next in line,
was carefully orchestrated to prepare senate and public opinion alike.
Tiberius came to power with a curriculum vitae which overwhelmingly
testified to his competence. He was already co-emperor in all but name
on the death of Augustus, and did not need the bestowal of extra powers
to confirm his rule.

Gaius Caligula, on the other hand, had demonstrated no personal
abilities other than a talent for survival and of being born of the right
ancestors. Far more than Octavian, he merited the taunt of his ancestor
Mark Antony, 'You, boy, owe everything to a name.' This must be qualified with the admission that a great deal was also owed to Macro, the
Praetorian prefect. Macro had paid the Praetorians a bounty of 2,000

sesterces to ensure their loyalty and had also guaranteed the allegiance of the governors and generals of Rome's Empire.

Macro was also instrumental in getting the will of Tiberius annulled by the senate. In theory, this meant that the property of Tiberius would be equally distributed among his direct or adopted descendants (i.e. Gaius and Gemellus). In fact, this annulment established the precedent by which all the possessions of a deceased emperor became the property of his successor. On 28 March AD 37 Gaius Caligula arrived in Rome.

He showed great deference to the senators on that occasion when knights and also some of the populace were present at their meeting. He promised to share power with them and to do whatever would please them, calling himself their son and ward. He was then five months and four days short of twenty-five years old.

Cassius Dio *History 59.3*

At this meeting the senate probably recognized Gaius Caligula as princeps by bestowing on him the powers of *tribunicia potestas, maius imperium* and the other offices which Augustus and Tiberius had only accumulated slowly throughout their imperial careers. This act of the senate was probably the basis of the *lex de imperio* by which Vespasian received his imperial powers after the civil war of AD 69. Gaius Caligula happily collected the other honours associated with the Caesars, becoming Pontifex Maximus and soon afterwards Pater Patriae ('Father of his country'). He styled himself Gaius Julius Caesar after his famous forebear, but he added to this the title of Augustus and his family name of Germanicus as reminders of his descent from these popular figures.

With Tiberius, Gaius Caligula behaved as a dutiful son. He requested that the late emperor be given the same divine honours as Augustus had been. (The idea was passed to a senatorial committee which tactfully dropped the subject.) Gaius Caligula again demonstrated his oratorical skills with a eulogy for Tiberius which moved him, at least, to tears. Tiberius' ashes were laid in the mausoleum of Augustus, and the legacies which Tiberius had left in his will were conscientiously paid off. Gaius Caligula also repaid the kindness of Livia by honouring her bequests as Tiberius notoriously had not.

There remained another act of *pietas* ('family duty') for the new emperor to perform. Despite the stormy springtime Mediterranean sea, he personally retrieved the remains of his mother Agrippina and his brother Nero from their islands of exile and interred the ashes in the family mausoleum. The remains of his brother Drusus could not be found, so Gaius Caligula instead erected a cenotaph in his memory.

Antonia Augusta was honoured with the privileges of a Vestal Virgin, and all the rights and honours once enjoyed by Livia. Sadly, Antonia died one month later on 1 May AD 37 at the age of seventy-three. Later historians claimed that Gaius Caligula had either poisoned her (mad emperors do not need a motive), or that Antonia committed suicide because Gaius Caligula ignored her and would not even receive her in private. This would have been most uncharacteristic in a lady who had always stayed out of front-line politics, and who can hardly have considered Gaius Caligula indifferent to his family when he had passed the last month of her life collecting her grandson Nero's remains and re-interring them with honour.

Antonia's son, the despised Claudius, was elevated to the senate and shared a consulship with Gaius Caligula, whose devotion to family had also a political dimension. Gaius Caligula had been the ward of Tiberius, and had been on good terms with him despite Tiberius' malign influence on the rest of his family. To dispel the charge of hypocrisy, Gaius Caligula had to show that he had always been secretly loyal to his family, and demonstrate this at the earliest opportunity. For the same reason Gaius Caligula claimed that once, desperate for vengeance, he had taken a knife to the bedchamber where Tiberius lay sleeping. However, he was overwhelmed with pity for the tired old man he found there and quietly left the room. In leaving, he saw that Tiberius had been awake all along. The pair never discussed the incident afterwards.

36 *Gaius Caligula addressing the troops. He is seen making the traditional orator's gesture (called* adlocutio), *and the eagles carried by the troops probably symbolize the Rhine legions with which his immediate family were closely associated.*

By such stories Gaius Caligula emphasized that he was the son of the heroic Germanicus. It was for the same motive that he had his sisters included in the annual oath of allegiance, and granted them the honours due to Vestal Virgins. (Although if he was truly enjoying carnal relations with them at this time, these honours also demonstrated Gaius Caligula's twisted sense of humour.)

Gaius Caligula also dealt with the problem of young Gemellus, the dispossessed grandson of Tiberius who had, theoretically, as strong a claim as Gaius Caligula to the Empire, and who was therefore a potential focus of opposition. Gaius Caligula adopted the young man, making him his son and (by implication through the honours heaped on him) heir, but also assuming the absolute power, the *patria potestas*, which a Roman father had over his son.

To the Romans it seemed as though Augustus at his most enlightened had returned to Rome.

As Augustus had done, he [Gaius Caligula] made public all the accounts of the treasury, which had been suppressed for the time when Tiberius was away from the city. He helped the soldiers to extinguish a conflagration, and rendered assistance to those who had suffered loss in it.

Cassius Dio *History* 59.4

Gaius Caligula announced that the *maiestas* treason trials were over. It is uncertain whether the charge of *maiestas* was abolished or merely that those trials currently in progress were halted. Certainly treason remained on the statute books, but the announcement probably signalled that being impolite about the emperor would no longer count as such. Gaius Caligula publicly burned records of the charges against the accused, announcing, 'I have done this so that, no matter how strongly I may some day return to my grudge against those who harmed my mother and brothers, I will not have any way to punish them.'

Those exiled by Tiberius were allowed to return, and censorship was lifted, allowing even such hostile critics of the regime as Titus Labienus to be published for the first time in a generation. Caligula promised that the abuses of the regime of Tiberius were at an end, and assured the senate that they would not be repeated in his reign. In a typically self-serving piece of flattery, the senate proposed that this speech be read out annually, both to show their awe at the new emperor's wisdom, and (more importantly) to regularly remind the emperor of his promise.

The senate was less comforted by Gaius Caligula's plan to restore elections to the people's assembly, since a return to having to court public favour would greatly increase the financial strain on many would-be magistrates. (Magisterial candidates had also been granted some relief in the past when Tiberius had restricted displays of munificence to the public, such as extravagant games. This was both to stop rivals from becoming popular and to prevent a return to the situation in the Republic when those desperate to bribe the voters had extorted the necessary funds from the unfortunate subjects of the Empire.)

Those who worried about such things noted that the young emperor was remarkably liberal with the public purse. At the games he scattered tickets among the crowd at random, and these could be reclaimed for expensive gifts. However, Tiberius had left the Empire in such good shape that some fiscal laxity could be tolerated.

After the death of Tiberius, Gaius became master of the whole earth and sea, a sovereignty gained not by political strife but established by law. East and west, north and south, all parts of his domains had been set in harmony and peace, the Greek in concord with the barbarian, the civilian with the soldier, enjoying and participating in the peace. I say that no one could not be totally amazed at this overflowing and indescribable prosperity. He had at his fingertips huge stocks of accumulated goods, the gold and silver of his patrimony...vast forces of infantry, cavalry, ships and money flowing in as if from a perennial stream.

Philo *Embassy to Gaius* 8–10

Then, some six to eight months into his reign, Gaius Caligula fell ill. Both the nature of the malaise and the precise dates are unknown. Malaria has been suggested as a cause of his collapse, but this is not probable – the collapse was in autumn when malaria was not prevalent in Rome. Rather, it may well be that, after spending a decade and a half under the sword of Damocles, Gaius Caligula understood that he was finally safe, and the realization precipitated a long-overdue nervous breakdown.

Whatever struck Gaius Caligula hit him hard. For a while the last son of Germanicus was believed to be on his deathbed. All over the Empire, people prayed and sacrificed for their emperor's survival. Some Romans, such as an equestrian called Atanius Secundus, dedicated themselves to fight in the arena as gladiators if the emperor lived, while others made equally extreme promises. After a month of suspense it was announced that Gaius Caligula had survived and would make a full recovery. At the time, this seemed wonderful news.

The Mad Emperor?

Joy…now pervaded the whole of the habitable world at the recovery of Gaius, and at his being able to regain his power and having completely got rid of his sickness. For they all rejoiced, from ignorance of the truth, …for the human mind is apt to be blind towards what is really expedient and beneficial, being influenced rather by conjecture and notions of probability than by real knowledge. Anyway, it was not long before Gaius – who was now considered a saviour and benefactor who would shower down fresh and everlasting streams of benefits upon all Asia and Europe…changed to a ferocious disposition, or, rather, displayed the savagery which he had previously cloaked with pretence and hypocrisy.

Philo *Embassy to Gaius* 19–23

Many later believed that despite his full physical recovery, the mind of the emperor was mortally affected by his illness, and for the remaining years of his reign he was basically a raving homicidal lunatic. Suetonius remarks, 'I am certain he was sick, both mentally and physically…there were times when he could hardly walk, stand, think or hold up his head due to sudden fits [of epilepsy].' On another occasion Suetonius writes,

I am persuaded that it was a malaise of the brain which explains the apparently contradictory vices of over-confidence and extreme fearfulness. This is the man who scorned the gods and yet shut his eyes and hid beneath the bedclothes at the sound of thunder in the distance, and if it came any closer he would abandon the bed and crawl underneath it.

Suetonius *Gaius Caligula* 51

Tales like this, and the far more extreme examples which follow, must be regarded with the same caution as the allegations of sexual excesses by Tiberius. The senate came to loathe Gaius Caligula with an almost visceral hatred, and later biographers (mostly senators themselves) followed the senatorial tradition. Gaius Caligula became, by his own declaration, an enemy of the senate. Senators treated him as such and (when Gaius Caligula was safely dead) unleashed on him the full range of Roman political invective, which traditionally compensated with colour and imagination what it lacked in veracity.

Even in the Republic, Cicero freely accused his enemies of drunkenness, parricide, violent robbery and unwholesome sexual practices, including incest. Yet these same men were often senators in good standing who remained so after Cicero's 'revelations'. Therefore we must be sceptical of allegations such as that Gaius Caligula 'drained the treasury', since the Empire was not in dire financial straits after his death, and anyway, even a huge amount of personal extravagance costs less than a modest war.

Gaius Caligula started his reign as a rather repressed young man who expelled notorious *spintriae* from Rome and could only with difficulty be prevented from drowning them. (The *spintriae* were originally male prostitutes, but the word could mean anyone who practised deviant sexual behaviour for money.) Yet over the next few years he reportedly developed an extensive sexual repertoire which did not distinguish between partners of different age, social class, gender or family relationship. Suetonius remarks that the emperor 'had not the slightest regard for chastity, either his own or anyone else's'.

There can be little doubt that Gaius Caligula enjoyed shocking the senatorial class and defying convention – he may well, for example, have dressed in female clothing simply to provoke outrage, though it caused the senate to leap happily to conclusions about his sexual preferences. Gaius Caligula was such a controversial figure that it is almost impossible now to distinguish truth from rumour, scandal and outright lies. But the venom of the senatorial tradition indicates that in Gaius Caligula's reign the struggle for power between senate and emperor flared to a new intensity.

One interpretation of Gaius Caligula's behaviour stems from his youth and childhood. He was an intelligent and sensitive boy who had seen his father murdered (or so his mother firmly believed), his mother exiled, beaten and starved, and his two brothers killed. His own survival against powerful enemies had largely depended on the indulgence of two aged ladies and the whim of the man partly responsible for the catastrophes which had struck his family. Gaius Caligula in his early youth was impotent to control his own fate and had to depend on (manifestly undependable) others for his survival. Small wonder that after a youth spent powerless and in danger, he came to associate absolute security with absolute power.

Few Romans truly believed the 'restored Republic' of Augustus to be any such thing, but Augustus had deliberately constructed the illusion of continuity with the ancient democracy to help with his political and personal survival. As Gaius Caligula rose from his sickbed, he had apparently decided that the issue had been fudged for long enough. It was time to make the distinction between emperor and subjects unambiguously clear.

This changed outlook of Gaius Caligula was stimulated by his illness. During the two months he had been ill the Empire had functioned smoothly without him. It was highly disturbing to his insecurity that his role might be considered optional, and he set about centralizing power on himself.

For this reason he decided to become a god. Politicking during the emperor's illness had been as fevered as Gaius Caligula himself had been. Discussion of his possible replacements had unsettled the young emperor, and self-deification was certainly one way of distancing oneself from potential rivals. Nor was doing so as evidently a sign of insanity as it is considered today. The Ptolemies of Egypt had insisted on semi-divine status, as had other Hellenic kings. Augustus and Julius Caesar, both ancestors of Gaius Caligula, were gods by decree of the senate, and Tiberius had been worshipped as a god in the Eastern provinces of the Empire even while he lived.

However, no amount of political naivety could blind him to the fact that a living god who centralized power on himself was anathema to the senate. This meant the death of Gemellus, and a nucleus about which opposition might form. Either through foresight or fortune, Gaius Caligula had at hand the perfect weapon to dispose of his rival: the *patria potestas.* As Philo wrote, 'Amid his lawless and unsanctified deeds Gaius remembered law and sanctity as a travesty of their true nature.'

He deceived both the public and the young man himself. The adoption [of Gemellus] was a snare to assure not the sovereignty which he expected, but the loss of that which he held already...for Roman laws assign absolute power over the son to the father, not to mention his irresponsible authority as emperor, since no one had the power or the courage to call him to account for actions of any kind.

Philo *Embassy to Gaius* 28

Gaius Caligula accused his adopted son of rejoicing at his illness and looking forward to his death – treason to an emperor, and lack of filial piety towards a father. Though the right was seldom exercised, Roman law allowed a father to kill his son for almost any reason at all. Rather than invoke the controversial charge of *maiestas*, Gaius Caligula disposed of his rival through *patria potestas* – which was legally, if not morally, defensible. Gemellus was ordered to kill himself, and a centurion was sent to ensure that he did the deed.

But the lad lacked the skill, for he had never seen anyone else killed and had not yet practised the martial exercises by which those raised to rule were trained. So he stretched out his neck to the emissaries and told them to kill him. When they could not bring themselves to do it, he took the sword himself and asked them what was the most vital spot so that he could accurately aim the blow that would end his miserable life.... Having received this first and last lesson on swordsmanship, he was compelled to become his own murderer.

Philo *Embassy to Gaius* 31

It was a good moment for Gaius Caligula to strike. He was still wildly popular, and public resentment of Tiberius meant that his grandson received little sympathy. Another who perished at this time was Marcus Silanus, a leading senator. Later historians have speculated that Silanus was suspected of plotting to seize power, or that he offended the emperor by pressing too hard his relationship as Gaius Caligula's former father-in-law. We know that Silanus was formally arraigned before the senate, since another senator was later executed for refusing to lay the charges, but the nature of these charges is unknown. Nor did Silanus face them, for he pre-empted his fate by cutting his own throat.

Next to fall was Macro, commander of the Praetorian Guard and the man who had done more than any other to bring Gaius Caligula to power. As might any sensible subordinate, Macro had explored with Gemellus what might happen if the emperor were to die. However, the deeply insecure Gaius Caligula considered that the man who had helped to create one emperor could create another. The childhood nightmare of Sejanus showed what happened when Praetorian prefects became too ambitious, so Macro was relieved as commander of the Praetorians on the pretext that he was to be made Prefect of Egypt. Then he was arrested and charged – thanks to Gaius Caligula's savage sense of humour – with pandering, in that Macro had supplied his wife for sexual services to another. After the death of Macro and his wife, Gaius Caligula appointed the commanders of the Praetorians in pairs to keep watch on each other.

Gaius Caligula ordered those who had offered their lives if he lived, or who had dedicated themselves to fight in the arena, now to fulfil their commitments. This has been variously interpreted as chastising flatterers (unlikely, as he loved being flattered) or as pure savagery, but the superstitious emperor may have feared that reneging on promises to the gods might cause them to retract their side of the bargain and take his life.

Certainly the gods were not kind to Gaius Caligula's family. On 10 June AD 38 he lost his favourite sister, Drusilla. Naturally, later tradition sought to link the emperor with her death, which probably occurred during childbirth. Marcus Lepidus, Drusilla's husband, shared Gaius Caligula's passion for chariot racing and wild living, and the brothers-in-law got on very well. Since Gaius Caligula was accused of incest with Drusilla, the senatorial tradition explained their friendship by suggesting a homosexual relationship, though even Suetonius, who is prepared to believe a lot, reports this as speculation. Gaius Caligula mourned Drusilla extravagantly, neither shaving nor cutting his hair (plate 19), and was too moved to attend her public funeral at which she was given the same honours as Livia had been given. A period of public mourning was called (a *iustitium*) and, at Gaius Caligula's prompting, Drusilla became the first Roman to be made a goddess by the senate.

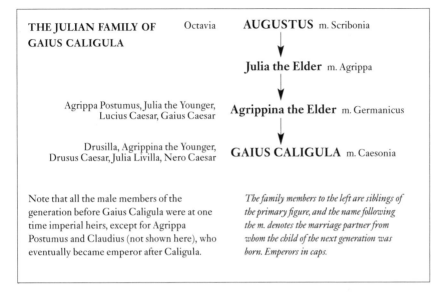

**THE JULIAN FAMILY OF
GAIUS CALIGULA**

Octavia

AUGUSTUS m. Scribonia

Julia the Elder m. Agrippa

Agrippa Postumus, Julia the Younger,
Lucius Caesar, Gaius Caesar

Agrippina the Elder m. Germanicus

Drusilla, Agrippina the Younger,
Drusus Caesar, Julia Livilla, Nero Caesar

GAIUS CALIGULA m. Caesonia

Note that all the male members of the
generation before Gaius Caligula were at one
time imperial heirs, except for Agrippa
Postumus and Claudius (not shown here), who
eventually became emperor after Caligula.

*The family members to the left are siblings of
the primary figure, and the name following
the m. denotes the marriage partner from
whom the child of the next generation was
born. Emperors in caps.*

Gaius Caligula's mourning for his family reminded the public of the distinguished bloodline that constituted his sole claim to rule. And the line of the Caesars was now running rather thin. Therefore as soon as the period of mourning was over, Gaius Caligula found a new wife. He had already briefly taken a second wife, a lady called either Orestilla or Orestina. This second marriage was basically a crude joke played on a certain Calpurnius Piso, who was about to marry the lady when Gaius Caligula stepped in and claimed the bride as his own. He soon tired of her, and her fate is uncertain. Tradition says that she and Piso were promptly exiled, but the records of the college of Arval priests to which Piso belonged show that he remained in Rome for several more years.

Gaius Caligula's third bride was only slightly more conventional. She was Lollia Paulina, a striking beauty who was married to Memmius, the governor of Macedonia. The emperor ordered her husband first to divorce her, and then to return to Rome to give the bride away. This was not merely a bizarre sense of humour at work, for Roman women usually had a guardian. If Lollia was in Memmius' *potestas* then, as Lollia's guardian, Memmius' attendance at the wedding was legally desirable. Afterwards Memmius returned to his province, where he remained until AD 44. This shows that although Gaius Caligula retained his trust in the man, he had no wish for his embarrassing presence in Rome.

Tyrant

The method of execution he preferred was to inflict numerous small wounds, none of them touching the victim's vital parts. His orders soon became familiar. 'Make him feel that he is dying' became a catchphrase. Once a mix-up of names resulted in the wrong man being executed, but he announced that the other had just as much deserved death. He often quoted a line from Accius: 'Let them hate me, so long as they fear me.'

Suetonius *Gaius Caligula* 30

The turning point in Gaius Caligula's reign came in AD 39. The prefect Flaccus had been recalled and executed, perhaps for mishandling Graeco-Jewish friction which had led to substantial unrest. Gaius Caligula knew that this further execution must have caused anger and unease among the senators, yet they remained as deferential and obliging as ever. The disillusioned young emperor realized that the senate might be plotting furiously against him, yet he would never know from the outward appearance of its members. Impetuously he stormed into the senate house and denounced the entire institution in a long furious speech. He accused the senators of having been in league with his enemy Sejanus, and said that his study of Tiberius' papers (which he once claimed to have burned) showed that the senate had collectively informed against his mother and brothers. He invoked the memory of Tiberius, claiming that the pernicious body of hypocrites in the senate had merited the former emperor's cruelty, and announced that libelling the emperor would again be considered *maiestas*, and trials were to recommence henceforth. Dio tells us that he added:

'If Tiberius really did do wrong, you ought not, by Jupiter, to have honoured him while he lived, and then, after repeatedly saying and voting as you did, now completely reverse your conduct. But it was not Tiberius alone that you treated in this fickle manner; Sejanus also you first puffed up with conceit and spoiled, then put to death. Therefore I, too, ought not to expect any decent treatment from you.'

Cassius Dio *History* 59.16

The stunned senate reconvened the next day and immediately proved the emperor's point by passing decrees praising his justice and mercy, especially invoking the goddess Clementia, and proposing further honours for the man who had just insulted and abused them.

There followed a period in which Gaius Caligula seemed to be testing the limits of his power. That September he arbitrarily removed both consuls from office, claiming that they had not celebrated his birthday (on 31 August) but the defeat of his ancestor Antony at the battle of Actium instead. In fact, says Dio, Gaius Caligula had confided to a friend that he would be rid of the consuls whatever they did, since had they not celebrated the battle, he would have taken umbrage on account of Augustus, who was also an ancestor.

We know of at least three senatorial victims of Gaius Caligula in the final months of the year. A Junius Priscus was arraigned on an unspecified charge and committed suicide, and when another senator called Carrinas Secundus delivered a speech against tyrants, he was banished to Athens where he killed himself. Sabinus, governor of Pannonia, was recalled. His wife was accused of impropriety with the soldiers in his camp, but the charges against Sabinus are unknown. In all probability the true charge was that he was close to Sejanus during the persecution of the family of Germanicus. Lucius Vitellius, governor of Syria and father of the future emperor of that name (AD 69), was also recalled, but he escaped the fate of Sabinus and his wife – who were forced to commit suicide – by grovelling before Gaius Caligula and worshipping him as a god.

It is significant that Vitellius not only escaped but became a favourite of the emperor in this way. Another who had done likewise was a man called Afer, whom Gaius Caligula prosecuted personally. Afer announced himself so overwhelmed by the brilliance of the prosecution that he was not even going to offer a defence, but simply to throw himself on Gaius Caligula's mercy. Gaius Caligula seems to have been terrified of opposition, and placated by absolute surrender. Afer was rewarded by being made consul in the place of one of those deposed in September 39.

It is also in AD 39 that Gaius Caligula married for the fourth and final time. Lollia Paulina had proved an unrewarding wife. It is quite probable that she had difficulty in coping with such an unpredictable and demanding husband, but Gaius Caligula's main complaint was her failure to produce an heir. On the other hand, Gaius' mistress, Milonia

Caesonia, was well advanced in her pregnancy with his child. It appears that Gaius Caligula waited until the last moment to see if Lollia might also conceive, but when Milonia entered the final month of her pregnancy Gaius Caligula put Lollia aside with the spiteful injunction that she was never to sleep with anyone again, and married Milonia who gave him a daughter a few weeks later. To the astonishment of everyone who knew the couple, their marriage was a happy one, and Gaius Caligula proved to be an indulgent father. Suetonius, for example, is evidently bemused and suggests that Gaius Caligula's new bride used a love-potion on him, so further addling his wits.

Caesonia was neither young nor beautiful. She'd already had three daughters by a previous marriage and was both over-sexed and madly extravagant. Yet he [Gaius Caligula] loved her passionately and faithfully, and often when reviewing the troops would ride out with her dressed in a helmet, cloak and shield. He would parade her naked before his friends, but would not call her his wife until she was with child; whereupon he announced the marriage and the birth at the same time. He called the infant Julia Drusilla. After doing a circuit of the temples of every goddess in Rome, he finally decided on Minerva, setting the child on her [the statue's] lap and entrusting her with his daughter's upbringing and education. The child's savage temperament had convinced him that he was the father – the infant on occasion tried to scratch out the eyes of her young companions.
Suetonius *Gaius Caligula* 25

And elsewhere,

There were times when he [Gaius Caligula] threatened that he would torture Caesonia to make her say why she was so devoted to him.
Suetonius *Gaius Caligula* 33

Again, it is evident that Gaius Caligula felt safe with Caesonia, in that he felt his power over her was absolute. He is alleged to have often kissed her neck, murmuring, 'And this could be cut through, the moment I give the word.'

However, Gaius Caligula did not linger to enjoy his married bliss. Soon after he had replaced the consuls of AD 39 he set off unexpectedly for the northern provinces, accompanied by at least an element of the Praetorian Guard. According to Dio, this is because he had exhausted the treasury in Rome and wanted to loot Gaul. In fact his target was Lentulus Gaetulicus, the governor of Germany. As with many of Gaius Caligula's victims, Gaetulicus had been a close associate of Sejanus. He had survived the latter's fall by vigorously protesting his innocence, and simultaneously hinting unsubtly that as commander of the Rhine garrison he could be a dangerous man if desperate. Gaetulicus, though incompetent in other ways, had assiduously courted the goodwill of his men and he could probably have raised his own four legions, as well as the two new legions created for the planned invasion of Britain (named *primigeniae* either in honour of Gaius Caligula's new daughter or – more probably – as they were meant to be the first of a new breed of legions).

Though Gaius Caligula travelled (as always) in great luxury, he also travelled at speed. Gaetulicus had little time to prepare for his distinguished visitor before Gaius Caligula descended on him (or at least Gaius Caligula's emissaries did – the exact whereabouts of the emperor at this time are uncertain, though he was certainly outside Rome). It is not clear exactly what happened in Germany during the late summer, but by 27 October Gaetulicus was dead, executed for treason. This may have been a preliminary step for the invasion of Britain, since Gaetulicus was blatantly unsuitable to command an invading force, yet would not have lightly stepped aside for another. Or it may have simply been Gaius Caligula striking at another enemy of his family whom he still considered a threat. Or indeed both, since the two factors are not mutually incompatible.

Another victim who died at this time was Lepidus, once the emperor's close friend. Gaius Caligula accused him of sexual misconduct with his sisters and had him executed. Possibly the charges were true, or perhaps Lepidus was suspected of conspiring against the emperor. Lepidus' ancestry and closeness to the imperial family made him a likely successor should Gaius Caligula die. Also, one of the alleged adulteresses, Agrippina the Younger, may already have been ambitious for her young son Nero – she certainly became so later. In any case, Gaius Caligula was very aware of the threat that other members of the dynasty posed towards his newborn daughter. (He had, after all, killed Gemellus precisely because he was a dynastic rival.) Agrippina was ordered to carry

Lepidus' remains back to Rome, after which she and her sister were exiled. Gaius Caligula occasionally amused himself by sending the exiles blood-curdling threats about his future intentions, but otherwise took no further action against them. Nor were the sisters' husbands harmed.

Gaius Caligula appointed a hard, competent soldier called Servius Sulpicius Galba to command the Rhine army, and the new broom immediately began to sweep away the indulgences with which Gaetulicus had pampered his troops, thus inspiring the Roman saying *Galba non est Gaetulicus* ('This is Galba, not Gaetulicus') to indicate dramatically changed circumstances.

Galba would have realized that there was little point in conducting a major campaign in Germany, especially as the slow build-up for a massive invasion of Britain was under way. But he could and did lead raids and incursions to toughen up the troops and improve discipline.

The emperor himself had conducted a rapid tour of Gaul while Galba sorted out the German frontier. When Gaius Caligula returned to check on his new appointee's progress, he was impressed. He complimented Galba, and went some way towards eroding Galba's improvements in discipline by showering his men with rewards and benefactions.

Then, in one of the most puzzling incidents of his entire bizarre career, Gaius Caligula led his army to the shores of the English Channel. He ordered his soldiers to line up on the seashore, fire their catapults into the water, and then gather seashells as the 'spoils' of the ocean. This was odd, even for a mad emperor. One theory is that Gaius Caligula actually intended to invade Britain, but his soldiers refused, so he ordered them to gather seashells as a way of mocking their cowardice. Another is that Gaius Caligula was avenging his father's mistreatment by Oceanus, the god whose sudden storm had sunk much of Germanicus' army while his fleet was transferring it up the German coast. Or it may have been that diplomatic considerations in Britain itself demanded that Gaius Caligula make a show of force on his side of the channel. (Gaius received the capitulation of a minor British king at this time.)

Dynastic infighting on the British side of the Channel had been particularly lively while Gaius Caligula was in Gaul, and what we know of the political situation in Britain suggests that an invading force would have landed in a country divided against itself. However, the English

Channel remained a formidable obstacle, and Gaius Caligula and his army arrived too early in the season for ocean sailing to be safe. Perhaps Gaius Caligula gambled on both his transports being ready, and on unseasonably clement weather to give him the sort of chance which so often presented itself to his ancestor and namesake Gaius Julius Caesar. If so, the gamble failed and Gaius Caligula's 'war on the ocean' was a demonstration of petulance against the sea which had failed to co-operate. In these circumstances the surrender of a British leader offered a chance to save face and give Gaius Caligula something to show on his return to Rome, where he was sure that the senate was up to no good.

Apotheosis and Assassination

He would pose as Neptune, because he had bridged so great an expanse of sea; he also impersonated Hercules, Bacchus, Apollo and all the other divinities.... Once a Gaul saw him get onto a high platform disguised as Jupiter and begin to spout oracles. When the man burst into laughter, Gaius had him brought before him, and demanded, 'What is it you think you see before you?' And the other answered with these exact words: '*Mega parlerema*' ('A huge bullshitter'). Yet nothing happened to the man, since he was only a shoemaker. It would appear that people of Gaius Caligula's rank can bear to hear truths from the great unwashed that would be intolerable from anyone of a respectable social position.

Cassius Dio *History* 59.26.5–9

The above incident suggests that Gaius Caligula's demand to be worshipped as a god stemmed more from his need for absolute submission from potential rivals than from a heartfelt belief in his own divinity. In the Eastern provinces, and probably in the municipalities of Italy, the emperor was routinely considered as divine, and even in Rome it was normal to make libations if not to a divine emperor, then to his 'divine spirit' or *genius*.

We have numerous accounts of Gaius Caligula dressing up as a god (and even more outrageously, a goddess) and demanding to be worshipped. However, the sources tend more towards scandalous and shocking stories than specific details. For instance we are told of one Apelles who came across Gaius Caligula standing next to a statue of

Jupiter. Apelles was asked which was the greater, Gaius Caligula or Jupiter, and when he hesitated, the emperor had him skinned alive. (Apelles means literally 'skin off', so his name either inspired his torture, or is the reason why this story was invented.)

There are few details of how the imperial cult was organized in Rome. Philo, who wrote an invaluable contemporary account of his part in the Jewish embassy to Gaius Caligula, does not say that Gaius Caligula-worship in the capital went further than ad hoc grovelling by senators and the placing of Gaius Caligula's statue among those of the gods. (Tiberius had permitted the same, but insisted that his statue be considered as merely a temple ornament rather than an object of worship.) Modern archaeologists in Rome have found evidence which supports Suetonius in his claim that Gaius Caligula extended the temple of Castor and Pollux in the forum to make the temple seem like a portico to his own palace.

As well as Gaius Caligula's vigorous promotion of himself as a deity, there were popular manifestations of imperial cult, but by and large these were extensions of similar honours performed for other members of the house of Caesar, and less than startling in an age when the boundaries between human and divine were blurred. From what we can garner from the sources, the general public rather enjoyed those aspects of emperor-worship which they did not take seriously, and Gaius Caligula's public standing was unharmed – if anything, rather the contrary. Those who were angered and humiliated by the charade were in the Roman senate, and this is exactly how Gaius Caligula intended it should be.

It is uncertain when Gaius Caligula returned to Rome after his busy year abroad, but he was certainly in the environs of the city well before he entered it officially to receive an ovation (a lesser form of a Roman triumph) in the summer of AD 40. As soon as he returned it was evident that Gaius Caligula intended to challenge the concept that the emperor was simply the first among equals in the Roman senate. He wanted to make it plain who was master, and any hint of opposition was mercilessly crushed. For the senate, this alone justified any of the later insults to his memory, though this abuse also reflects the guilty realization that during Gaius Caligula's reign the senate did not acquit itself well. The more it was abused and humiliated, the more its members fell over themselves to offer Gaius Caligula more and greater honours. Few senators allowed even a dignified interval before rushing to prostrate themselves before their god-emperor and kissing his sandals. This rite was known as *prosky-nesis*, and was an honour done to the kings of the Persian empire.

There were exceptions. The philosopher Canus easily outmatched the emperor in debate, and when Gaius Caligula vindictively ordered his execution, Canus coolly replied, 'Thank you, you wonderful prince', and took his leave. He was executed ten days later.

His malice, insolence, pride and destructiveness were unleashed on men of every era. Augustus had once moved the statues of some famous men to the Campus Martius to make more room on the Capitol. Gaius Caligula had these thrown down and shattered and the inscriptions destroyed so completely that they were beyond recovery. Thereafter his express permission was required before the setting up of a statue or bust of a living person.... Gaius Caligula stripped the noblest scions of Rome of their ancient family icons. Torquatus lost his golden collar, Cincinnatus his hair, and Pompey his nickname of 'the Great'.

Suetonius *Gaius Caligula* 34–35

There is method discernible in this madness. The feud between the Julio-Claudians and the senate which had spluttered for three genera-tions was now outright warfare. If Gaius Caligula wanted to break the senate, he had to destroy its history and tradition as well as the will of its current members.

Unsurprisingly, some senators collaborated enthusiastically with this project, and equally unsurprisingly, there was resistance hidden under the guise of the deepest servility. Gaius Caligula was caught in a descending spiral. As he became more savage and merciless, he created more and better-hidden enemies to be yet more savagely and mercilessly rooted out, creating a new and greater crop of foes.

Only recently Gaius Caesar scourged with the whip and tortured Sextus Papinius, whose father had been consul, and Betilienus Bassus, his own quaestor and the son of his procurator, and others, both Roman senators and knights, all in one day – and not to extract information but for amusement. Then he became so impatient at postponing his pleasure – a pleasure so great that his cruelty demanded it instantly – that he decapitated some of his victims by lamplight.... He had them tortured by every unhappy device in existence – by the cord, by the rack, by fire...three senators, as if no better than worthless slaves, were mangled by whip and flame at the behest of a man who contemplated murdering the whole senate.

Seneca *On Anger* 3.18

At least here Seneca has named the victims. Generalizations abound, such as 'his frenzy knew no limit' or 'he executed forty men with a single death warrant while Caesonia was taking a nap', but in terms of actual names, we know of fewer than thirty people whom Gaius Caligula executed or forced to suicide, and this is the total over the whole of his five-year reign. Of this number, at least half a dozen may have been justifiably accused.

One whom contemporary accounts describe as guilty as charged was Quintillia, a beautiful actress who suffered horrific tortures so stoically that an impressed Gaius Caligula spared her life and gave her a small fortune in cash as compensation for her suffering. Among those present at the torture was the man who was later to assassinate Gaius Caligula, but Quintillia reassured him by a secret sign that she would endure without betraying him.

At this point, with Gaius Caligula at his worst, the Jewish embassy of Philo arrived from Alexandria to put the Jewish point of view about unrest between Greeks and Jews which had recently disrupted civic life in that city. Given the young emperor's current reputation, participating in the delegation must have seemed a suicide mission. Its members were sent to where Gaius Caligula was inspecting some houses which he wanted renovated to his demanding standards.

While he was talking to us, he went on with his survey of the houses, the different chambers, men's and women's, the ground floors, the upper floors, all of them, with some he criticized structural defects, and for others he made his own plans and ordered them to be made more magnificent. We were compelled to follow him up and down, mocked and insulted by our adversaries.... But after giving some of his orders about the buildings, he put to us this earth-shattering question, 'Why do you refuse to eat pork?' The question was greeted by an outburst of laughter…intended to make the remark seem witty and sprightly. The laughter was so great that some of the servants following him were annoyed at it, since it seemed disrespectful to an emperor with whom even a carefully judged smile was unsafe.

Philo *Embassy to Gaius* 361

Someone remarked that one might as well not eat lamb, and Gaius Caligula commented, 'Well, you shouldn't, it's not a nice thing to do.' It was evident from the tone of the meeting so far that the carefully rehearsed speeches of the delegates would not be delivered.

When he had a taste of our pleading and recognized that it was by no means contemptible, he cut short our preliminary points before we could bring in the stronger ones, and dashed at high speed into the large room of the house where he ordered the windows all round to be restored with transparent stones, which, in the same way as white glass, do not obstruct the light but keep off the wind and burning sun. Then he advanced casually and said in a more moderate tone, 'What is it that you say?' and when we launched into the next points in our argument he ran again into another room and ordered the original pictures to be put up there. So with the presentation of our case so mangled and disjointed…we gave up.

Philo *Embassy to Gaius* 365

It would have appealed to Gaius Caligula's sense of humour to have a gaggle of breathless elders choking and gasping in his wake as he charged about the building, and this tactic evidently forced the delegates to condense their argument to essentials. Rather to their surprise, no one was executed afterwards.

He relaxed into a softer mood and said just this, 'They strike me as being sadly misguided rather than wicked; and foolish in refusing to believe that I have got the nature of a god,' and saying this he went off, ordering us to be gone too.

Philo *Embassy to Gaius* 368

How Gaius Caligula would have ruled is unknown, since he died before reaching a decision. However, he does not seem to have been anti-Semitic in principle, and got on well with individual Jewish aristocrats and rulers. He famously antagonized the Jewish peoples everywhere by ordering that his statue be set up in the Temple in Jerusalem, but this order was never carried out (see below).

Gaius Caligula was twenty-eight years of age in AD 41. The fourth year of his reign brought with it a new crop of conspiracies. The one which finally succeeded was led by Gaius Caligula's Praetorian tribune, Cassius Chaerea. Chaerea had been a soldier in the Rhine army and his loyalty to the imperial cause had distinguished him during the mutinies which marked the beginning of Tiberius' reign. Evidently this had led to his promotion to the Praetorians, where he came to the attention of Gaius Caligula because of his high, lisping voice. The emperor nick-named him 'Lassie', and whenever he gave the watchword for the night's guard to Chaerea he chose something like 'Venus' or 'Priapus' (a god usually depicted with an outstanding erection). When extending his hand to be kissed by Chaerea, Gaius Caligula would turn his fingers at the last moment to an obscene gesture, causing much hilarity among Chaerea's colleagues, and igniting a slow-burning but profound hatred in the man he was humiliating.

Gaius Caligula was warned, allegedly by an omen, but possibly by a spy, that a 'Cassius' was plotting his downfall. His suspicions fell natu-rally on Cassius Longinus, who not only commanded several legions on the eastern frontier, but who came from a family with previous form in assassinating Julio-Claudians – a Cassius had led the conspiracy with Brutus to murder Julius Caesar.

In his *Jewish Antiquities* the historian Josephus describes in detail how the assassination of Gaius Caligula was planned and carried out. He adds the interesting detail that Chaerea had been lax in his tax-collecting duties, either through sympathy with those being heavily taxed (Jose-phus' suggestion) or through corruption on his part (more probable). To avoid a reckoning with an emperor not famed for his mercy, Chaerea was eager to deal with Gaius Caligula as soon as possible.

An opportunity arose during a show on the Palatine. The emperor was fond of spectacles and theatre (his liking for the actors' company was another annoyance to the senate), and in this case he decided to attend even though he was still hungover from the previous night. Perhaps for this reason Gaius Caligula was in no hurry to leave for his lunch.

And now Gaius was in doubt whether he should stay on to the end of the shows…. Minucianus [another conspirator], who sat by Gaius, was afraid that they might lose their chance, because he saw Chaerea was not present, so he got up to hurry out and make sure that Chaerea was ready; but Gaius took hold of his clothes and said to him in a friendly way, 'Hey, hero, where are you off to?' So in order to show respect to the emperor, he had to sit down again. But his worries got the better of him and he again got up to go, and this time the emperor allowed him, perhaps thinking that he had to answer a pressing call of nature.

Josephus *Jewish Antiquities* 19.13

It was planned to assassinate Gaius Caligula in one of the narrow passageways leading from the theatre, where his guards would find it hard to come to his assistance. The emperor took a shorter route than normal, passing a troupe of child performers from Syria who were practising their act. He conversed briefly with the youngsters, but was interrupted by the arrival of Chaerea and his fellow conspirators.

So Chaerea asked him for the watchword; and when Gaius gave another ridiculous word, Chaerea promptly cursed him, and drawing his sword gave him [Gaius] a fearsome, yet not fatal blow…. Gaius was stunned by the pain from his wound. The sword had hit him exactly between the shoulder and the neck, and the first bone on his chest stopped the blade from going any further. He was so shocked that he did not cry out. He did not call for his friends either, perhaps because he did not trust them, or possibly because he was totally confused. He groaned from the pain, and dived forward to escape. But Cornelius Sabinus had already decided what to do next, and shoved him down on to one knee. Then all of them surrounded him, stabbing with their swords, and shouting encouragement to each other to keep stabbing.

Josephus *Jewish Antiquities* 19.14

Gaius Caligula died immediately, but the bloodshed went on. His German bodyguards were mortified at their failure to protect their master and rushed back to slay those assassins tardy at disappearing from the scene, along with some innocent bystanders paralyzed by shock. Meanwhile the vindictive assassins vented their fury on the rest of Gaius Caligula's family, slaying Caesonia and dashing the baby Drusilla's brains out against a wall.

The senate met in triumph to discuss the restoration of the Republic.

Outside the meeting the Roman people loudly and publicly demonstrated their anger, showing considerable affection for their dead emperor and marked antipathy to the return of senatorial rule. Likewise, the Praetorian Guard immediately disowned their tribune and secured the palace against both senate and conspirators. It had quickly occurred to them that they owed their privileges to being guards of the emperor, and without an emperor they were redundant. In some quarters at least, the death of Rome's mad tyrant was already a cause for regret.

Of Bridges at Baiae and Horses as Consuls

It is typical of perceptions of Gaius Caligula that his reign is best known for something which certainly never happened. Gaius Caligula had a horse named Incitatus, and this was undoubtedly a very pampered beast indeed.

To prevent Incitatus, his favourite horse, from growing restive he always picketed the neighbourhood with troops on the day before the races, ordering them to enforce absolute silence. Incitatus owned a marble stable, an ivory stall and a jewelled collar; also a house, furniture and slaves – to provide suitable entertainment for guests whom Gaius Caligula invited in its name. It is said that he even planned to award Incitatus a consulship.

Suetonius *Gaius Caligula 55*

But Incitatus was never made a consul of Rome. Dio alleges that Gaius Caligula would have done so had he lived, which is possible, given the deterioration in the emperor's conduct in his last months. But more probably Gaius Caligula had commented (with some justification) that his horse would have done a better job than the consuls of the day, and his remark was wilfully misinterpreted. The acts of a mad emperor inspire the imagination more than the bizarre humour of a power-drunk youth.

37 *Two handsome charioteers. Chariot racing was a dangerous but exciting sport which Caligula, like many Romans, followed passionately. These mosaics are two of a set of four which depict the different colours of the teams that raced in the Circus Maximus. They are now in the National Museum in Rome.*

Not everyone hated Gaius Caligula. His life story was recorded for posterity by the Roman elite, who quite reasonably loathed him for the humiliations heaped upon their class. At the time however, seeing the senate suffer rather appealed to the common people of Rome. Nor did all senators suffer equally. As indignantly as they denied it later, a substantial number of senators enjoyed Gaius Caligula's favour and prospered under his rule. Some of his victims were probably genuine conspirators or – equally treasonable in Gaius Caligula's eyes – refused to defer properly to his superior rank and commands, however unreasonable those might be. Others were former associates of Sejanus, the bogeyman of Gaius Caligula's youth.

It was on the neck of Rome's aristocracy that the jewelled sandal of Gaius Caligula pressed most heavily; but even if we double the number of Gaius Caligula's named victims, we still fall short by dozens of the number of Roman nobles slain by Octavian the triumvir or by Caesar in the civil wars. Octavian slew his half-brother Caesarion, and young Agrippa was killed at the start of Tiberius' reign, so Gaius Caligula was hardly alone in killing his kinsfolk. As we have heard, Augustus himself had commented that 'one can have too many Caesars'.

The true crime of Gaius Caligula was not homicidal mania, but pushing the trend of the past century to its logical conclusion to show the Caesars as the autocrats they had become. This was not so much mad as several centuries premature. Gaius Caligula's bid for absolute power was certain to fail, because first-century Roman senators were essential to the

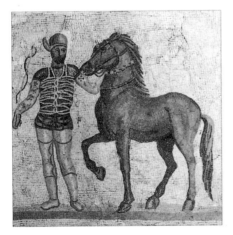 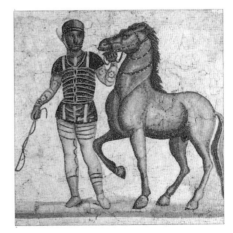

trade in favours and privileges, which defined social life at every level in the Roman world. Individual senators could be replaced or killed, but senators in general were vital to Roman society. What the senate failed to realize until Gaius Caligula's death was that the same was now true of Roman emperors.

The senate's proposed return to the Republic was doomed to failure for another reason. The Roman Empire which had prospered under Augustus and Tiberius continued to do so under Gaius Caligula. Modern economists are far less appalled by Gaius Caligula's financial behaviour than were Rome's senators. The emperor certainly extracted huge sums from the treasury, and extorted equally large sums from the aristocracy. But the money did not stay in his hands. Gaius Caligula was wildly extravagant. In the 1920s some of his pleasure boats were found where they had been scuttled in Lake Nemi. They had mosaic floors, lead piping for the water, and columns of African marble. 'There were sterns set with precious gems, heated baths and banqueting halls, multicoloured sails and fruit trees,' Suetonius adds helpfully.

Gaius Caligula was a keen builder, who planned a number of structures around the Empire, from a lighthouse in Boulogne (which stood until the sixteenth century) to a proposed canal across the isthmus in Greece. He also set about rearranging the Palatine hill to reflect a more imperial theme (which is why the residences of rulers are still referred to as 'palaces'). This expenditure benefited the jewellers, artisans and craftsmen of the Empire. Gaius Caligula also paid the common people more directly too, with disaster relief (after a major fire in Rome), benefactions (such as finally paying out the provisions of Livia's will, which Tiberius had suppressed) or direct distribution, on one occasion throwing so much gold and silver to the public that dozens were killed in the crush to retrieve it. These actions would be referred to today as 'increasing the velocity of the money supply', and boosted the economy in much the same way as modern governments attempt by tax rebates, for example, or staging the Olympic games.

Totally unintentionally, this is also what Gaius Caligula achieved with his famous bridge at Baiae. This 'bridge' was in fact a pontoon of boats three miles' long built at huge effort and expense across the bay at the holiday resort of Baiae. Once the bridge was built, Gaius Caligula crossed it, once on a warhorse, and once on a chariot pulled by two famous racehorses. By the end of the second day the event had become a huge drunken party, including the general public who had gathered on the sea shore, some of whom drowned during the festivities. This show-manship and lavish expenditure both raised the morale of the Roman people and made it plain to everyone that Gaius Caligula was firmly in charge. Suetonius says much the same thing.

Some believe that he built the bridge as a marvel of engineering to overawe the Germans and Britons [and incidentally the Parthians, who had at least one representative at the spectacle]...but my grandfather told me when I was a boy that, according to those intimate with Gaius Caligula's inner circle, there was only one reason why the bridge was built. When Tiberius could not decide on a successor, and was considering the grandson who carried his name, he was informed by the astrologer Thrasyllus that Gaius 'could no more become emperor than he could ride a horse across the Gulf of Baiae'.

Suetonius *Gaius Caligula* 19

It was not so much Gaius Caligula's expenditure which affected the national budget as the fact that at the start of his reign he had reduced taxes (another reason for his popularity). As stated earlier, Gaius Caligula's very expensive tastes were balanced by his disinclination to go to war. Overall, his combined extravagances probably cost less than one of his father's campaigns in Germany. Despite later accusations that Gaius Caligula drained the treasury, there was little sign of economic austerity under his successor. This was partly because of Gaius Caligula's exactions from the aristocracy, and partly because he instituted new taxes later in his reign to balance the books, including a tax on brothels and taverns. Since direct taxation was almost unknown in Italy at that time, this inspired one of the few popular demonstrations against Gaius Caligula, allegedly causing the emperor to snarl back defiantly, 'I wish you Roman people had just one neck, so that I could cut it through at a blow.'

A factor which much less affected Gaius Caligula's popularity was the fading away of the last semblances of democracy. At the start of his reign Gaius Caligula restored to the people the right to elect the magistrates of

Rome. This had been curtailed by Caesar, made a sham by Augustus, and transferred to the senate by Tiberius. In reality, the people very soon realized voting had become a meaningless gesture. Even when the power to elect magistrates was restored to them, either the senate or the emperor worked behind the scenes to ensure only their preferred candidates were available for each office.

The lack of any real choice of candidate, combined with the total inability of those elected to affect the Roman state for good or ill, evoked such overwhelming and embarrassing apathy from the voters that Gaius Caligula reluctantly transferred the choice of magistrates back to the senate, although in reality, by manipulating who stood for office, the senate had never really lost control of the process.

Gaius Caligula seems to have been competent in his selection of provincial governors. Galba was an excellent choice for Germany, while in the East both Vitellius and his successor proved adept at dealing with both Parthians and provincials. In fact, the Empire was mainly tranquil under Gaius Caligula. During his reign Mauretania was incorporated into the Empire. Until then the region had been divided into the Roman province of Africa, and the kingdom of Ptolemy in the region of modern Morocco. This Ptolemy was a distant relative of Gaius Caligula, being descended from Mark Antony's liaison with Cleopatra. Consanguinity did not save him, for he was summoned to Rome and executed. Ptolemy was the only Roman client king to be executed, though Mithridates of Armenia was imprisoned and later exiled.

Ptolemy's crime may have been that he was a bad ruler, and experience with the rebel Tacfarinas had taught the Romans that an unruly and unstable kingdom to the west of their province of Africa threatened their interests. One of the governors of Africa in the late AD 30s was Calpurnius Piso, the son of the Calpurnius Piso suspected of poisoning Gaius Caligula's father Germanicus. This would suggest that Gaius Caligula followed the senatorial tradition that, whatever the sins of the elder Piso, the son was certainly innocent.

There was (as ever) skirmishing on the Rhine frontier with the Germans, but within the provinces the most significant problem Gaius Caligula encountered was with the Jews. As with most Romans of this period, there is little sign that Gaius Caligula was anti-Semitic. Indeed, when anti-Jewish riots broke out in Alexandria in Egypt, Gaius Caligula recalled the governor, Flaccus, and had him executed. It did not help Flaccus that he had been involved in the exile of Gaius Caligula's mother, but certainly his offence included incompetence in allowing the riots to happen in the first place.

There were serious riots between Jews and Greeks in Judaea, where the Greeks erected an altar to Gaius Caligula, and the Jews tore it down. Gaius Caligula reacted furiously to the news, and decreed that the Temple in Jerusalem was to be converted for use by the imperial cult, and that a huge statue of himself should stand in the sanctum. Petronius, the governor of Syria, had military responsibility for Judaea, and on receiving this news he immediately began to make both military and diplomatic preparations for the measure, which would almost certainly spark a revolt.

Petronius, when he had read the letter containing his orders, was in a quandary. He was afraid to query the instructions he had been given, for he had heard of the emperor's implacable wrath not only against those who did not follow orders, but also against those who did not follow them instantly. On the other hand, he did not see how he could easily execute his instructions either, for he knew that the Jews would, if it were possible, willingly die ten thousand times rather than submit to seeing any profanity perpetrated against their religion; for all men are eager to preserve their own customs and laws, and the Jewish nation above all others.

Philo *Embassy to Gaius* 210

Petronius ordered the sculptors making Gaius Caligula's statue to take their time, and simultaneously tried to persuade the Jews to accept the idea and Gaius Caligula to abandon it. In the end Gaius Caligula's close friend, the Jewish king Herod Agrippa, brokered a diplomatic compromise whereby Gaius Caligula did not press his claims to be worshipped in the Temple as long as the Jewish people refrained from interfering with emperor-worship elsewhere. Philo's more hostile tradition claims that Gaius Caligula would not be swayed, and ordered the death of the temporizing Petronius, who was only saved by the news that the emperor had been killed.

CHAPTER 7

CLAUDIUS:
THE UNEXPECTED EMPEROR

*The crux of the matter is (how best to put this?) whether he has full command
of his faculties. If he is going to be physically or mentally handicapped, he
(and therefore we) might easily become a laughing stock. There are going to be
constant problems if we have to keep deciding if he can officiate here, or
carry out duties there. What we need to decide is whether he is basically
competent to perform in a public capacity.*
(Letter of Augustus to Livia) Suetonius *Claudius* 4

Caligula's death raised the question of how far the Julio-Claudians had
succeeded in taking over the Roman Empire. Opinion was divided on the
issue. When Julius Caesar first took power, the idea that Rome should be
subject to an autocrat was intolerable to the senate, and even now the
idea rankled. The petty nobility of Italy, on the other hand, had rather
warmed to the idea. Excluded and ignored by the elite in Rome, they discovered the Caesars as champions against the power and influence which
the great families had wielded with such greedy self-interest. Another
group that supported the Caesars was the common people of the Empire
who appreciated good government in Italy, relative freedom from extor-
tionate exploitation in the provinces, and everywhere the stability of
imperial rule. Since the common people supplied the soldiers in the
legions, they were not a constituency to be lightly ignored.

Furthermore, Roman society had adapted itself to the presence of
emperors. Emperors had become the controlling factor in the power
struggles of the elite, the channel by which influential provincials were
introduced to the top echelons of the government, and above all the only
part of the aristocracy capable of keeping the army under control.

This slowly dawned on the senate when it met shortly after the death of Caligula. It had convened on the Capitol, a site chosen for its venerable religious and political significance, but above all because it was easily defended. The people suspected the senate of complicity in Caligula's death and were angry, confused and dangerous.

After debating earnestly whether the Republic could be restored, the senate finally came to the pragmatic decision that it could not, but if Rome must have an emperor, he should at least be one of the senate's own. Unfortunately most senators had clear but incompatible ideas about whom this should be.

But for those outside the senate, the only acceptable candidate was Tiberius Claudius Nero Germanicus, known today simply as Claudius. This popular support shows how deeply the people appreciated the stability of the long reigns of Augustus and Tiberius, and also shows that their experience of Gaius Caligula had not severely dampened enthusiasm for Julio-Claudian rule.

That Claudius was chosen indicates how far the pressures of imperial rule had decimated the ruling family, and how strongly the public wanted almost its last surviving member as emperor, notwithstanding his evident disabilities. Even Claudius' own kin had considered him unpromising material: 'Capricious and wool-gathering.' 'Heaven help the Roman people if he were to become emperor!' 'Something half-formed and then abandoned by nature.' These opinions were uttered respectively by Augustus, by Claudius' sister Livilla, and by his mother Antonia. The last also criticized someone as being 'almost as stupid as my son'. That Claudius became emperor despite these harsh judgments on his character shows that the Julio-Claudian takeover of Rome was now so complete that Caligula might well have succeeded in his alleged intention of making a consul of his horse – had he first formally adopted the beast into the imperial family.

38 *Antonia Augusta, mother of Claudius. Antonia stayed well out of the front line of Roman politics, and showed no interest in promoting the career of Claudius, rather regarding him as an embarrassment to be kept from the public eye.*

The son whom Antonia so despised was born in 10 BC while she accompanied her husband Drusus the Elder in Gaul. The event was parodied by the philosopher Seneca.

I tell you, he was born at Lyons...he was born at the sixteenth milestone from Vienne, a native Gaul. So of course he took Rome, as a good Gaul ought to do. I pledge you my word that in Lyons he was born, where Licinus was king so many years.

Seneca *The Pumpkinification of Claudius*

Young Claudius laboured under a number of disadvantages. A childhood illness – perhaps cerebral palsy – had left him with shaky arms and head, a dragging leg and a harsh croaking voice which Seneca later unfavourably compared with a sea-monster's. Rather like his uncle Tiberius, he was somewhat ponderous, wayward in learning, but good at what he learned, and whimsical in his personal attachments. This, together with his habit of digressing and losing track of what he was saying, gave an impression of reduced mental capacity. His family seems to have quickly regarded Claudius as an imbecile – not an unusual attitude in a society intolerant of the physically handicapped. And since at the time of Claudius' childhood the Julio-Claudian line was flourishing, there seemed no need to inspect him for hidden qualities.

As is evident from his name, Claudius was a Claudius Nero. His brother Germanicus was next in line for the imperial succession until his

39 *Two members of the imperial family, believed to be Antonia Augusta and her husband Drusus, on the Ara Pacis. Claudius himself is relegated to the background, and indeed probably only appears on Augustan statuary at all because his absence would be yet more conspicuous.*

untimely death (p. 141). After Germanicus, his three sons were next in line for the purple and Gemellus, the son of the emperor Tiberius, also had a powerful claim. Claudius himself was well down the line of succession and no one imagined that he had the personal qualities to jump the queue. He lacked the quick wit and ambition of the Julians as completely as he lacked the charisma of his brother Germanicus, but it turned out that instead he had the far more valuable knack of staying alive.

From the beginning Claudius' public appearances were rare. When he did appear at the games, he was often well wrapped up and seated somewhere inconspicuous. In statuary groups from before AD 41 he is a minor figure sandwiched between the wives and children of peripheral family members. The emperor Augustus put his disappointing relative in the care of a teacher-cum-mentor whom Claudius bitterly described as a semi-literate mule driver who beat him whatever he did. Augustus further displayed his disdain by virtually ignoring Claudius in his will.

To impress his family Claudius turned to scholarship. Despairing of his shaking right hand, he learned to write with his left, an effort which was totally wasted.

Though he applied himself earnestly to literature while a child, and showed his ability in several of the samples which he published, this failed to inspire his family to more hopeful plans for his future, or to aid his hopes for public office.

Suetonius *Claudius* 3

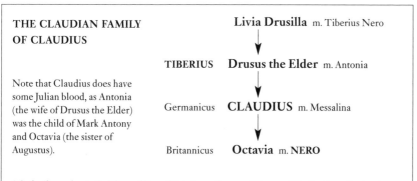

THE CLAUDIAN FAMILY OF CLAUDIUS

Note that Claudius does have some Julian blood, as Antonia (the wife of Drusus the Elder) was the child of Mark Antony and Octavia (the sister of Augustus).

Livia Drusilla m. Tiberius Nero

TIBERIUS Drusus the Elder m. Antonia

Germanicus CLAUDIUS m. Messalina

Britannicus Octavia m. NERO

The family members to the left are siblings of the primary figure, and the name following the m. denotes the marriage partner from whom the child of the next generation was born. Emperors in caps.

In fact, when Claudius wrote to his uncle, the emperor Tiberius, asking permission to begin his senatorial career by standing for election as quaestor, he was rudely rebuffed. Tiberius told him to be content with his honorary priesthoods, and to spend his money on idle amusements.

Claudius threw himself deeper into his studies. The writing of history was a suitable occupation for a gentleman, as the disappointed politicians Thucydides and Sallust had demonstrated. Claudius may also have received encouragement from the great historian Livy before the latter's death in AD 17 (or AD 12 as some have argued). Writing in Greek, Claudius produced an extensive Etruscan history, and reputedly made himself one of the last speakers of Etruscan in the process. He also wrote a history of Carthage, and another of near-contemporary Rome (though he diplomatically omitted the blood-soaked years of Octavian's triumvirate).

When not engaged in literary pursuits (none of his works has survived), Claudius passed his time drinking and gambling in the company of disreputable friends – something of a Julio-Claudian family habit, and one that Claudius retained until the end of his days. Nevertheless, he was respected both by the general public and the senate, who voted him to a priesthood in the Augustan cult and offered to rebuild his house at public expense when it was destroyed in a fire. Since Claudius was not permitted public office he could not be a senator, but he was the foremost member of the equestrian order, and their chosen delegate in representations to the emperor. 'As a mark of respect, the entire equestrian order would rise and take off their cloaks when he appeared in the theatre or amphitheatre', Suetonius tells us, adding that Claudius frequently attended literary salons and readings.

Though he might have considered Claudius useless as a person, Tiberius did not neglect his nephew's potential for his dynastic plans. Claudius was married first to Urgulanilla, from a family traditionally allied with the imperial house, and later to the highly aristocratic ladies Aemilia Lepida and Livia Camilla. Claudius outlived all these brides, and also his own son by Urgulanilla. His wives all died naturally, which tells us something of mortality rates in ancient Rome, while his son (who was engaged to be married to the daughter of Tiberius' second-in-command Sejanus) died by choking on a pear which he had thrown into the air and tried all too successfully to catch in his mouth.

In March AD 37 Claudius' life of quiet study was changed forever by the death of his uncle Tiberius and the accession of his nephew Gaius Caligula. Gaius' sole claim to imperial power was that he was a Julio-Claudian. Accordingly he strove to reinforce public respect for his family to strengthen his hold on power. As a son of the popular hero Germanicus, Gaius Caligula had to show respect for Germanicus' brother (who was also entitled to call himself Germanicus, for the designation was a hereditary family name).

Thus Claudius finally entered the senate at the age of forty-six, and in so doing proved that one can start a job at the top, since he joined as fellow consul of the emperor. It was not a comfortable job, for Gaius Caligula was a bully and impatient with Claudius' deficiencies. If it is true that Gaius Caligula habitually asked Claudius for his opinion last of all the senators, this was certainly an insult to his consular uncle; but it also meant that other senators could express themselves without being constrained by an opinion from the imperial household. Given Gaius Caligula's nature, he was probably aware of both these factors. As a final act of nastiness, the emperor made Claudius a priest of his cult, forcing him to pay most of his estate for the dubious honour.

Nevertheless, it is a mark of Claudius' increased status, as well as a sign of the ever-increasing scarcity of eligible Julio-Claudian spouses, that Claudius now put his relatively obscure current wife aside, and married the young Valeria Messalina in AD 38. Messalina had connections with the Claudius Pulchers through her aunt and more distantly with the Marcellan branch of the clan. She was also a descendant of Valerius Messala, who had been a ruthless henchman of Augustus. Messalina and Claudius had a daughter, Octavia, born AD 39, and a son, Germanicus (later renamed Britannicus), who was born in AD 41. In securing her children's future and her own grip on power, Messalina showed herself without scruple or mercy to a degree that would have struck her grim ancestors dumb with horrified admiration.

Meanwhile as Gaius Caligula mistakenly began to feel more secure as emperor, Claudius became ever more vulnerable. Some of the emperor's lackeys began to test the imperial attitude by launching petty lawsuits against the increasingly isolated Claudius, and it is reasonable to surmise that had Gaius Caligula lasted much longer, Claudius would not have.

A Different Emperor, a Different Empire

It is interesting yet futile to speculate how far Claudius was involved in the assassination of Gaius Caligula. Possibly he let it be known through his subordinates that he would accept the action, and imperial power thereafter. Possibly powerful factions imagined setting him up as a drooling figurehead while they got on with ruling the Empire. Possibly the conspirators had no fixed plan apart from a powerful desire to be rid of Caligula or, more probably, they each had their own incompatible ideas about what to do next. Messalina was quite possibly actively involved, or had at the least made contingency plans with Gaius Caligula's powerful freedman Callistus.

That Claudius left that fateful theatrical event ahead of Gaius Caligula suggests that either he or those about him knew that the locality was about to become extremely unsafe. But Claudius returned to the palace, apparently unaware that it was the second most dangerous place in Rome after the assassination site itself. The palace was occupied by those intent on finishing off the dynasty altogether, and by others intent on preserving it. The extirpationists found Caesonia and her daughter first, killed them, and went in search of Claudius. The historian Josephus takes up the story.

The highly agitated Claudius sought to save himself by hiding in a small room, though the only thing of which he was guilty was his high birth, but everywhere there was consternation, the palace was filled with the soldiers' madness and the guards were in the grip of fear and disorder no less than the civilians. But Gratus, who was one of the palace guards, discovered him. Actually, he did not know who he had found in the shadows but it was plain that the person had put himself there with a purpose [i.e. to hide]. He came close, and when Claudius tried to get away, he recognized him at once. So he said to his companions, 'This is a Germanicus; come on, let us choose him as our emperor.'

Josephus *Wars of the Jews* 3.1

Claudius was escorted from the palace to the relative safety of the Praetorian camp. There he met delegates from the senate who first blustered and threatened, but with their political power waning almost as fast as their military power (the swiftly defecting urban cohorts), later delegates were left to beg only that Claudius accept supreme power at their hands rather than from the soldiers. It was a decisive moment in the history of the Empire. Henceforth the power of the Caesars openly rested on the soldiers and was expressed through the emperor's courtiers. The senate remained as a consultative body which formalized legislation and acted as a pool from which administrators and generals were drawn. It was still immensely important, but perceptions had irrevocably shifted. Rome was now an autocracy which happened to have a senate rather than a senatorial government which happened to have an emperor.

Once everyone was clear on this point, the formalities went ahead. The senate officially gave Claudius his imperial powers, and Claudius celebrated his access to the imperial purse-strings by giving the Praetorian Guard a substantial cash bonus (called a donative, which became traditional on the accession of a new emperor). Coins from this occasion still exist showing Claudius frankly recognizing that he owed the Empire to the Praetorians.

Almost the last of the Julians were the sisters of Gaius Caligula. These were restored from the safety of exile to where the jealous Messalina awaited them in Rome. Meanwhile Claudius appended the Julian name of Caesar to his own. Roman tradition allowed this, in that Claudius was related to Augustus (his grandmother was Augustus' sister) and more distant relatives could take a distinguished family name if its immediate bearers became extinct. Nevertheless, this marked the point at which Caesar became less a name than a job description. Until now imperial power had passed directly down the paternal line through an unlikely series of adoptions. But Claudius did not become emperor because he was a Caesar, he became a Caesar because he was emperor.

There was a further development. Augustus and his successors had companions and a retinue. Claudius had a court. And with this came the obscure internecine scheming and jockeying for position which were an integral part of such institutions. This suited two parties in particular. One was Messalina and her successors, for an imperial wife could influence her husband and be persuaded to influence him for others. The other group was the freedmen of the imperial household. As their names imply, freedmen were ex-slaves who could be handed positions of responsibility in the household of their former master. Since the private persona of the emperor was not separated from his public role, the imperial household in a manner of speaking was the Roman Empire.

That the Empire was being partly managed by women and freed slaves outraged the senate, who had once had the job to themselves. Those whom the senate particularly loathed were Narcissus, the secretary, and Pallas, the treasurer. Claudius was able to give both huge power and responsibility because he knew that they were both dependent on him and totally incapable of taking power for themselves. Both men became so rich that it was jokingly suggested that the financial problems of the Empire would be resolved overnight if Claudius' freedmen took him into their partnership.

What caused the deterioration of Claudius was above all the freedmen and the women with whom he associated. More obviously than any of his peers, he was ruled by slaves and by women.

   Cassius Dio *History* 60.2

It also helped that unpopular but politically expedient actions could be carried out by these freedmen, or even Messalina, yet they could be disowned if the backlash proved too strong. In short, Claudius had wittingly or unwittingly created a powerful faction dedicated to his well-being, not through loyalty but self interest, and to which he owed no reciprocal loyalty and could abandon if it suited him.

This was demonstrated by the execution of Cassius Chaerea, the assassin of Gaius Caligula. This death had brought Claudius to power, and probably saved his life. Yet Claudius, through circumstance or design, was seen as so remote from the plot that he could execute its perpetrators without any accusation of ingratitude. This execution calmed popular pressure for justice for Gaius Caligula and clearly signalled that assassinating emperors, for whatever reason, could not go unpunished. However, those awaiting trial for *maiestas* were released, and shown the charges against them for the first time. In a further step away from the policies of his predecessor, Claudius took care to assure the senate of his complete non-divinity, and showed the same respect to Rome's magistrates as Tiberius and Augustus had done.

In reviewing the *maiestas* trials, Claudius demonstrated, not for the last time, a keen interest in legal proceedings. He personally went through all the outstanding cases to determine which actually had merit, and which were Caligula's caprice.

In a nice (and typically Claudian) touch, the dancers with whom Gaius Caligula had stopped to chat were asked to complete the performance for which they had been rehearsing when he was assassinated. Afterwards they were rewarded with Roman citizenship.

In AD 42 the new regime faced an early challenge from the governor of Dalmatia, L. Arruntius Camillus Scribonianus. This Scribonianus was brother to one of Claudius' former brides, a lady who had actually died on her wedding day. Thereafter Scribonianus seems to have converted to republican sentiments. His demand that Claudius stand down and hand power to the senate was ignored by both the government in Rome and by Scribonianus' own soldiers, forcing the governor to flight, capture and death. The event caused the legions concerned to be renamed Claudia Pia Fidelis ('faithful and true'), but also reminded Claudius that as the brother of Germanicus his reign rested in part on a tradition of military glory which had captured the imagination of the troops. Fortunately the reign of Claudius started with a series of military successes.

His freedmen persuaded Claudius to accept triumphal ornaments as though he had gained a success in Mauretania, though this was not the case, for in fact the war had ended before he came to power. But that same year, Sulpicius Galba defeated the Chatti, and Publius Gabinius the Chauci and, to top it all off, recovered a Roman eagle – the only one still in enemy hands after the Varian disaster. Thanks to these two men Claudius now received and well deserved the title of imperator.
Cassius Dio *History* 60.8

In North Africa Suetonius Paulinus, an ex-praetor, had taken Roman arms to the foot of Mount Atlas, yet it was probably the successes in Germany that made Claudius greedy for more. Accordingly plans for the invasion of Britain, abandoned since the farcical attempt of Gaius, were dusted off and re-examined.

Meanwhile in Rome, the political temperature was rising. Messalina successfully undermined the position of the newly returned Julia Livilla, the sister whom Gaius Caligula had exiled in AD 39. The tired old charge of adultery was wheeled out again, and Julia Livilla found herself back on an island, allegedly guilty of consorting with Annaeus Seneca (who was also exiled, which explains his later attitude to the Claudian regime). With Julia Livilla out of sight and out of Claudius' mind, Messalina turned her potential rival's exile into a more permanent condition by having her killed. Not unnaturally, this put Agrippina, the surviving sister, well on her guard, and throughout their subsequent bitter feud Messalina was unable to land a significant blow.

Claudius himself was engaged in rooting out the supporters of Scribonianus in Rome, even resorting to the torture of free men, something he had sworn to abjure. The accused were tried in the senate, which allowed that body to relish the tart reply of Scribonianus' freedman when asked by Narcissus what he would have done had his master become emperor: 'I would have stood behind him – and kept my mouth shut.' Another memorable comment was by Arria, wife of one of the accused. Angered by her husband's feeble attempts to commit suicide, she finally demonstrated the correct process by emphatically stabbing herself. Then while dying, she handed over the sword with the comment, 'Paetus, it doesn't hurt.'

Claudius now had anyone coming into his presence searched for weapons – not an unreasonable measure since a nameless would-be assassin was caught outside his chambers with a knife, and two equestrians were found lurking in ambuscade when he went to sacrifice at the temple of Mars. In a slightly more organized conspiracy one Asinius Gallus and Statilius Corvinus, both of respected families, suborned several freedmen of Claudius' household before they were caught.

Home and Abroad: Britons and Messalina

We know that Jupiter is king in heaven because we hear his thunder roll;
Augustus [Claudius] shall be considered a god on earth for adding to our
Empire the Britons and dreaded Parthians.

Horace *Odes* 3.5: 1–4

As is evident from the above quotation, the invasion of Britain was not, as often advertised, a quick fix by which Claudius established his military credentials, but a project which the Romans had been mulling over for generations. Julius Caesar had conducted something between an invasion and a reconnaissance in force, but events in Gaul and later in Rome had claimed his attention. Augustus had been similarly distracted by Varus' huge defeat in Germany. Tiberius had neither the need to establish a military reputation, nor the inclination to let anyone else do so. Gaius Caligula's attempt ended as a shambles, all of which left Claudius with the motive, means and opportunity to make Rome master of the fabled and distant island.

Claudius, the historian, had learned from the experience of Julius Caesar. He gathered four legions to Caesar's five (II Augusta, IX Hispana, the twentieth and XIV Gemina), but thousands more auxiliary cavalrymen from Gaul and the Rhinelands.

Despite having had three generations to prepare, the British response to the Roman threat was inadequate and in many cases half-hearted, but this is not to say the invasion was an easy business. The Romans were poor sailors. In previous campaigns they had lost more men to storms at sea than to the combined warriors of Britain and Germany, and as their record in the Punic Wars shows, this was not an unusual proportion of casualties for a Roman maritime campaign. Claudius' soldiers were so reluctant to take to sea that his freedman Narcissus attempted to sway them with a speech. At first affronted at taking orders from a freedman, the soldiers jokingly decided that Saturnalia had come early and embarked in good spirits. (At the Saturnalia festival, slaves could order their masters about.)

The Romans probably landed at Richborough in late May of 42, and after meeting bitter resistance at the Medway and the Thames crossings, they were poised to take London by July. At this point Claudius himself joined the fray. Dio's account that the general leading the army was afraid to advance any further is correct, but only insofar as he was afraid to disobey orders to call for Claudius after a secure bridgehead had been established. Claudius arrived in all haste – eager for the glory of leading the invading army, but reluctant to be away from Rome so early in his reign. His lightning campaign is well summarized by Dio:

He crossed over to Britain, where he joined the legions that were waiting for him near the Thames. Taking command, he crossed the river and engaged the barbarians, who had gathered at his approach. He defeated them and captured Camulodunum [Colchester; see plate 25 for Claudius' temple], the capital of Cunobellinus. Thereafter he won over numerous tribes, some by negotiated surrender, others by naked force. He was saluted as imperator several times, which was unprecedented for this title should only be given once during the same war. He disarmed the conquered and handed them over to Plautius, ordering him also to subjugate the remaining lands. Claudius himself now hastened back to Rome, sending ahead the news of his victory.

Cassius Dio *History* 60.21

The campaign was successful partly because it was meticulously organized. Claudius would have heartily endorsed the modern dictum, 'Good generals do tactics, great generals do logistics.' Claudius, as Caesar probably did before him, brought the first elephants to tread British soil since the woolly mammoth. Since Britain was strange and wonderful to the Romans, the reasoning was that the Romans should appear equally exotic and terrifying to the Britons. Furthermore, the sight and smell of elephants terrified inexperienced horses, and this mitigated the effect of the British light chariots which had harassed and frustrated Julius Caesar.

Claudius was away from Rome for less than nine months, but achieved enough to genuinely merit the triumph he celebrated in AD 44. A further sign of his satisfaction is that Aulus Plautius, the Roman field commander in Britain, was allowed to celebrate an ovation (a minor triumph) when he returned in 47 – the first general outside the house of Caesar to do so since the time of Augustus. After Plautius, a series of commanders (including the future emperor Vespasian) inched Roman control northwards in a series of gruelling campaigns. The British found a worthy leader in Caractacus, son of Cunobellinus, and even after he was captured and paraded in Rome in AD 51 the war continued. It remained a background theme to the rest of Claudius' reign, a source of pride and glory (Claudius even renamed his son Britannicus to celebrate his achievement), but also a steady and unrelenting drain on the treasury. It would be centuries before the island repaid the cost of conquering it.

Meanwhile, back in Rome, the household of Claudius had to grapple with the growing problem of Messalina.

…The good old sluggard [Claudius] but began to snore,
When from his side up rose the imperial whore…
To the known brothel-house she takes her way;
And for a nasty room gives double pay;
That room in which the rankest harlot lay.
Prepared for fight, expectingly she lies,
With heaving breasts, and with desiring eyes.
Still as one drops, another takes his place,
And baffled still succeeds to like disgrace. …
    John Dryden *Messalina*

It takes a certain degree of character to become remembered as the most depraved and murderous nymphomaniac in antiquity, but Messalina (plate 26) earned her place in Dryden's fevered imagination. She used adultery both as a political instrument and a recreational device, and had not the slightest hesitation in killing anyone who crossed her. She was in her late teens or early twenties when she married the fifty-year-old Claudius, who was her second cousin – Messalina's great-grandmother was Octavia, sister of Augustus.

Messalina was for a long time allied with Claudius' freedman Narcissus, as each of the pair used the trust of Claudius to further their own power. Ancient historians such as Cassius Dio depict Messalina as a lust-crazed young woman with little interest in politics, but many of her early killings had a clear political dimension. Claudius himself was secure in his power (when there was a rumour that he had died in Ostia, the public almost rioted), but he was elderly and had a history of poor health. If he were to die unexpectedly, the outlook for Messalina and her offspring was bleak unless potential rivals were speedily disposed of.

With Agrippina on her guard, Messalina's malign attention turned to junior members of her clan. Appius Silanus had close connections to the Claudians (as is indicated by his name Appius), and his daughter had once married into the Julian family. Claudius considered Silanus sufficiently dangerous to recall him from his governorship in Spain, and marry him to Messalina's mother. Both Messalina and Narcissus considered this precaution insufficient. Silanus was summoned to the palace, allegedly by the emperor, but in fact without his knowledge. While he was *en route*, Narcissus burst into the imperial bedchamber maintaining that he had dreamed that Silanus was coming to assassinate Claudius. Messalina promptly announced that she had been disturbed by the identical dream. When a bemused Silanus arrived at the palace, he was promptly arrested and later executed.

That Claudius was duped by his wife and freedmen is a constant in all our sources. When Messalina decided to destroy a woman named Poppaea as part of a larger plot, Tacitus assures us that Claudius was blithely unaware of anything amiss.

At great speed she [Messalina] applied herself to Poppaea's destruction. She hired agents to drive her to suicide by making her believe she was about to be thrown into prison. [Claudius] Caesar meanwhile was so unaware of all this that a few days afterwards he asked her husband Scipio, who was dining with him, why he had come to the meal without his wife. Scipio replied that she had paid a debt to nature.

Tacitus *Annals* 11.2

Modern historians are rather more cynical. Claudius was hardly the amiable old buffer of his caricature. During his reign he proved a shrewd and ruthless politician. Suetonius tells us he took a keen technical interest in torture, and thoroughly enjoyed the bloodletting of the arena. That his wife and freedmen were cutting a swathe through his political and dynastic rivals probably did not distress him unduly, especially as the opprobrium for these dark deeds fell upon others. Dio is probably correct to claim that Messalina incited or coerced noble ladies into sexual liaisons, but this was more than simply to cover her own misdeeds. Adultery was a threat Messalina could hold over these ladies and their lovers, with the threat of death or banishment if the crime was revealed.

However, some of Messalina's affairs, such as with the actor Mnester, seem to have been purely self-gratification and a juvenile delight in taking risks. Messalina may have calculated that her personal hold on the emperor as his wife and the mother of his children should buy her immunity. But she reckoned without her husband's finely honed instinct for self-preservation and overlooked Claudius' freedmen, who would not countenance the undermining of the man on whom their fate depended.

Early in AD 47, Messalina successfully disposed of the venerable and respected Valerius Asiaticus, apparently for no better reason than that she wanted his famous Sallustian Gardens on the outskirts of Rome. Any deeper motive is uncertain – for the most part, palace intrigues were almost as opaque to contemporary outsiders as they are to historians today. In any case, the death of Asiaticus did not go down well with the senate or Claudius' aristocratic supporters. This was partly because Asiaticus appeared patently innocent (one witness even picked out the wrong man, having been briefed only that the accused was bald), but mainly because the trial was held *intra cubiculum*, in the emperor's private chambers, with the imperial household as judge and jury.

When Polybius, a freedman of Claudius, fell out of favour, his colleagues attributed this to the machinations of Messalina, completing her set of enemies in every stratum of the court. Fast becoming a political liability to Claudius, Messalina was uncomfortably aware that her overheated libido had made her acutely vulnerable. Instead of mending her ways, Messalina promptly launched into an affair with the handsome young consul-designate C. Silius. Perhaps she hoped for the support of the well-connected aristocrat. She may have been contemplating a legal separation from her elderly husband, in the desperate hope that Claudius, with his love of legalism, might not oppose a divorce which formally severed his ties with her. It was a rash move, but time and support were slipping away, and Messalina was justifiably desperate. Alternatively, as Tacitus suggests, her lust simply overruled her common sense. For whatever reason, while Claudius was visiting the nearby Roman port of Ostia, Messalina and Silius decided to wed.

I know that, no matter how obtuse his audience, no storyteller could credibly relate this. That in a city which sees everything and where concealment is impossible, two people, no, a consul-elect and an emperor's wife, came together before witnesses duly summoned and solemnized a marriage. She listened to the words of the bridegroom's companions, sacrificed to the gods…and passed a night in the license of the marriage bed. I tell this story not to stretch your credulity but simply as what I was told, and what our fathers have put on record.

Tacitus *Annals* 11.27

Two questions obsessed an appalled Rome. Who was going to tell Claudius, and what would he do about it? There was a risk that the Roman aristocracy would gather about two of their own, for the families of both Silius and Messalina were of the highest rank. If such a group could bring the Praetorian Guard over to their cause, then Claudius and his Empire stood at risk. Undoubtedly almost as the wedding was being celebrated, every Roman senator was anxiously gauging his position and sounding out opinions. Consensus was quick to form. Claudius was popular with the people and the army. Even most senators felt they could do worse than with the present emperor. In fact, if they supported the newly-weds' cause, they probably would do worse, since Silius was so easily influenced by his murderous spouse. Inevitably the aristocracy withheld their support. This was tantamount to condemning the pair to death, which was exactly what Messalina's many enemies in the senate desired.

If the senate was passively hostile, Claudius' freedmen were actively so. Narcissus took the initiative, and persuaded two of Claudius' concubines to break the news to their imperial paramour. Tacitus and Dio both give credit to Claudius' freedmen, especially Narcissus, but whoever was in control, the government reacted swiftly and decisively to Messalina's treason. Loyal allies were gathered, and since the commander of the Praetorians was not among these, he was suspended for the duration of the emergency. The emperor set off at speed for Rome.

Meanwhile Messalina was sliding ever further into excess. Ensconced in her new home, she oversaw the mid-autumn preparation of the new vintage. The vats overflowed as the presses were trodden. Women dressed in skins danced in a kind of Bacchanal frenzy. Messalina with her hair unbound...and Silius beside her, crowned with ivy, nodded to their lascivious tune. One Vettius Valens climbed a high tree for fun, and when they asked him what he could see from up there, he replied, 'A terrible storm coming from Ostia.'... It was a prophecy, for messengers soon arrived with the news that a vengeful Claudius knew everything and was on his way.

Tacitus *Annals* II.31–32

Any hope of reprieve for the couple was lost when the Praetorians rallied strongly behind Claudius. Silius did not even offer a defence, pleading only that his end be swift. Messalina took refuge in the gardens of Lucullus, and from there sent a stream of pleas for mercy to the palace. It is uncertain whether Claudius knew when executioners were sent to the 'poor creature' (as he now referred to his ex-wife), but he certainly did not stop them. Over the following days, says Tacitus, 'he showed neither hatred, joy, anger nor sadness. In fact, not a single human emotion, either when he looked on his wife's triumphant accusers or on her weeping children.' It was as if Messalina had never existed.

Emperor at Work

Whether Claudius was running the Roman state, or (as was popularly believed) the task fell to others in his household, it was undeniable that the state was rather well run. In part this was because the administrative machinery born under Augustus was gaining shape and maturity. As power centralized about the imperial court, a rudimentary civil service was coming into being.

In the name of administrative efficiency, Claudius took control of the fleets, the Roman roads and the treasury. In AD 53 jurisdiction on financial questions in the provinces was transferred from the proconsul to the imperial procurator, who was not a senator, but an equestrian. Although most of the decisions made by Claudius' appointees were sound, the aristocracy was seriously irked that decisions and appointments were not being made by themselves. Also Claudius' officials were loosely supervised, and allowed considerable latitude; on hearing that his officials had executed a man on his authority, Claudius replied that he had not known of the matter, but no doubt the man had deserved to die.

For most of its history, Rome had a smaller full-time administrative team running its Empire than would today be considered decent for a small modern city. Rome's administrative deficit was partly compensated by the considerable autonomy of the network of the city-states which made up most of the Empire, but even so Claudius could not run the Empire single-handed. While the senate and equestrian order were happy to accept top jobs such as governor, legate or treasurer, there were many other posts which the emperor preferred to keep under his direct control, or which required consistent long-term attention. Therefore, like any Roman aristocrat who took up public office, Claudius and his predecessors delegated many of their official tasks to their own households.

The power of imperial freedmen sprang directly from this latter fact. Freedmen were men who had once been slaves – 'talking tools', Cato the Censor had once called them – and were despised by many aristocrats for their origins, especially when these freedmen seemed to become more powerful than the aristocrats themselves.

Being entirely governed by his freedmen and, as I have already said, by his wives, he [Claudius] was a tool to others, rather than an emperor. He distributed offices, or the command of armies, pardoned or punished, according as it suited their interests, their passions or their caprice; and for the most part without knowing, or being aware of what he did. I won't go into the precise details here about the revocation of grants, the reversal of judicial decisions, obtaining his signature to fictitious appointments, or the bare-faced alteration of them after signing.

Suetonius *Claudius* 29

Despite such opinions, the Romans were fond of pointing out to their subjects that while the benefits of imperial rule extended everywhere, the disadvantages were felt disproportionately by the elite in Rome. Whoever was ruling the Empire and making appointments, cities and provinces benefited from a shrewd grasp of financesthe intricacies of internal and foreign policy, and an understanding of how to handle the fractious and scheming aristocracy.

Therefore if it was Messalina, Narcissus *et al.* who allocated the top jobs in government, it was still in their interest to pick competent placemen. Many appointees were either good with money (or they could not pay the necessary bribes), or excellent at personal relationships or they would not have become protégés. In short, the pool of administrative candidates was self-regulating, and the criteria for selection were in line with the requirements of the job.

Overall, the most dysfunctional part of the entire Roman body politic was the imperial family itself, partly because of the huge pressures that imperial rule imposed upon those doing it, but also because Claudius

17 (*right*) Tiberius as a young man.
Through much of the principate of
Augustus, Tiberius was one of the
Empire's most senior generals, and his
importance as a commander became even
greater after the death of Agrippa. After
spending his youth campaigning on
Rome's northern frontiers, Tiberius
never left Italy again once he was made
emperor.

18 (*below*) Part of a Roman sword sheath
showing Germanicus in military dress
greeting Tiberius. The emperor
reclines on his throne, resting his hand
on a shield bearing the caption 'the
felicity of Tiberius'. The female
figure behind him is probably that of
Victory. Note the artistic
convention which makes the seated
emperor almost as tall as the
standing Germanicus.

19 (*right*) A head found in the Tiber believed to depict Gaius Caligula. The hair on the back of the neck is grown long in the Claudian style, but for reasons of self-preservation the sculptor probably exaggerated the amount of hair remaining on top of Caligula's head.

20 (*below*) The Grand Camée de France. This sardoynx is from the early first century AD. Because the cameo was reworked, probably in the fourth century, it is difficult to establish which Julio-Claudian emperor was originally depicted. The theme (common, as we have seen, in imperial propaganda) is of an emperor receiving his conquering general. The conquered peoples are shown below, while the gods of Rome watch approvingly from above.

21 (*left*) A racing chariot takes a corner at the Circus Maximus. Gaius Caligula was a dedicated follower of the races, and most of Rome shared his passion. Between the races it was not uncommon for prisoners to be executed, or for there to be displays of acrobats and animals, and it is from these latter shows that the word 'circus' is derived.

22 (*right*) Agrippina the Elder, wife of Germanicus and mother of Gaius Caligula. This Agrippina was one of the few Julio-Claudian women who was universally believed to have been faithful to her husband. The damage to her statue may have been contemporary with Agrippina's fall from favour and subsequent exile.

23 (*below*) The sisters of Gaius Caligula. According to popular report, the young emperor committed incest regularly with all three sisters, but turned against the remaining two on the death of his favourite Drusilla. The sister on the left is Agrippina the Younger, the mother of Nero.

24 (*left*) Claudius overcoming Britannia. Before the Roman conquest Britain was seen as a fabulous, semi-mystical island at the edge of the world. Claudius' conquest was intended not only to establish his military reputation, but to control both sides of cross-channel trade and remove the seditious influence of Druidism from the peoples of Gaul.

25 (*below*) A reconstruction of the temple of Claudius at Camulodonum (Colchester). Though designed to awe the Britons and help to secure their loyalty, the cost of building the temple fell squarely on the local aristocracy, and it became a symbol of all that was oppressive in Roman rule. When Boudicca stormed the city, the temple – turned into an impromptu fort – was the last redoubt to fall.

26 (*left*) Messalina. The two children shown in this cameo were the son and daughter of Claudius, and represented the strongest part of Messalina's influence over her husband. After her fall, Claudius married Agrippina, whose son Nero murdered Messalina's son, and married but later disposed of her daughter.

27 (*below*) Claudius as Jupiter. Depicting the physically infirm Claudius as mighty Jove no doubt struck some Romans as ironic, but it helped the common people to identify Claudius with the city and its gods. Note the eagle which gives extra support to the statue's base, and the *patera* (a dish used during sacrifices) in Claudius' hand.

28–30 Scenes from Nero's Golden House, one of the most sumptuous buildings ever raised in antiquity. Everything was overlaid with gold and encrusted with gems and mother-of-pearl. There were dining-rooms with fretted ceilings of ivory, whose panels could turn and shower down flowers, and fitted pipes which sprinkled the guests with perfume. The main banqueting hall (*below*) was circular and constantly revolved in time with the day and night. The Colosseum later took its name from the gigantic statue of Nero which once stood beside it near the site of this palace.

31 (*below*) Statuette of Nero in military dress. Nero never commanded an army personally, and the major military achievement of his reign was the suppression of the rebellion of Boudicca in Britain. Because Nero's memory was condemned in Rome after his overthrow in AD 68, many of his statues were destroyed, and his image has been less well preserved than any other Julio-Claudian emperor except Gaius Caligula.

32 (*top*) Cameo of Agrippina the Younger. No other Roman could boast her pedigree. Augustus' great-granddaughter and Gaius Caligula's sister, she went on to marry her uncle Claudius, and was the mother of the emperor Nero. She was exiled under Tiberius, and again under Caligula. After surviving the intrigues of Messalina, she helped her son to become emperor, only for him to order her death.

33 (*above*) A bust believed to be of the stoic philosopher Seneca. Together with Burrus, the Praetorian commander, Seneca is generally credited with restraining Nero in the early years of his rule. However, Nero eventually turned on everyone close to him, and in due course Seneca too was obliged to commit suicide.

lacked the iron grip of his predecessors. It is only regrettable that the Claudian regime's selection of wives for the emperor did not have the same happy results as its selection of administrators for the Empire.

Under Claudius, extensive building projects were launched, with an emphasis on utility rather than grandeur. The Roman public expected good service from their emperors. When there was a bread shortage, a crowd pelted Claudius with mouldy crusts to bring his attention forcibly to the grain supply. Since his power rested on popular support, Claudius swiftly eased the price of grain, and guaranteed the cargoes of the merchants who risked their fortunes on the dangerous voyage of grain ships from Egypt to Rome. Another improvement for Mediterranean seafarers was the construction of a proper harbour for Rome at Ostia, which had previously been an unsatisfactory shallow bay.

Considering this, Claudius undertook to construct a harbour [at Ostia]. When he asked the architects how much it would cost, they answered confidently 'More than you would want to know', assuming that the huge sums would put him off the project if he knew the exact figures. Nevertheless Claudius wanted something worthy of the dignity and greatness of Rome, and he accomplished it. Firstly, he excavated a very considerable expanse of land, built retaining walls on every side, and then let the sea into it. Then, in the sea itself, he constructed huge moles on both sides of the entrance to enclose a large body of water. He set an island in the middle and gave it a tower with a navigation light.

Cassius Dio *History* 60.11

As an incidental benefit, when Claudius instructed an engineer to make part of the underwater structure of concrete, the engineer found it easier to invent a concrete that set underwater than to tell the emperor that he could not do it.

40 *Coin of Nero showing Claudius' harbour works at Ostia. Wharves and warehouses are shown on each side of the coin while ships throng the space between them. The top of the coin shows a statue which stood at the harbour mouth, while a river god, possibly a personification of the Tiber, reclines at the bottom.*

Another of Claudius' enterprises was an aqueduct (started by Gaius Caligula) to serve the growing city. (Under Claudius the *pomerium*, the sacred boundary of Rome, received one of its rare extensions.) Suetonius praises the 'cool and plentiful' waters brought by this aqueduct and grudgingly concedes it to have been hugely beneficial.

A further project was the draining of the Fucine Lake, a large lake in central Italy which appeared to have no visible outlet. The effort, which involved tunnelling through a mountain, was laborious, time-consuming and ultimately futile. It is also interesting as an early example of a public-private partnership, 'Undertaken as much for profit as for the honour of the enterprise; some parties offered to drain it at their own expense, if they were consequently given title to the land that was thus exposed' (Suetonius).

That Claudius was able to undertake extraordinarily expensive projects, as well as the costly invasion of Britain, testifies that Gaius Caligula had left a healthy treasury which had since been competently managed. Undoubtedly good management brought its own rewards – Gaul, Asia Minor and Spain were now thoroughly integrated and prosperous, a fact reflected in their tax returns. Augustus' inheritance tax was still heartily loathed almost a century after its imposition, but paid for much of the cost of discharging soldiers from the army – and the army was always Rome's biggest expense. Another problem was the growing size and power of the imperial fisc (the emperor's private funds) relative to the anaemic state treasury. Like emperors before and after, Claudius had to make substantial transfers from fisc to treasury, something which more substantially emphasized the shift in power from state to emperor than any grovelling decree from the senate.

The growing prosperity of the Empire was reflected in an internationalization of its outlook, and Claudius was ahead of the trend. He published an edict allowing religious freedom for the Jews, and apparently exempted them from obligations to the imperial cult. But he forbade them to proselytize, and may have expelled them from Rome in AD 49 after a number of violent clashes 'caused by Chrestos', perhaps one of the earliest references to Christianity in Rome.

Secure in his unimpeachable pedigree as a Roman, Claudius was relaxed about allowing others that title. Being a historian, Claudius was aware that chauvinism and narrow-minded jealousy had almost destroyed Rome in the Italian war of 90 BC when Rome's exasperated allies had demanded Roman citizenship – even if they had to burn down Rome to get it. Consequently Claudius championed the cause of those provincials wanting to participate in government and sit in the senate. Tacitus has preserved this remarkably sensible speech by Claudius:

My ancestors, the most ancient of whom was made simultaneously a citizen and a noble of Rome, encourage me to govern by the same policy of transferring to this city those who obviously deserve it, wherever they come from. And indeed I know, as facts, that the Julians came from Alba, …that new members have been brought into the senate from Etruria and Lucania and the whole of Italy…. What was the ruin of Sparta and Athens, but this, though mighty as they were in war, they rejected as aliens those they had conquered? On the other hand, our wise founder Romulus fought as enemies and then greeted as fellow-citizens several nations on the same day. Strangers have ruled over us. That freedmen's sons should be entrusted with public offices is not, as many wrongly think, a sudden innovation, but was a common practice in the old commonwealth…. They [the Gauls] have preserved an unbroken and loyal peace. Now they are united with us by custom, education and intermarriage, so let them bring their gold and their wealth to us rather than enjoy it by themselves. Everything, senators, which we now consider of the greatest antiquity, was once new…. This practice too will establish itself, and what we are today justifying by precedents, will be itself a precedent.

Tacitus *Annals* 11.24

Though Claudius was keen to maintain good relations with the senate, he had a low opinion of its ability as a deliberative body. Once he presented the senate with a proposal saying, 'If you do not like it, find another solution, but you must do it right now.' Later he chided that 'It is not enough, when the consul has given his opinion, for everyone to stand up in turn and say "I agree" and then sit down thinking that the matter has been properly debated.' Claudius was slightly disingenuous in this criticism, since he was in part responsible for the senate's keen risk-avoidance. Even under his relatively benign rule some three dozen senators lost their lives, confirming that senatorial service was among the Empire's most dangerous jobs.

In AD 47–48 Claudius took reform of the senate's composition further by getting himself appointed Censor, an office dormant since the early days of Augustus. Unfortunately Claudius' quirky approach and over-reliance on paid informants undid his good intentions. For example, he was persuaded by friends to expunge the black mark against one man on the senatorial record, but insisted that the erasure should show. On another occasion he was about to strike someone off the rolls because he had been informed that the man had attempted suicide with a dagger when the accused ripped off his robe and demanded, 'Then show me the scar!' As guardian of public morality (another of the Censor's jobs), Claudius showed his distaste for an extravagantly expensive chariot by purchasing it, and then having it publicly hacked to pieces.

In the same way, Claudius' personal characteristics overshadowed some useful reforms to judicial administration, not least the rearranging of the judicial calendar and the expediting of cases so they came to trial faster. But Romans noted only odd decisions such as a man accused of having falsely assumed Roman citizenship, who had to wear a Greek tunic while accused, and a Roman toga while defending himself. Claudius was fond of judging cases personally, and this was generally popular, though Suetonius adds that 'his erratic behaviour [in court] brought him open and general contempt'.

Everyone knows of the time when a Roman knight was falsely accused by totally unscrupulous enemies of unnatural behaviour with women. When that man saw that Claudius was admitting the evidence even of common street-walkers, he flung his stylus and wax tablets at the emperor's face, shouting 'Damn you and your cruel stupidity!' Claudius suffered a severe gash on his cheek.

Suetonius *Claudius* 15

History does not record what became of this particular knight, but Claudius was harsh with the equestrian order as whole – he is accused of ordering the deaths over two hundred knights for one reason or another. Claudius himself confessed to being prone to both anger and ill-temper, distinguishing between the two by saying that the latter never lasted for long, and the former was never unjustified. To his faults may be added resentment over the ill-treatment he had received when young. He banished without a hearing a man who had insulted him in a court case before his accession, and a senator who had ill-treated some of his tenants. But he promoted the campaign for office of another young man because, 'When I was young and ill, this man's father was the only one who saw fit to bring me a cooling drink.'

Claudius' sympathy with the underdog extended to the considerable numbers of sick and worn-out slaves abandoned by their owners on the island of Aesculapius in the Tiber (Aesculapius was a god of healing). Claudius freed these slaves, and ruled that any abandoned this way were not to return to their former masters if they recovered. He also decreed that anyone who killed a slave simply because that slave was sick would be guilty of murder.

Claudius shared a genuine empathy with the common people of Rome. Senators were appalled by his habit of exchanging jokes and badinage with the crowd, and getting so excited on public occasions that he forgot his imperial dignity. His fondness for the good things in life was well known, and he seldom left a table less than replete with food and wine. Once, during a technical discussion in the senate about the regulation of taverns and eating houses, the emperor suddenly exclaimed, 'But I ask you, who does not sometimes enjoy a good snack?'

When sitting or standing still he had a certain dignity about him, if he kept his face impassive. He was tall, good-looking and well built, with a sturdy neck and a full head of white hair. But his knees were weak and he stumbled when he walked. If he became worked up by either business or pleasure, he showed several disagreeable characteristics including his habitual ghastly, uncontrolled

41 *Bust of Claudius. Even to contemporaries, Claudius was an enigma. Did his eccentric character and physical disabilities conceal a shrewd and ruthless politician? Many modern historians are inclined to believe so.*

laugh. When in the grip of anger he would slobber at the mouth and his nose would run. He would stammer, and his constant twitching movement would be so exaggerated when he was under strain that his whole head would toss from side to side.

Suetonius *Claudius* 30

Despite this unappealing description, imperial power exercised its own charms. After the death of Messalina, Claudius found himself the most eligible male in the Empire.

Agrippina and Mushrooms for Dinner

'If I marry again, you can kill me on the spot.'
(Claudius to the Praetorians during the Messalina crisis)

Despite Claudius' fervent declaration to the contrary, after the Messalina affair, it was essential that the emperor remarry, and soon, a suitable spouse. Messalina's infidelity had weakened Claudius' political strength and personal prestige. He was in his fifties, with a history of poor health, yet his son Britannicus was still too young to succeed him. If he were to die a succession crisis would result. Undoubtedly, the more powerful and ambitious of Rome's elite were even now considering their options.

There was one almost ideal choice: Agrippina the Younger, sister of Gaius Caligula, daughter of the revered Germanicus. Through her marriage to the late Domitius Ahenobarbus, Agrippina had a son who could be groomed in tandem with Britannicus as a potential successor, much as Augustus had advanced both his grandsons Gaius and Lucius (p. 102). Agrippina was revered by the Praetorian Guard as the daughter of their beloved former commander. She also had a strong following among the common people who had followed her turbulent life with interest. (A life which included glory while Germanicus lived, eclipse

42 Gemma Claudia: *Claudius is on the left with Agrippina's profile behind. Agrippina faces her mother Agrippina the Elder, whose husband Germanicus faces his brother Claudius. The heads sprout from cornucopia (horns of plenty) with the eagle of Jupiter and Rome between.*

and danger under Tiberius and Sejanus, restoration and promotion followed by disgrace and exile under Caligula, and a further restoration under Claudius.) Also, of all the Julio-Claudians, Agrippina had the most prestigious pedigree, in some ways superior even to Claudius', since she was descended from Augustus via her grandmother Julia, Augustus' daughter. She also had an emperor for an uncle, and this was the problem; for that emperor was Claudius, the brother of Germanicus. By Roman tradition, this consanguinity was too close for a legal union.

That such a union was even contemplated shows how far the Julio-Claudian clan had moved from their adventurous exogamous unions of the early first century BC. Then the clan had cheerfully made family alliances with parvenues and established families alike. Now, admitting outsiders into the imperial circle created potential rivals in a clan already decimated by dynastic struggles. To the Claudian court, Agrippina and her son had always been foci about which hostile alliances might form. After the weakening of Claudius' prestige after the Messalina debacle, these descendants of Germanicus became an intolerable threat. Either they were to be brought into the imperial household or they were to be eliminated altogether. Agrippina was fully aware of the stakes involved in these considerations, and did her bit to influence the decision. 'She had a

niece's privilege of kissing and caressing Claudius, and exercised it to noticeable effect,' Suetonius observed drily.

It only remained to put the matter to senate and people. After the senate had been carefully primed, one of Claudius' cat's-paws, Vitellius – father of the future emperor of that name – put the matter to its members, arguing,

'It will be said that marriage to a brother's daughter is completely new to us. This is true, but it is a fact of life in many other countries, and is not forbidden by law...customs change according to the circumstances, and this new development will soon become accepted.'

There were even some senators who rushed out of the house vehemently exclaiming that if the emperor hesitated to make this match, they would force him to it. An unruly crowd assembled shouting that the whole Roman people prayed for the same thing. Without a moment's delay, Claudius went to the forum to receive their congratulations and from there to the senate to ask them to decree that marriages between uncles and nieces should in future be legal.

Tacitus *Annals* 12.7

Agrippina was no giddy young heiress as Messalina had been. She was as unhesitatingly ruthless as her former rival ('terrifying in her hatred', Tacitus says of her), but more self-disciplined and devious. She was thirty-three years old when she married Claudius in early AD 49, and she promptly set about removing any potential threats. The fiancé of Claudius' daughter Octavia was the first to go. Accused of incest with his sister, he committed suicide on the day of Claudius' marriage, thus clearing the way for the union of Octavia and Agrippina's son Nero. Lollia Paulina, the former wife of Gaius Caligula, had been considered as a spouse for Claudius, and this caused her to be exiled on a pretext, with the inevitable assassins following after a decent interval. It is said that when Lollia's head was brought to Agrippina she did not recognize it. To make sure the killers had got the right victim she personally opened the mouth to check the teeth, since Lollia had certain dental peculiarities.

Even the great Domitia Lepida found no safety in the fact that she was Agrippina's former sister-in-law. As the maternal grandmother of Britannicus and a great-niece of Augustus she was a formidable rival and potential wife for Claudius, all the more so when her good looks and huge wealth were taken into account. Tacitus says that the emperor in a less than sober moment once growled that it was his misfortune to have to tolerate the misbehaviour of his wives before he punished it, with the inference that Agrippina was considered replaceable. If Tacitus heard this report, no doubt Agrippina did as well. This hastened the end of Domitia who was certainly a potential replacement. (It also possibly hastened the end of Claudius as well.)

Domitia was accused of witchcraft, and Nero (who had spent some time in her household) was one of the leading witnesses for the prosecution. Narcissus, the freedman who had masterminded the downfall of Messalina, strongly opposed the trial but his influence was waning. Narcissus was a supporter of Britannicus, which was in itself enough to make an enemy of Agrippina. Claudius continued to protect his former favourite, but Narcissus was on the defensive, unable to influence policy as before. Domitia was sentenced to death.

A further sign of Agrippina's influence was the recall of the philosopher Seneca from exile, and his appointment as tutor to Nero. In February AD 50, Nero was adopted as the son of Claudius, becoming Nero Claudius Caesar Drusus Germanicus. It is noticeable that four of these five names are from the Claudian line, but since Nero was a Julian by direct descent in the maternal line, Claudius may have felt that he needed to highlight his branch of the family, not least because Agrippina and Nero were probably more popular than he was – and certainly more so amongst the aristocracy. Agrippina was given the title of Augusta, a boost to her personal prestige, and by reflection to the prestige of the imperial house as a whole. Claudius was using the prestige of the descendants of Germanicus to patch up the damage done by Messalina. He proclaimed the fact through statues and coins, apparently to good effect. The capture and parading of the British leader Caractacus in a Roman triumph at this time also reminded the populace that Claudius was a successful war leader.

But however much he might have resented it, Claudius was to some degree dependent on Agrippina after his marriage. He certainly could not afford to dispose of her until his own prestige had recovered, especially as Agrippina's position was from the beginning stronger than Messalina's had been, and it increased greatly thereafter. Pallas, the freedman who had risen in importance even as Narcissus had declined, was as much a creature of Agrippina as he was of Claudius. Agrippina also managed to persuade Claudius that the Praetorians were divided in their loyalties between their two current commanders, whereas in fact she was worried that they were united in their loyalty to Britannicus. Consequently she had command of the Praetorians transferred to one of her placemen, Burrus. Typical of many imperial appointments, he owed his promotion to favouritism within the palace, but was well-deserving of that favouritism, being loyal (albeit in the first instance to Agrippina), hard-working and highly competent.

As soon as Agrippina had come to live in the palace she gained complete control over Claudius. Indeed, she was very clever in making the most of opportunities and, partly by fear and partly by favours, she won the devotion of all those who were at all friendly towards him.... She accomplished these ends partly by getting the freedmen to persuade Claudius and partly by arranging beforehand that the senate, the populace and the soldiers would join together in shouting their approval of her demands on every occasion.... She was amassing untold wealth for him [her son Nero], overlooking no possible source of revenue, not even the most humble or despised, but paying court to everyone who was in the least degree well-to-do but also murdering many for this very reason.

Cassius Dio *History* 61.32 passim

It was a sign of Agrippina's growing influence that a new colony in Germany was named after her ('Colonia Agrippiniensis', modern Cologne) and she took to travelling to the capitol on a chariot, a practice once permitted only to priests and sacred images. She also (which was unheard of for a woman) received embassies from abroad in her own right, meetings which were not informal presentations but official diplomatic occasions recorded in the proceedings of the senate.

Furthermore, these meetings at the very least did no harm. Several tricky diplomatic issues involving client kingdoms in the East were satisfactorily resolved, and restlessness in Judaea was at least temporarily assuaged by the governor of Syria – another exceptionally competent appointee of the Claudian regime.

In all this the eclipse of Britannicus by Nero was noted, and the corresponding conclusions accordingly drawn. When Claudius was consul in 51 he took the opportunity to give Nero his *toga virilis* several months early. Nero received proconsular authority outside the city and was allowed to address the senate. Britannicus, three years younger and still in the toga of a minor, had to see his rival (whom he still bitterly referred to as 'Domitius') hailed at the games and everywhere considered Claudius' natural successor. In AD 53, when he had barely passed his mid-teens, Nero married Claudius' daughter Octavia. Suetonius tells us that Claudius was in the habit of taking Britannicus aside every time he suffered one of these slights by seeing his stepbrother advanced, and telling him that one day he would see why things had been done in this way.

Why Nero was so overtly favoured has ever since been a matter for debate, but one credible reason is that Claudius felt that it was essential to keep Agrippina firmly attached to his cause until he had recouped enough personal influence to strike. Perhaps Claudius nursed plans of removing Agrippina and her supporters at a single stroke, even as Tiberius had uprooted Sejanus, though by now Agrippina was so firmly rooted in the imperial household that Tiberius' task might have seemed easy in comparison.

Nevertheless, Agrippina too might have realized that she was becoming less essential as time went on. In 54 Britannicus would soon receive his *toga virilis* and become a credible alternative to Nero. The latter was still Claudius' adopted son and had proconsular imperium, but the children of the elder Agrippina had also been raised high before they were thrown down. Claudius had been on the throne for thirteen years, and the effects of the Messalina affair were fading into the past. Claudius might have begun to feel the time was right to reassert his authority.

That October, Narcissus – perhaps feeling the strain of his unsuccessful attempt to save Domitia Lepida – either went, or was sent, to recuperate by the salubrious waters of a resort conveniently distant from Rome. Agrippina had an opportunity to strike. Tacitus presents the case for the prosecution.

The deed would be betrayed by a sudden, instantaneous death, while if she chose a slow and lingering poison, there was a fear that Claudius, when near his death, might, on detecting the treachery, return to his love for his son. She decided on some rare compound which might derange his mind and delay death. A person skilled in such matters was selected, Locusta by name, who had lately been condemned for poisoning.... By this woman's art the poison was prepared, and it was to be administered by an eunuch, Halotus, who was accustomed to bring in and taste the dishes.

Tacitus *Annals* 12.67

Not only was the food taster suborned, but also the doctor.

The poison was in some mushrooms, a favourite delicacy [of Claudius], and its effect was not immediately apparent, due to the emperor's lethargic, or possibly intoxicated, condition. He also emptied his bowels, and this seemed to have saved him. Agrippina was thoroughly dismayed. Fearing the worst, and defying the risk of the deed being too immediate, she took advantage of the complicity of Xenophon, the doctor, of which she had already made sure. Under pretence of helping the emperor's efforts to vomit, this man (it is generally believed) introduced into his throat a feather smeared with some rapid poison.

(ibid.)

Motive, means and opportunity – Agrippina had them all, yet the prosecution's evidence remains circumstantial. Claudius was then sixty-four years old and his health was always fragile. The mushroom which produces symptoms such as those described by the ancient historians is one easily confused with the edible variety, and it certainly would have required neither the intervention of poisoner nor physician to do its work. The alleviation of the patient's symptoms before death was not a victory for the body's defences, but rather a sign that they had given up the fight. Thus, if Claudius was killed by a mushroom (and even this is by no means certain), the offending fungus might have got into his meal by either accident or design. It is therefore possible that Claudius was killed not by a poisoned mushroom, but by a poisonous one, and the poisoning need not have been done deliberately. But if it was an accident, it was a thoroughly fortuitous one for Agrippina. Events could not have fallen out more smoothly had she planned them, which is the best reason for believing that she did in fact do so.

Dynastic Considerations

Claudius did not marry Agrippina for love. Though lust may have played a part, the marriage was mostly due to cold political calculation. The major weakness in the public perception of Claudius (emphasized by the name by which he is now known) is that he was not a Julian. By marrying Agrippina he both tightened his family's alliance with the Julians and offered sentimentalists the prospect of further Julio-Claudian offspring.

The Roman aristocracy took a deep interest in matters of heredity, and were well aware of Claudius' intentions. Though children were above all the progeny of the father (who usually got custody after a divorce, and whose characteristics the child was mainly supposed to inherit), the mother's input was generally seen as improving or weakening the bloodline. The choice of a wife had eugenic and dynastic implications as well as immediate political consequences for any senator, but exponentially more so in the case of an emperor.

To a very large degree Gaius Caligula came to power because of the successful marriages of his forebears. He was not only the son of the great Germanicus, the flower of the Claudian line, but also the child of Agrippina the Elder, granddaughter of Augustus himself. It is a reflection of how strongly Gaius Caligula himself felt about his distinguished ancestry that he bitterly resented having the relatively lowly Agrippa as his maternal grandfather and preferred to believe that his mother was the fruit of an incestuous union between Augustus and his daughter Julia.

In short then, marriage was a tool for enhancing the political potency of the dynasty. Once the business of producing heirs had been dealt with, Roman society permitted the husband numerous outlets for his sexual energy away from the conjugal bed. Wives were traditionally permitted no such license, though according to most observers of contemporary Rome they went ahead and enjoyed it anyway. (Note that Claudius divorced his first wife for 'scandalous behaviour' and had her child from the marriage delivered to her door, since he suspected a freedman called Boter of having fathered it. Messalina was less than an improvement, and Augustus' progeny were hardly models of fidelity.)

Love and fidelity mattered on a personal level, but imperial and aristocratic marriages were about politics and the production of offspring.

On the political level, children were powerful peacemakers. Many elite Romans had ancestries going back half a millennium, and were keenly aware of their duty to keep the line going. When a marriage had produced children it muted enmity between the family groups within the marriage, since the political destruction of the in-laws was bound to have a negative effect on the children – not least by depriving them of half of their inheritance.

When we consider that thousands of lives (including Mark Antony's own) were spent in a struggle over whether he or Octavian should rule the Empire, it is ironic – but predictable from a Roman perspective – that power should end up with the joint heirs of both. This came about through the marriage of Augustus' sister Octavia to Mark Antony at a time when the triumvirs were trying to keep from each other's throats. The daughter of Antony and Octavia married the son of Augustus' wife Livia, and so, through the distaff line, the blood of the Julio-Claudians became co-mingled with that of Augustus/Octavian's arch-enemy, and the surviving members of the Antonine faction were appeased by the blending of their leader's bloodline with that of the imperial family.

Such were the uncertainties of birth and death in Rome that descendants were to be treasured, even if fifty per cent of them came from someone who later turned out to be a mortal enemy. In fact, as with Octavia, such children could even be helpful, since children with mixed bloodlines could be married to members of other factions, thus drawing them into the family orbit. Thereafter, meetings at family occasions could be used to cement these ties and make allies out of potential foes.

Finally there were those whose relatively obscure birth meant that they had little realistic chance of gaining power for themselves. A good marriage, such as that of Agrippa with Julia or Sejanus with the daughter of Tiberius, was a way of deferring the hopes of a loyal subordinate to the next generation and so avoiding jealousy among the prickly aristocracy.

While the Roman aristocracy were not exactly redundant, they had certainly less to do since the advent of the imperial Caesars. During the Republic, the aristocracy had been the main source of patronage, and had supplied the commanders for Rome's armies. The aristocracy had been active in the courts and in legislation, and their households had provided most of the manpower in Rome's rudimentary civil service.

By the time of Claudius, much had changed. Imperial patronage overshadowed all other forms, and those who could in any way appeal to Caesar did so, bypassing lesser aristocrats in their search for favour. With the Caesars exercising a near monopoly on military glory, a career in the army was now less attractive. Since the common people were by now effectively disenfranchised, a successful campaign could not be easily converted into a strong political position, and indeed, too great popularity with the Roman people or the army was positively unhealthy.

The Caesars showed an increasing preference for giving tasks of particular importance or prestige to members of the equestrian order. Since at that time it was unthinkable that an emperor should be anything other than a senator, equestrians could not threaten the imperial throne no matter what their achievements. This was even more true of freedmen, a fact which gave rise to a situation – bitterly resented by the aristocracy – where an emperor's senior freedmen were often the most important people in the state after the emperor himself.

Claudius did what he could. He attended the senate regularly and ostentatiously deferred to its wishes, particularly when those wishes did not matter much anyway. He was modest in the number of consulships he held, and made a point of yielding them early to allow deserving cases to hold the position. Nevertheless, throughout the rule of the Julio-Claudians (including under Claudius himself) the number of consulships held by descendants of the republican aristocracy declined steeply and steadily, with their share of consulships at about fifty per cent under Augustus and about fifteen per cent under Nero.

Overall though, Claudius seems to have pulled off the delicate trick of giving the aristocracy enough power and honours to keep its members satisfied, but not enough to allow anyone to seriously threaten his own position.

With dynastic affairs there was a similar balancing act. Claudius was the first emperor not to be a son of Caesar. Caesar had adopted Augustus, who had adopted Tiberius, who was Gaius Caligula's grandfather (by Germanicus' adoption). But Gaius had not adopted Claudius. By taking the name Caesar in any case, Claudius tried to achieve the same effect, but it was not the same and everyone knew it. Yet at the same time, there were advantages in not being the adoptee of Gaius Caligula (which would not have been legally possible anyway given the age differences involved). His non-adoption gave Claudius the ability to distance himself from his predecessor without seeming disloyal, though this still left the challenge of repudiating the acts of Gaius Caligula without bringing the Julio-Claudians as a whole into disrepute.

Under the guise of healing the state Claudius was able to pass an amnesty for many who had conspired against Gaius Caligula without needing to admit that the conspirators may have had a point. He refused to allow Gaius Caligula's statues to be destroyed, as this would dishonour his own house, but he made sure that they were quietly removed from public display. Nor did he make a great fuss about the anniversary of his succession to power, as this would also be celebrating the assassination of his predecessor. That Gaius Caligula had not seriously eroded the enormous fund of goodwill among the people and army towards the Julio-Claudian clan is shown by the haste with which Claudius espoused Agrippina, the great-granddaughter of Augustus and daughter of Germanicus, in order to repair the damage caused by his failed marriage to Messalina.

Likewise his adoption of Nero helped to straighten the kink which Claudius' reign had put in the line of succession. Claudius became Nero's adoptive father, but Nero was through his maternal line the great-great-grandson of Augustus. This made Nero a Julian, and by his descent from Germanicus also a Claudian. Furthermore, by Nero's betrothal to Octavia, Claudius' daughter, the promise of a Julio-Claudian succession seemed assured. The adoption of Nero was thus so highly expedient that after Claudius' marriage to Agrippina it was politically unavoidable. Claudius was gloomily aware that until he could change the situation, his own son Britannicus was left in an extremely vulnerable situation. That the Julio-Claudians were famously ungentle with their kin was a leading factor in the family's ever-quickening march towards extinction.

Of the Julio-Claudians still standing at the death of Claudius, the most senior were Agrippina and her son Nero, closely followed by Claudius' son and two daughters. Apart from these, the only branch of the family which had appeared to flourish was that of the Silani. Agrippina had a cousin, Aemilia Lepida, who had married the aristocratic Silius Torquatus, and the pair had four children – all of whom shared with Nero the distinction of direct descent from Augustus through the maternal line. In terms of heredity, this was a factor as deadly as any genetic defect. We have already seen how Lucius Silanus compounded the felony of his birth by becoming a rival of Nero for the hand of Claudius' daughter Octavia. Junia Calvina, his sister, was banished. Their father had so far stayed alive despite his perilous marriage to Augustus' descendant by maintaining a posture of such genial inoffensiveness that Gaius Caligula nicknamed him 'the golden sheep'. Innocence and harmlessness were sufficient protection against Caligula and Claudius, but Agrippina was to prove again that among the Julio-Claudians, the female could be at least as deadly as the male.

CHAPTER 8

NERO:
THE DEATH OF A DYNASTY

Gradually Nero's vices took control of him. His banquets now lasted from
noon to midnight, apart from the occasional dip into a warm bath, or,
in summer, into snow-cooled water.... Whenever he cruised down the Tiber
to Ostia, or offshore past Baiae, he would have temporary brothels erected
in a line along the shore, staffed with noblewomen as madams waiting
to solicit him as a customer.
Suetonius *Nero* 27

The name of Nero held an honourable place in Roman history for hundreds of years before its last bearer made it synonymous with tyranny.
The first Nero on record in Rome was one of the sons of Appius Claudius
the Censor in 312 BC, but if we are to believe the grammarian Aulus
Gellius the name goes back to the clan's Sabine origins, meaning in that
language 'strong and energetic'. The most famous Nero was the general
who defeated the brother of Hannibal on the banks of the Metaurus river
in 207 BC.

> What you owe, O Rome, to the Neros
> The river Metaurus and defeated Hasdrubal
> Can testify.
> Horace *Carmina* 4.4

The emperor Tiberius was a Nero, son of the Tiberius Nero who was the
first husband of Livia, the later wife of Augustus. Tiberius' brother
Drusus Nero passed the name of Nero to his son Germanicus, who gave
it to his brother, the emperor Claudius (properly Tiberius Claudius

Nero Germanicus). When Claudius adopted the son of Agrippina, this was the very first time anyone had ever been adopted into the Claudian house. The adopted son took the name he was so comprehensively to dishonour – Nero.

Until his adoption, Nero had been called Lucius Domitius Ahenobarbus, a name appropriate to the Domitian clan of his father. This clan, literally 'the Bronze Beards', could claim an ancestry almost as ancient and distinguished as either Julians or Claudians. In traditional Roman nomenclature the Domitian name would have been included in Nero's names after his adoption. Nero should have styled himself as 'Domitianus' with the -anus suffix denoting adoption from the family preceding the suffix, just as Octavian gets that name from Octavianus which means 'adopted from the family of Octavius'. However, just as Octavian never used that name, but took *in toto* the name of his adoptive parent, so Lucius Domitius Ahenobarbus disappeared on his adoption, becoming Nero Claudius Drusus Germanicus.

Those who comment that being adopted by Claudius somehow means that Nero was not a 'true' Julio-Claudian overlook one of the principal reasons for his adoption in the first place. In his maternal line, Nero was a direct descendant of the emperor Augustus. His mother Agrippina was the granddaughter of Julia, daughter of Augustus. There was also a connection on the other side of the family tree, for Nero's great-grandfather had married an Antonia, one of the two daughters of that name resulting from the marriage of Mark Antony and Augustus' sister Octavia. Apart from the extra infusion of Julian blood, this also meant that Nero could claim Mark Antony as a great-great-grandfather, something which later Roman historians relished in pointing out.

Agrippina, after bearing a son, Lucius Domitius, to Ahenobarbus, was married to Claudius Caesar, who adopted Domitius, giving him the name of Nero Germanicus. He was emperor in our time…and with his madness and folly [he] came not far from ruining the Roman Empire, being Antony's descendant in the fifth generation.
Plutarch *Life of Antony* 87

Suetonius is equally unflattering about Nero's father, Ahenobarbus:

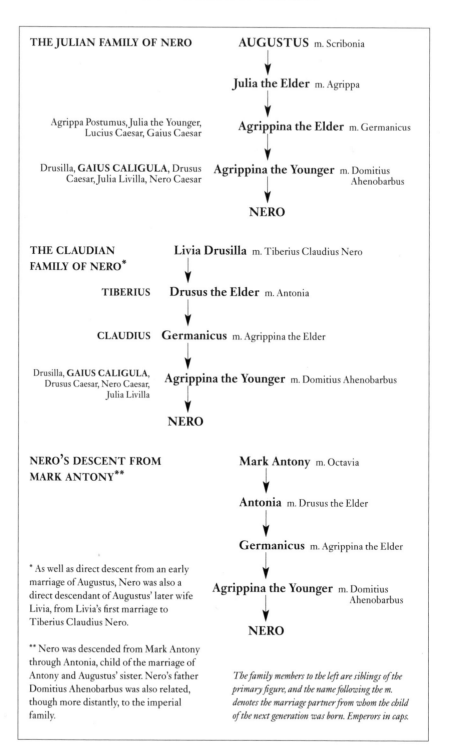

THE JULIAN FAMILY OF NERO

AUGUSTUS m. Scribonia

Julia the Elder m. Agrippa

Agrippa Postumus, Julia the Younger,
Lucius Caesar, Gaius Caesar

Agrippina the Elder m. Germanicus

Drusilla, **GAIUS CALIGULA**, Drusus
Caesar, Julia Livilla, Nero Caesar

Agrippina the Younger m. Domitius
Ahenobarbus

NERO

**THE CLAUDIAN
FAMILY OF NERO**[*]

Livia Drusilla m. Tiberius Claudius Nero

TIBERIUS **Drusus the Elder** m. Antonia

CLAUDIUS **Germanicus** m. Agrippina the Elder

Drusilla, **GAIUS CALIGULA**,
Drusus Caesar, Nero Caesar,
Julia Livilla

Agrippina the Younger m. Domitius Ahenobarbus

NERO

**NERO'S DESCENT FROM
MARK ANTONY**[**]

Mark Antony m. Octavia

Antonia m. Drusus the Elder

Germanicus m. Agrippina the Elder

[*] As well as direct descent from an early
marriage of Augustus, Nero was also a
direct descendant of Augustus' later wife
Livia, from Livia's first marriage to
Tiberius Claudius Nero.

Agrippina the Younger m. Domitius
Ahenobarbus

NERO

[**] Nero was descended from Mark Antony
through Antonia, child of the marriage of
Antony and Augustus' sister. Nero's father
Domitius Ahenobarbus was also related,
though more distantly, to the imperial
family.

*The family members to the left are siblings of the
primary figure, and the name following the m.
denotes the marriage partner from whom the child
of the next generation was born. Emperors in caps.*

…an utterly despicable character. When he had gone to the East on the staff of the young Gaius Caesar [Caligula], he killed one of his own freedmen who refused to drink as much as he was ordered, as a result of which Gaius ceased to count him as a friend. This did not make him any more law-abiding. On the contrary, in a village on the Appian Way, he whipped up his horses and deliberately ran over and killed a boy. And right in the Roman forum he gouged out the eye of a Roman knight who was too outspoken in his criticism of him.… He made a significant comment when accepting the congratulations of friends [on the birth of Nero], namely that any child born of himself and Agrippina was bound to have a detestable nature and become a public menace.

Suetonius *Nero* 5 & 6 passim

Nero was born at the seaside resort of Antium (modern Anzio) in December AD 37. Gaius Caligula (who may also have been born at Antium) attended the ceremony when his nephew received his name. Agrippina, seeking to flatter her imperial brother, suggested that he choose what the child should be called. Gaius Caligula, aware of Agrippina's intent, looked slyly at his despised uncle who was also in attendance, and said 'I name him Claudius'. The naming was prescient, but Agrippina ignored it.

From the start, Agrippina was ambitious that a son of hers should inherit the imperial purple. If there is any truth in Gaius Caligula's imputation of adultery by Agrippina with Lepidus, then Tacitus is probably correct to claim that Lepidus' proximity to the line of succession constituted his principal attraction. Being born a sister of Gaius Caligula and sharing his vicissitudes of fortune and danger in childhood had convinced Agrippina, no less than her brother, that security was to be found in power.

Once Agrippina had been banished, Nero ended up in the house of another of the Lepidus clan – Domitia Lepida, Agrippina's former sister-in-law and a great-niece of Augustus. Nero's father had died when he was three, and with his mother in exile, Nero was for a short time practically an orphan. His fortunes were soon restored when Gaius Caligula was assassinated, and his mother returned from exile, but in returning to his mother's household Nero was promptly drawn into an atmosphere of scheming and suspicion which was to endure for the rest of his life.

On her return, Agrippina was immediately locked in a power struggle with Messalina, wife of the new emperor Claudius, and the daughter of Nero's erstwhile mentor Domitia Lepida. Needing allies, Agrippina sought a new husband. She settled on the millionaire Sallustius Crispus, descendant of a former henchman of Augustus. The pair stayed married just long enough for Sallustius to make Agrippina and her son his heirs. Then Sallustius died unexpectedly, a fact which came to be considered in a new light after the equally well-timed demise of Claudius a few years later.

Messalina correctly divined that Nero was a possible threat to the succession of her own son Britannicus. Agrippina alleged that Messalina sent assassins to kill Nero, but these were driven away by a snake which unexpectedly darted out from under his pillow. The skin of the snake was later found sloughed off nearby, and Agrippina had this made into a bracelet which Nero ostentatiously displayed at every opportunity.

It became popularly reported that Nero had snakes to guard him in his cradle, as imaginative a tale as was ever invented for more exotic lands. Nero, never one to do himself down, used to say modestly that at most, only one snake was seen in his rooms. His popularity with the people was a legacy from the memory of Germanicus, whose only surviving male descendant he was, and of public sympathy for his mother Agrippina which was increased by the cruelty of her enemy Messalina.

Tacitus *Annals* 11.11–12

Soon afterwards Messalina overreached herself with her marriage to Silius, an act (as we have seen) of near-lunacy which resulted in her death and a severe weakening of Claudius' own position. Agrippina had already secured the alliance of the influential Vitellius in the senate and the freedman Pallas in the imperial court. These now pressed the argument that only an alliance with another of the Julio-Claudian family could shore up Claudius' crumbling prestige – arguments which his niece Agrippina bolstered by her proximity to Claudius which allowed her to suggest how much more pleasant that proximity would be if she were a wife.

The marriage of Agrippina and Claudius took place in AD 49 while Nero was in his early teens and Claudius was approaching sixty years old. Shortly thereafter, Nero was betrothed to Claudius' daughter Octavia, and took another huge step towards becoming Claudius' acknowledged successor. There was now a powerful faction backing Nero. Not only had Agrippina secured the most loyal followers that money could buy, but those who had played a large part in the overthrow of Messalina were understandably reluctant to see power pass to her son Britannicus. The exception was Narcissus, the freedman most involved in Messalina's downfall. He had supported a rival candidate as wife for Claudius and knew that Agrippina was unlikely to forgive him. Accordingly he allied himself with Britannicus, and the young man accepted him simply because he was desperately short of supporters.

Little happened in the following years to encourage Britannicus' partisans. At the age of thirteen, at least a year younger than was usual, Nero took the *toga virilis* and received the title of 'Prince of youth'. The senate hastened to grant him all the privileges which had been awarded to Augustus' grandsons, Gaius and Lucius, when they were being groomed as his successors. Britannicus could only watch impotently as Nero collected prestigious titles and priesthoods. When the two appeared at the theatre, the one in his robes of office, the other in a child's toga, or Nero delivered speeches in the senate to which Britannicus did not even have entry, there could be little doubt who was the more likely to succeed Claudius.

In 53 the pre-ordained marriage with Octavia went ahead. Because she would otherwise be marrying her brother by adoption, Octavia was transferred by adoption out of the imperial family as expeditiously as Nero had entered it.

By now Nero's education had been entrusted to the senator and famed writer and philosopher Annaeus Seneca. Seneca had been exiled for his supposed part in the adulterous affair of one of Agrippina's sisters, and loathed the Claudian regime as heartily as he supported Agrippina. Rapidly discerning how the political wind was blowing, Seneca shaped Nero's curriculum into something suitable for a future emperor, while the tutors of Britannicus were dismissed and replaced by freedmen reporting directly to Agrippina.

Nero was drawn towards the arts early in his life. He had one of the best lyre players in the Empire summoned to play for him, and afterwards took up the study of the instrument himself. The hostile senatorial tradition alleges that his voice was weak and husky, though Nero worked hard to strengthen it by a variety of exercises and potions. We have the following description from Suetonius in which the biographer tries to maintain a semblance of impartiality – mainly to give his later condemnation greater force.

As a boy, Nero followed the usual course of study, apart from philosophy, which Agrippina had forbidden as unsuitable for a future emperor. He did not do much rhetoric either, as Seneca kept the works of earlier orators from him so that he himself could be admired all the more. Instead Nero took up poetry, which he was soon able to compose with little effort. Although it is claimed that his best work was plagiarized from others, I have in my possession notebooks and scrap papers with some of Nero's best-known poems. They are in his handwriting and the number of crossings-out, corrections and substitutions above the line clearly show that he was thinking things out himself and neither copying nor taking dictation. Nero also took more than a dilettante's interest in painting and sculpture.

Suetonius *Nero* 52

Contemporary statues show a bull-necked, rather baby-faced youth of average height and build. His hair is described as 'tawny', so his Domitian forebears may have bequeathed him reddish-blond hair, which he tended to keep rather long and artfully arrayed in ringlets. He had blue eyes, and an earnest expression, which, if Suetonius' spiteful description is accurate, was ravaged by acne.

43 *The young Nero as an orator. Whatever his later detractors claimed of him, none denied that Nero's lifelong attachment to the liberal arts was both deep and genuine.*

44 *Nero as a young man. Though now remembered as one of history's most infamous despots, young Nero's career was full of promise. When he succeeded to the* imperium, *many Romans confidently hoped for the dawn of a new golden age. As with Gaius Caligula, the bright star turned out to be illusory.*

Nero was a few months short of his seventeenth birthday when Claudius suddenly became ill and died. This was a fortunate development, since there were signs that Agrippina was falling out of favour, and the emperor had been talking of taking serious steps to advance the career of Britannicus, who had been eligible to receive the *toga virilis* since February that year. It is uncertain what further steps the emperor would have taken to promote Britannicus, or if he stated these intentions in his will. The will itself was suppressed by Nero and Agrippina, leaving later generations to draw their own (predictably anti-Neronian) conclusions.

If Agrippina did poison Claudius, the old man proved tougher than expected. By the time the emperor relinquished his hold on life, the omens were uniformly bad for his successor. Agrippina accordingly suppressed the news of Claudius' death until the astrologers could come up with something better. The senate and priests were offering prayers for the emperor's recovery even as his lifeless body lay cooling under the blankets, and Agrippina and Burrus, head of the Praetorian Guard, were locked in hurried conference.

At last, at noon on 13 October [54], the palace gates were unexpectedly thrown wide, and Nero and Burrus headed for the cohort which was on guard as custom dictated. There, prompted by their commander, the men greeted Nero with joyful shouts and raised him on a litter. It is said that some looked around asking where Britannicus was, but since there was no one to oppose Nero, the men took what was on offer. Nero was taken to the Praetorian camp. He said something suitable for the occasion, and promised a donative as generous as his [adoptive] father's had been. Then he was unanimously hailed as emperor.

Tacitus *Annals* 12.69

The Good Years

With rays direct your radiance to your city of Rome.
…and let that part of heaven
Where Caesar sits, be evermore serene
And smile upon us with unclouded blue.
Then may all men lay down their arms, and peace
Through all the nations reign, and shut the gates
That close the temple of the God of War.

    Lucan *Pharsalia* 62–71

Whether Lucan, a friend of Nero from youth, sincerely meant these lines, or whether his earlier friendship was already tainted with bitter irony, many believed his sentiment that the brutality of the civil wars and the horrors of the triumvirate were now balanced by the serenity and prosperity of imperial rule.

Despite problems with the fractious Britons, and occasional strife on the borders, most of the Mediterranean world basked in the *Pax Romana* which stretched unbroken from the Thames to the Euphrates. After the whimsy and fickleness of the reign of Claudius, the Roman people felt they had now a young leader, disciplined and determined, and guided by some of the wisest heads in the state.

…Afranius Burrus, and Annaeus Seneca. These two men guided the youthful emperor with a unity of purpose seldom found when power is shared. Though totally different in their accomplishments, they had equal influence. Burrus was a disciplined soldier with a severe manner, Seneca taught eloquence, dignity and courtesy, and with these qualities they worked shoulder-to-shoulder against their emperor's youthful vices.

    Tacitus *Annals* 13.2

45 *The temple of Janus, the doors of which were only closed when Rome was at peace. This coin proclaims, 'The peace of the people of Rome being everywhere on land and sea, the doors of the Janus temple are closed.' This probably reflects the conclusion of Corbulo's successful campaigns in the East.*

Apart from imperial vices, Nero's mentors had to contend with Agrippina. Germanicus' daughter was not like Livia Drusilla, who had guided Augustus in confidential family chats. She intended to take a more hands-on role in government, and is generally blamed for the first killing of the new regime. That the genial Marcus Junius Silanus was a great-great-grandson of Augustus inspired less than family feeling in Agrippina. She had already destroyed his brother Lucius so as to leave Claudius' daughter without a fiancé and available for Nero to wed, and regarded the rest of that branch of the family as unfinished business. Tacitus tells us that Agrippina's henchmen poisoned Silanus at a banquet without much troubling to hide what they were doing. Silanus was not the only victim of the change of regime. Narcissus had long been an opponent of Agrippina. That he also was doomed went without saying. He killed himself to save Agrippina the trouble.

Agrippina had on her side a powerful nexus of connections built up over time, and the advantage of a son accustomed to taking her orders. The senate quickly gave Agrippina the rank of Augusta, and Nero allocated her a squad of Praetorians as a personal guard. Nero often chose 'the best of mothers' when giving the Praetorians their watchword for the night. It is also interesting that the moneyer who produced the coins of 54 to honour the now-deified Claudius had Agrippina and Nero both displayed on the obverse, but with Agrippina's titles given prominence.

Agrippina's style of government was through secret consultations with preferred favourites – the accepted form under Claudius, yet one which clashed with her son's declared policy of open government shared between emperor and senate. A policy which, it became distressingly clear to Agrippina, her son did not intend as a mere propaganda exercise. 'The senate shall keep its ancient powers,' Nero declared, indirectly criticizing his predecessor by adding that he would not allow a

46 *Coin showing a young Nero practically nose-to-nose with his mother. There were several issues of these coins, the artwork of which is exceptionally fine, and each bore around the edge an inscription honouring Agrippina as the mother of Nero.*

few favourites to become dangerously strong and run the state. A sceptical senate heard that treason trials for libelling the emperor were, yet again, to be abolished. They had heard this lie from Gaius Caligula and Claudius on their ascent to the throne, so cynicism in Nero's case was excusable, and only eroded by the years during which he kept his promise (until AD 62). Two cases were referred to the emperor soon after his succession both involving men who had too loudly expressed a preference for Britannicus as emperor. Nero ostentatiously refused to follow up either charge.

Nor did Nero take Claudius' interest in the law courts. He presided personally over fewer trials, and at this time he was much more restrained with the death sentence than his predecessor had been. Where Seneca commented of Claudius, 'He kills more easily than a dog sits down,' Nero when about to sign the death sentences of a pair of convicted bandits remarked sadly, 'I wish I had never learned to write.' Also, to great senatorial relief, Nero did away with the notorious trials *intra cubiculum*, where the emperor tried cases in his own rooms with his intimates acting as judge and jury.

It seems that Nero delegated more power of decision to the senate. Until AD 61 the leading consuls of the year were of distinguished families of the republican era, and we note from Tacitus an increase in the number of senatorial decrees from this period, and that they dealt with more weighty matters. It was the senate, not Nero, which responded decisively to rioting after gladiatorial games in Pompeii, exiling the ringleaders and the organizer and banning games in the town for ten years. Up until AD 60 we hear of provincial governors, the last being the governor of Mauretania, tried before the senate, and on occasion convicted of abuses while in office. The exception was the brother of the freedman Pallas, who avoided punishment for misbehaviour in Judaea through the influence of Agrippina, with whom Pallas was closely allied.

In foreign affairs Nero mulled over the idea of pulling out of Britain, which had failed to repay its early promise, and which was proving an unrelenting drain on the treasury. When trouble intensified in the East due to the continual rivalry between Rome and Parthia for influence in Armenia, Nero acted promptly. He made sure that troops were on hand, and gave them a competent commander in the crusty general Corbulo, notwithstanding that Corbulo had once loudly praised the independence of republican generals when Claudius sharply reined him in after he ventured too deep into enemy territory beyond the Rhine.

In foreign affairs as in domestic administration, Agrippina proved a nuisance.

When envoys from Armenia came to put their case before Nero, Agrippina was seen to be about to seat herself alongside the emperor and preside over the tribunal with him. While everyone else was frozen with alarm and embarrassment, Seneca made a quick gesture to the emperor that he should rise and go to greet his mother [and lead her away]. Thus did the guise of filial duty serve to avert a scandalous scene.

Tacitus *Annals* 13.5

Yet again, the imperial household was the most dysfunctional part of an otherwise smoothly running Empire. It rapidly became apparent to Nero's intimates that his marriage to Octavia was not working out. In AD 55 Nero began an affair with a theatrical performer called Acte, a liaison which Burrus and Seneca saw as a harmless diversion of Nero's sexual energies, but which Agrippina interpreted as a direct threat to her relationship with her son.

Agrippina, indignant at this and other things, first attempted to admonish him, and gave a beating to some of his associates and got rid of others. But when she found herself accomplishing nothing, she took it greatly to heart and told him, 'It was I who made you emperor' – just as if she had the power to take away the sovereignty from him again.

Cassius Dio *History* 61.7

Agrippina's hostility prompted Nero into an unprecedented show of force against his mother. He removed her creature, Pallas, from his post as financial secretary, something that Agrippina could hardly protest about publicly since the move was highly popular and seen as a sign that Nero was serious about reducing the influence of the freedmen, one of the most despised facets of the Claudian regime.

The woman who had faced down Messalina was not so easily cowed.

Agrippina started to pay much more attention to leaders of the Praetorian Guard, and Britannicus suddenly found himself basking in his stepmother's favour. Agrippina seemed set on making good her threat to replace Nero, a threat which was all the more realistic as now, in AD 55, Britannicus was officially about to become an adult. But Nero had learned from his mother, and he unhesitatingly upped the stakes once more, displaying a ruthlessness that boded ill for the future. As the day Britannicus was to receive his *toga virilis* approached…

…Britannicus was dining, and what he ate and drank was always checked by a food-taster…the food taster had tried it. When he refused it [a drink] because it was too hot, poison was poured in with the cold water, and this went through his body so fast that he lost his voice and breath. This caused a stir among those present; some ran about aimlessly in their surprise, but those keener in their judgment focused their attention on Nero, who seemed totally unconcerned, remarking that this was obviously a return of childhood epilepsy, and the fit would soon pass. From the way that Agrippina was struggling to keep terror and confusion from her face it was evident she was as ignorant as Octavia, Britannicus' sister…. Even Octavia, notwithstanding her youthful inexperience, had learnt to hide her grief, her affection and indeed every emotion.

Tacitus *Annals* 13.16

The more cynical members of Nero's court were not surprised when the 'temporary fit of epilepsy' proved fatal. Claudius' son and Nero's main rival was given a speedy burial on a rain-swept day which reduced the number of spectators, though Dio remarks that the same rain cleaned off the gypsum with which the body had been coated, clearly revealing the lividity caused by the poison.

Agrippina was still not cowed, and turned her attention to well-born senators with sons who might make suitable husbands for Octavia. Nero responded by removing her Praetorian escort and expelling her from the palace. Agrippina's many enemies scented blood, and a charge was laid before Nero that Agrippina was scheming to have him replaced with a distant relative called Rubellius Plautus. The accuser was a Junia Silana, and the accusation not unexpected after all that her family had suffered at Agrippina's hands.

The realization that she was in very real peril finally forced Agrippina to back down, but the incident left marked stresses in the imperial household. When he first heard Silana's accusation, Nero had wanted his mother killed, and was taken aback by the opposition of Seneca and Burrus. He recalled that both men were his mother's former protégés and thereafter he trusted them less.

Meanwhile, the work of government went on. There was discussion of the rights of freedmen, a demarcation dispute between tribunes and praetors where the former were accused of overstepping their powers, the prosecution of corrupt officials, and changes in the tax rates. Much of this business was done through the senate, causing Tacitus to remark that 'some shadow of a free state remained'.

But Nero was slipping out of his mentors' control. He had developed the habit of leaving the palace disguised as one of a gang of thugs, and took an oafish delight in attacking passers-by returning to their homes at night. One senator defended himself with particular ferocity until he realized that he was beating up his emperor, at which point he stopped and begged for mercy. He was forced to commit suicide nevertheless.

In AD 58 Nero took a new lover, the beautiful Poppaea Sabina, causing a new explosion of jealousy from Agrippina, who strongly criticized the impropriety of the relationship since Poppaea was already married to Otho, a confidant of Nero. Nero had Otho sent off as governor of Lusitania, and contemplated an even more drastic solution for Agrippina. Agrippina too was in a mood for desperate measures.

When Nero was replete with wine and feasting, which often happened even before noon, more than once she [Agrippina] would dress attractively and offer herself to him, showering wanton kisses and caresses on his intoxicated body, with all the signs of an impending scandal.

Tacitus *Annals* 14.2

Seneca acted quickly, sending Nero's former favourite Acte to explain to the emperor that nothing would alienate the people and army more swiftly than the relationship which Agrippina was apparently encouraging. Nero responded by forcing Agrippina to withdraw from the court to Tusculum (near modern Frascati). Nero knew Agrippina was now an enemy, and he of all people was aware of his mother's political staying power, malice and ability. Seneca and Burrus were not to be trusted, so Nero turned to the commander of the fleet at Misenum, a former tutor who still smarted at his dismissal from Nero's service when Agrippina replaced him with Seneca. The pair cooked up a scheme to lure Agrippina into a sea voyage and a watery grave.

While Agrippina was reclining on the couch on her specially constructed trireme, the ceiling above her gave way. Specially weighted with lead, this was intended to crush her to death, as indeed it crushed some of her attendants. However, Agrippina's couch was of good Roman workmanship, and buckled but did not break. Seeing the empress crawl free, the crew panicked, and attempted to sink the ship by broaching it in a violent turn. They could not coordinate the manoeuvre properly, and succeeded only in having the ship subside slowly beneath the waves. One of Agrippina's servants screamed to the sailors for help, and the sailors, mistaking the servant's use of Agrippina's name for the lady herself, promptly beat the girl to death with oars. Agrippina, the hardened survivor, took note and silently slipped away to begin the long swim to safety.

Word of Agrippina's survival threw Nero back into the arms of Seneca and Burrus, whom he called for an emergency meeting. He told them that Agrippina was pretending that the whole affair had been a tragic accident, but he had no idea what desperate plans she was even now hatching. After a thoughtful pause, Burrus remarked that the Praetorians were too close to the family of the Caesars to be trusted, and Seneca agreed that it should be left for the prefect of the fleet to 'deliver what he had promised'.

At first Agrippina could not believe that Nero had so blatantly ordered her execution, but thereafter she faced death unflinchingly. After receiving a number of wounds she saw the centurion preparing for the final thrust and, rolling over, bitterly directed him to 'stab into the womb'.

The Slide into Tyranny

The end of Rome's rule will come with the end of obedience. It is no wonder that emperors, or rulers, the guardians of public order, whatever they are named, are loved even more than those who are intimate to us. If the public well-being comes before personal considerations for men of good sense, then no one can be more loved than the man on whom the state depends. The Caesars and the state have been mixed together for so long that one cannot be separated from the other without them both being destroyed.

Seneca *On Clemency* 1.4

In speeches and writing, as in the excerpt above, Seneca had argued that the Caesars *were* the state. Now he had to put the argument to the Roman people that Nero's matricide (officially called a suicide) was a family affair completely separate from his function as ruler. Whatever the internal problems of the imperial house, Seneca insisted, the Caesars were good for Rome. Evidence to support Seneca's argument was to be found in the East where war had broken out with Parthia. Thanks in no small part to Nero's precautions, the Romans under Corbulo were winning. Although his work for this period exists only in epitome, Cassius Dio seems to have agreed, claiming that though Nero's character was never anything but vicious, Burrus and Seneca between them kept private vice separate from public virtue. For Dio, this relatively happy state of affairs ended with the killing of Agrippina in AD 59. Tacitus is more inclined towards AD 62, the year that Burrus died (apparently of natural causes) and the treason trials began anew.

Nero was becoming more wayward even before this. His high opinion of himself as an artiste caused him to regale his guests with the lyre at dinner, and his passion for watching chariot races at the hippodrome inspired him to attempt charioteering himself. Seneca and Burrus deplored both lyre and chariot as unseemly in an emperor, but conceded if he must do one, it should be the chariot. Soon huge crowds attended Nero's 'private' practice sessions.

Yet Nero (or his advisors) reacted with good sense when the ever-restive Britons flared into open revolt under Boudicca in either AD 60 or 61. The rebellion was of extraordinary intensity, and Rome came nearer to losing a province than it had since the Varian disaster of AD 9 lost Germany to the rebel Arminius. Despite his reservations about Britain's long-term viability, Nero supported his general Paulinus through the campaign. Afterwards he intervened in favour of his procurator who had decided that Paulinus' desire for revenge was interfering with the work of reconstructing the shattered province. Unfortunately the agent of Nero's intervention was a freedman, Polyclitus, whose decadent love of luxury evoked scorn among the Britons and reminded the Romans of the worst excesses of Claudius' household.

In AD 60 a comet appeared, which many considered to presage a change of ruler. This reminded Nero of Rubellius Plautus, a man of Julian descent. Ever since he had been courted by Agrippina to remind Nero that Rome had other alternatives for an emperor, Plautus had assumed a profile so low as to be practically subterranean. Unfortunately, as Nero's excesses became ever more extravagant and tasteless, some senators began to see Plautus' timidity as modest decorum and restraint. When Nero suggested that the Roman air might be unhealthy for him, Plautus agreed with alacrity and moved to Asia Minor with the apparent intention of being as far from Rome as was possible while remaining within the Empire.

When the treason trials were restored in AD 62 it was because of some gratuitously anti-Neronian verses composed by the praetor Antistius. The senate convened and at the urging of the principled senator Paetus Thrasea, chose exile rather than death for the offender. Nero was unhappy with the result, but accepted it with apparent good grace, informing the senate they could even acquit the wretch if they felt like it.

When Burrus died, the shape of the regime was less to Seneca's liking, the philosopher asking permission from the emperor to quit the imperial service. Nero refused, though mainly to avoid the blow this would give to his prestige. He had for some time been paying little heed to Seneca's counsel, and more to that of Tigellinus, Burrus' replacement. It was probably at Tigellinus' urging that Sulla was assassinated, another whose crime was to be more closely associated with the imperial house than was safe.

Nero had decided that it was time to divorce Octavia and marry Poppaea, not least because the former had proved barren and the latter was pregnant with Nero's child. Removing his connection with the Claudian house caused the emperor a twinge of insecurity, which was assuaged by another murder, that of Plautus, who found that distance was after all no refuge. Nero unconvincingly denied involvement in the killing, but ordered that the head of Plautus be brought to him and sarcastically asked it, 'Well, did you want to be Nero?'

The old chestnut of infidelity was used against Octavia to justify the divorce, but the girl's handmaiden could not be persuaded to testify to this even under torture. Instead trusty Anicetus, the freedman in charge of the fleet at Misenum, was prevailed upon to testify to his intimate relations with the emperor's wife. He was exiled in luxury to Sardinia, while Octavia was sent to Pandateria, the delights of which island had been sampled by every generation of Julio-Claudian women since Augustus' daughter, Julia.

For Octavia, her marriage day had been a kind of funeral. She had been brought into a house filled with nothing but mourning where her father and…later her brother were snatched from her by poison, a slave girl [Acte] raised higher than her mistress…and to end it all an accusation more dishonourable than death itself…. This girl, surrounded by soldiers and with her doom already sealed, received the order for her death a few days later.

Tacitus *Annals* 14, 63–64

The near-contemporary play *Octavia* which is (probably wrongly) attributed to Seneca, reflects some of the popular revulsion at this murder, and marked the beginning of Nero's fatal estrangement from the Roman people. Also, those aristocrats loyal to the Claudian house now withdrew their support for the man who had murdered both of Claudius' offspring. On the other hand, those who would have applauded the killings belonged to the faction created by Agrippina, and they had their own grudge against Nero.

The Great Fire

The year AD 64 saw one of the defining events of Nero's principate when Rome was devastated by a huge fire. The blaze itself was no surprise. Rome had long been a fire-trap of enormous proportions, and indeed, one of the distinguishing features of Augustus' forum was that it also served as a firewall. But as the city grew and prospered, its overcrowded and rickety timber buildings were pushed ever closer together. Even the marble-fronted houses of the wealthy had timber-framed roofs, inflammable furnishings, and were surrounded by wooden kiosks and small workshops.

In any case, Tacitus tells us that the fire began near the Circus Maximus where there were 'no houses fenced in with solid masonry or temples surrounded by walls'. A powerful wind drove the fire between the Palatine and Caelian hills and from there spread to the poor quarters on the Esquiline. In the end, three of the fourteen districts of Rome were almost completely destroyed, and only four left untouched. Rome's inadequate fire-prevention measures were utterly overwhelmed, and numerous lives and small businesses incinerated.

Nero was some 35 miles (56 km) away at Antium when the blaze broke out, but he hurried to Rome and took charge of the fire-fighting, ordering huge fire-breaks to be smashed through Rome's ancient buildings, and quite probably also the lighting of backfires to give the main fire nothing to feed upon. 'He knocked down several granaries, solidly built in stone, and set the interiors ablaze,' says Suetonius, probably accurately, though he (wilfully?) misinterprets Nero's motives, which Tacitus understood well enough: 'The fire was met by clear ground and open sky.'

Yet even as the fire was being defeated, the flames burst out once more in a different part of the city. They may have been carried by the wind, but the confused and angry Roman people began to suspect a more human agency. Rumours went around of

threats from a number of people who prevented any attempt to put out the flames, and others who openly spread them by hurling firebrands, who shouted that they were authorized to do this, either because they were obeying orders, or seeking a cover for their plunder.

Tacitus *Annals* 15.38

Again Nero seems to have acted sensibly by keeping people out of the devastated areas to prevent looting, and opening undamaged properties on the Campus Martius to accommodate the homeless. He took charge of the corn dole, suspending the regular distribution and opening the warehouses to supply the needy. He allocated a chain of barges to carry the debris of the fire to the port of Ostia, and appointed new commissioners for the water supply, since one of the problems during the fire had been a shortage of water – pipes had been illegally diverted from the public supply to feed private houses.

Nero saw an opportunity to undo the damage done by the near-random rebuilding after Rome's last fire in 387 BC. Then it had been invading Gauls who, by what many saw as more than coincidence, had done the deed on the very same day – 19 July. The new streets were to be broad thoroughfares, with colonnades on each side. A compensation scheme was established, with the monies claimable after the claimants had rebuilt their houses. Furthermore these houses were not to have wooden beams, and were to be built of stone imported for this purpose.

So grand was the reconstruction scheme that it allowed Nero's enemies to claim that the fire had in fact been the first stage in an ambitious secret scheme for urban redevelopment. Far from fighting the fire, Nero was alleged to have secretly watched the conflagration from a tower, dressed in a tragedian's costume and singing the epic song *The Fall of Troy* from beginning to end. Nero's artistic pretensions were sufficiently known to give the caricature its bite, and even today this slander is one of the best-known images of his reign.

Accepting the impossibility of quashing the rumours, 'Nero laid the blame on a class hated for their abominations, whom the common people called Christians, believers in a most mischievous superstition' (says Tacitus). Nero devised extreme punishments, burning some alive and crucifying others. Some were covered with animal skins and torn apart by dogs, raising the suspicion that exemplary punishment had become an excuse for wholesale sadism. Many modern historians accept that some Christians *were* involved, in instigating the fire or helping its spread. The pattern of the fire suggests human help, even as eyewitness accounts claim. At a time when most Christians were Jews, Rome was hated in Judaea, which rose in revolt two years later. Early Christianity was an apocalyptic religion which believed in the imminent end of the world. Therefore it is possible that some deranged individuals might indeed have tried to hasten that end.

However, it was the Romans who established the principle *cui bono?* ('who benefits?') when investigating a crime, and here the beneficiary was undoubtedly Nero. He began construction of perhaps the most magnificent residence in antiquity – the *Domus Aurea* or 'Golden House', the beauty and expense of which were directly proportional to the opprobrium it caused to be heaped upon his head (plates 28–30).

47 Damnatio ad Bestias ('Condemned to be fed to wild animals'). Though this mosaic was made two centuries later than the punishments inflicted by Nero, this tried and trusted means of execution had changed little since Scipio adopted it for punishing deserters in the Carthaginian wars of the mid-Republic.

Parts of the house were overlaid with gold and precious stones. The dining rooms had ceilings of fretted ivory, and panels which could slide back to disgorge a rain of petals or allow perfume from hidden sprinklers to fall upon his guests. In the circular main dining room the roof revolved slowly in time with the day or night outside. Sea water or sulphur water was on tap in the baths. After the whole palace had been decorated in this lavish style, Nero dedicated it with the words, 'Now I can at last begin to live like a human being!'

Suetonius *Nero* 31

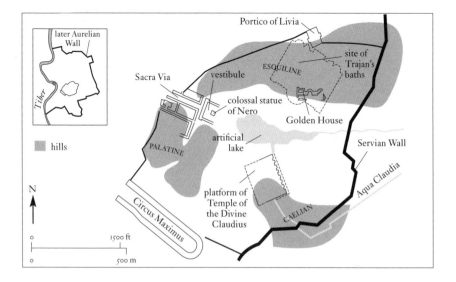

Outside this palace, he constructed a huge lake ('more like a sea', remarked Suetonius) surrounded by pleasant woodlands and overlooked by a gigantic gold statue. This was apparently of Nero himself and somewhat blasphemous, as colossal statues were reserved for the gods. Certainly Vespasian rededicated the statue to the sun god, Helios, when he drained the lake and constructed the Flavian amphitheatre on the site. Though the statue is long gone, the name it gave the area now attaches to Vespasian's building – the Colosseum.

An Emperor Out of Touch

> The palace is spreading and devouring Rome;
> We'll flee to Veii and make that our home
> Yet the palace is growing so incredibly quick
> It will swallow up Veii to the very last brick.
> (Popular doggerel about Nero's palace) Suetonius *Nero* 39

The common people supported the Caesars because they saw in them a champion of their own cause against the excesses of the aristocracy. The danger of Nero's palace was not the incredible expense, but that the Roman people saw this expense lavished on something which was not just for Nero's sole benefit, but was actually inimical to the interest of the Romans as it denied them space in the middle of their own city. 'An arrogant park which deprived the poor of their houses,' the poet Martial called it.

Also it was precisely because the people supported the Caesars that they cooled towards Nero. What true Caesar would murder his adoptive father, Claudius, and then his son and daughter? Nero was evidently a Domitius at heart. After all, what more convincing way to repudiate one's Julian blood than slaughtering the mother from whom it was inherited? That Rome saw Nero as the butcher of his family was emphasized by one comedian who launched into the popular song *Goodbye Father, Goodbye*

---

48 Nero's Golden House was in fact a 125-acre (50.5-ha) regal park and residential complex. As well as extending and embellishing existing imperial properties on the Palatine and Esquiline hills, Nero added new buildings and porticos, built mainly in the Hellenic style.

Mother by miming the actions of eating and swimming. A statue of Agrippina was covered with a veil and carried the tag, 'I am shamed by your shamelessness.'

The conspiracy against Nero which took shape in AD 65 reflected the spectrum of Roman society that Nero had alienated ('Every class, rank, age and sex, whether rich or poor', says Tacitus). At the core were Praetorian Guards, still loyal to the memory of Agrippina. They were joined by those who hated Nero's depravity and extravagance. Others were aristocrats whom the emperor saw as literary rivals and whose works he banned or lampooned. The conspiracy was perhaps given some urgency by the fact that Poppaea was pregnant again. Her first child, a daughter, had died soon after birth, but this time she might yet give Nero an heir.

The focus of the plot was Calpurnius Piso, a nobleman of an ancient house. He was tall and handsome, and in his serious, courteous demeanour he seemed to be everything that Nero was not. Piso's house was to be the venue for the assassination, as Nero was in the habit of visiting there without his guards. But Piso refused to countenance the murder of a guest under his roof, so it was decided to do the deed at the games. Then Piso would be escorted into the Praetorians' camp accompanied by Antonia, Claudius' sole surviving child.

When a freedman betrayed the plot to Nero, the emperor responded with a predictably violent overreaction. That Piso and the principal conspirators were executed or committed suicide goes without saying, yet others were caught in the net when their names were either blurted out under torture, or revealed by informers with a private grudge. Nero even turned on his old advisor Seneca, and forced him to commit suicide. Nero also made a purge of the Praetorian Guard, expunging those loyal to Agrippina's memory, and rewarding the rest with a large donative.

The failure of the plot left Rome cowed and resentful, with enough innocent victims of Nero's fury to ensure that their families formed the nucleus of any future plot. Nero was now trapped in the same downward spiral as had ruined Gaius Caligula. The more violently he tried to seek out and destroy potential assassins, the more hatred and fear he created, and the more likely his assassination became. Nero tried to buy popularity with public spectacles and lavish games which he called the Neronia. However, seeking a solution here merely worsened the situation elsewhere. Nero's massive extravagance was fast depleting his personal treasury, and this was a matter of state concern as the public finances were usually kept afloat by wholesale subsidies from the imperial purse.

The whole point of a fortune, he felt, was that it should be spent. 'It is the sign of a noble man to be careless with money,' he used to claim, saying that only penny-pinchers kept close track of their finances. He used to admire his uncle Caligula for getting through most of Tiberius' huge fortune. He himself never hesitated to waste or give away money…he never wore the same clothes twice, he would go fishing with a gold net with purple and scarlet thread. On his travels, it was a rare thing they say if he took less than a thousand carriages with him, the mules all shod with silver.

Suetonius *Nero* 30

In fact the Empire could easily afford such personal extravagance. But the costs of rebuilding the city, especially the Golden House, was another matter, especially as there was also the matter of rebuilding Britain after the devastation of Boudicca's revolt, and the cost of the Parthian war in the East.

The coins of Nero's reign are among the most beautiful ever minted in Rome, but they were also debased. They now contained slightly less silver than before, and both gold and silver coins were slightly smaller. Nero's successors picked up this useful trick and so started the slide of the value in Roman currency that peaked with the runaway inflation of the third century AD.

In a desperate attempt to balance the books, Nero decreed that those condemned who did not leave a substantial amount of property to him in their wills risked having him confiscate the lot, leaving nothing for the family. This hardly endeared him to the aristocracy. Nor did the growing and probably justified suspicion that many

49 *Coin of Nero. Good living seems to have bloated the once handsome features of the emperor and left him with a fine collection of chins. The legend on the coin simply states Nero's two dynastic claims to power: he was a Claudian Nero and a Julian Caesar.*

of those killed in the aftermath of the Pisonian conspiracy had been guilty only of having money or property that the emperor wanted to get his hands on.

In AD 66 Poppaea died, probably from complications with her pregnancy. Given Nero's obvious affection for his wife, and the fact that she was carrying his child, even the most jaundiced sceptic had to rule out poison in this case. Instead popular opinion decided that Nero had kicked her to death in a fit of anger when she criticized him for coming back late from the games.

It is from this point, having lost touch with senate and people, that Nero began to lose contact with reality. The arbitrary arrest and execution of senators gathered pace, with Nero apparently abandoning Seneca's dictum of 'No matter how many you kill, you can't kill your successor.' A Cassius was executed more or less on the grounds that he had a tyrannicide for an ancestor, and the remaining members of the Silanus family were killed in succession. Thrasea Paetus, the most respected senator of his day, received his death warrant apparently because he showed insufficient enthusiasm for the current regime, and probably because Nero had developed a suspicion of the Stoic philosophy of which both Thrasea and Seneca were adherents.

Nero abandoned all inhibitions about performing as an artiste in public. In fact, attendance at imperial performances on the stage became mandatory for the aristocracy. Dio is bitterly sarcastic about this.

So there he stood, this Caesar. On the stage, dressed as a lyre-player, this emperor proclaimed: 'My lords, kindly listen a moment.' And then this Augustus carolled on his lyre something called 'Attis' or 'The Bacchantes', or whatever, under the gaze of many of the soldiers, and as many people as could be crammed into the theatre. Yet it is said that his voice was so weak and indistinct that the audience ended up half laughing and half crying.

Cassius Dio *History* 62.20

The most dangerous moment in the career of the future emperor Vespasian came not while he was on campaign in Britain or Judaea, but when he was caught catching a quick nap during one of Nero's more tedious moments on stage. No one was allowed to leave the performances, and rumours spread of women who gave birth in the audience, and others who pretended death so that their 'corpses' could be carried outside.

The outbreak of peace with Parthia gave Nero a chance to indulge in the spectacular showmanship which he so enjoyed. Tiridates, the Parthian ruler of Armenia, was invited to Rome and entertained at spectacular games, the lavishness and expense of which were spoken of with awe for generations afterwards. These games so impressed the Parthians that King Volageses, when he later sent ambassadors to Rome, specifically asked the senate to honour Nero's memory.

Nero seems to have believed himself politically secure in Rome, with his principal danger being from individual assassins. Therefore he decided to absent himself from the capital for a trip to the Eastern provinces. His love of the arts had made Nero a natural convert to philhellenism, and now seemed an opportune moment to indulge. Nero was sped on his way by yet another plot, this one apparently involving Corbulo, the general who had performed so well against the Parthians. The early accord with the senate was now a forlorn memory, and Nero had as precedents the fate of Julius Caesar and Gaius Caligula. Both had made enemies of the senate, and neither had survived the experience. On the road to Greece, one of Nero's cronies amused him with the wisecrack, 'I hate you Caesar, because you are a senator.'

Another who accompanied Nero to Greece was Sporus, the son of one of Nero's freedmen who bore a resemblance to Poppaea. Nero had the lad castrated, and then 'married' him, an act which caused revulsion among the conservative Romans, and gave rise to the comment that it was a pity Nero's father had not chosen that kind of wife instead of Agrippina.

Nero and the Greeks were suited to each other. The Greeks proved adroit at flattering the emperor, and had no republican inhibitions about hailing him as absolute monarch and 'Nero Zeus, god of freedom'. After Nero abolished the oracle at Delphi for being insufficiently complimentary, the Greeks quickly established a corollary between the extravagance of the flattery bestowed on Nero and the munificence of the gift he bestowed in return, and accordingly abandoned all restraint. The emperor took part in every artistic festival he came across, including a large number arranged or rescheduled for his benefit, and won them all.

At the Olympics he took part in the chariot races, where he fell out of his chariot and then retired before the end of the race. Nevertheless, the judges decided to award him the victory, something that so delighted Nero that he had the Roman city wall breached when he returned to Rome – this being the traditional manner of greeting an Olympic victor.

At Corinth, Nero inaugurated work on a canal which he hoped would transect the Isthmus of Corinth, breaking the ground himself and carrying away the first basket of earth. The visit culminated in Nero repeating Flamininus' famous decree at the Isthmian games of 196 BC, when he relieved the Greeks of direct rule and taxation from Rome. Both measures did not long survive Nero himself. The fractious nature of Greek politics swiftly gave his successors grounds for reinstating direct rule, and the parlous state of the treasury made Greece's tax exemption unfeasible. In fact Nero's successors even demanded the return of his wilder cash gifts. So missed was Nero in the Greek-speaking part of the Empire that for years after his death there were a number of short-lived rebellions led by pretenders calling themselves by his name.

The End

And there are seven kings: five are fallen, and one is, and the other is not yet come; and when he cometh, he must continue a short space.

The Revelation of St John 17:10 (sometimes seen as a reference to the fall of Nero)

While Nero was in Greece, he had left Italy and Rome in the care of one of his freedmen. Given his relations with the senate, he could hardly entrust the state to one of its members, yet being ruled directly by a freedman was seen as a national insult. Nero raised senatorial hackles yet further by pointedly omitting the senate from his proclamation that the canal across the Isthmus of Corinth would be of great benefit to himself and the Roman people.

No other emperor, announced Nero grandly, had truly understood the extent of his power. The truth was though, that Nero had fatally overestimated his own strength. The aristocracy might tolerate its members being picked off individually, especially as much of the butchery involved those families foolish enough to have allied themselves with the Julio-Claudians in earlier generations, but Nero's threat to abolish the senate altogether and rule directly through his minions was intolerable.

With Nero still in Greece, the Jewish people ignited the torch of rebellion. This was a blow to Nero's diminishing credibility as a ruler, since the provinces, which had been peaceful under his predecessors, had now twice flared into serious rebellion. According to the historian Josephus, the Jews were upset less with Nero than his governor Florus, who had been appointed partly on the strength of his wife's friendship with Nero's wife Poppaea. There were more fundamental problems in Judaea than misrule by a single individual, but the appointment of Florus certainly did not ease the situation.

Yet if the tide was turning, Nero's strength remained formidable. While the Roman senate was sullen and rebellious, two failed conspiracies and the subsequent purges had left it cowed. With its leading members executed, the survivors needed to be sure that Nero would go before they would participate in his overthrow. The people may have been coming to accept that Nero was a bad ruler (a serious food shortage that year helped to reinforce this belief), but they loved Nero's showmanship and the fact that he seemed to be genuinely at ease with them. The murder of his immediate family was undoubtedly a crippling blow to Nero's credibility, but the Roman people had always expressed a preference for their rulers to be Julio-Claudians, and Nero's assiduous efforts had ensured that he was the only Julio-Claudian on offer.

Generations of rule by the Julio-Claudians had not only gradually turned the Roman state into a family possession, it had accustomed the Roman people to think of their state in this way. 'L'état, c'est moi,' said Louis XIV, and Nero could well have remarked the same. Nero's principate marked the end of the road down which Julius Caesar had embarked when he caused outrage by not rising to greet a senatorial delegation over a century before. The Caesars did not call themselves kings, but as Seneca said, they were Rome's masters, whatever appellation they chose.

If there was to be a challenge to Nero's rule it would come from the provinces. Britain and Judaea had shown the way, and increased taxation to pay for Nero's excesses had made the others restless. The crucial issue was whether the army could be persuaded to abandon its generations-old allegiance to the sons of Caesar. The matter was first put to the question in March AD 68, when Nero was thirty years old. Vindex, the governor of Gallia Lugdunensis (central and western Gaul), wrote to his colleagues seeking support for a rebellion. When most of these letters were promptly forwarded to Nero in Rome, Vindex had no choice but to start the rebellion on his own. Dio recounts the rebel governor summing up Nero's failings in a single pithy speech:

'He has pillaged the whole Empire, and destroyed the best of the senate. He debauched and murdered his mother, and he now does not even pretend to be capable of ruling. Many murders, robberies and outrages, it is true, have at times been committed by others, but the atrocities of Nero are truly indescribable. I have seen him, comrades and allies, believe me, I have seen that man – if you can call someone married to Sporus a man –…in the circle of the theatre, actually in the orchestra, sometimes holding the lyre and dressed in loose tunic and buskins…. How can someone like that be called Caesar, or emperor or Augustus? Impossible! Those sacred titles were held by Augustus and by Claudius, and cannot be so degraded…. Therefore finally rise up against him! Save yourselves, save the Romans and free the whole world!'
    Cassius Dio *History* 63.22

Vindex did not claim the Empire for himself – he knew that his Gallic origins and relatively low birth excluded him as a candidate. Instead he claimed to be acting on behalf of the seventy-one-year-old Galba, the respected and aristocratic senator who was governor of Spain. It was a shrewd move. Whatever Galba's feelings towards Nero, if Vindex's rebellion gained any kind of momentum, Galba would be seen as a credible rival to Nero and, no matter how much he protested his loyalty thereafter, his meeting with the executioner would be inevitable.

Nero took the news of Vindex's uprising with apparent calm. Possibly he knew the forces available to Vindex were few and that Rufus, commander of the legions on the Rhine, was loyal. Rufus marched his troops from Germany and defeated the rebels at Vesontio (modern Besançon). But then Rufus' troops proclaimed him *imperator*, and declared their intention of making him emperor by putting his name on their standards. Rufus fervently declared his loyalty to Nero and had his name rubbed off again, but this act by the soldiers sent a frisson through the entire Empire. Nero no longer commanded the loyalty of the legions. Once this knowledge was out, Nero's end was just a matter of time.

The next to feel safe to declare against the emperor was Macer, governor of the province of Africa. Four of the province's leading members had recently been executed by Nero, presumably because of their vast landholdings, and Africa's strategic position as a supplier of grain to Rome enabled Macer to put pressure on Nero by restricting the capital's food supplies. Equally important, Macer's action contributed to the general feeling that Nero's grip on power was slipping.

News that Galba had abandoned his loyalty to Nero came as a body blow to an emperor already well on the way to panic. Galba did not at this time raise the standard of revolt (he had precious few troops with which to do this anyway), but he simply informed the senate that he was at its disposal. Given Nero's relations with that body, this did not bode well, even though the senate dutifully obeyed Nero's orders and declared Galba a public enemy.

As soon as he heard of the rebellion, Nero is alleged to have dreamed up a number of characteristically appalling ideas for handling it. First he considered recalling all his army commanders and provincial governors and having them executed on a charge of conspiracy. Then he would do the same with exiles anywhere in the Empire lest they join the revolt, and then add the Gallic population of Rome, since these were automatically suspect. While he was at it, he would give the army leave to pillage Gaul, while he poisoned the entire senate at a banquet.

Suetonius *Nero* 43

While Suetonius is probably wrong about the details, there was certainly something of the headless chicken in Nero's response to the emergency. Some actions were appropriate and decisive. Nero made himself sole consul for the year, summoned troops from Illyricum and Britain, and raised a legion from the fleet at Misenum. But Nero could not leave Rome and his back unguarded, especially as his Praetorian prefect, Tigellinus, was too ill to take command. In any case, the loyalty of the Praetorians was wavering. This left Nero with the dilemma that whoever he sent into the field was just as likely to turn straight around and depose him. Indeed, the first part of the army, sent out under a commander called Petronius, had marched straight to Galba and joined him. Then

50 *The Praetorian Guard received privileges and pay which inspired envy and contempt from the average legionary. Within Rome the Praetorians were almost a law unto themselves, thanks to the emperor's dependence on them for personal security and his unwillingness to offend them.*

the troops from Illyricum declared for Rufus, making plain the army's opinion of Nero's artistic triumphs and his marriage to Sporus.

This was the first time Nero had been tested by a challenge from outside his family, and this time he lacked the counsel of Burrus or Seneca. In desperation Nero considered appealing directly to the Roman people to exploit any remaining affection for his family. Unfortunately, at that point a ship arrived from Alexandria, bearing not grain for the hungry city, but a cargo of sand which Nero had ordered for the imperial wrestling rings. Nero now abandoned his hopes of popular support and recalled that he was still loved in the East. He actively began to consider trying his fortunes in Egypt. Perhaps he could negotiate from a strong position there. If the Roman people really intended to abandon him, perhaps he might become prefect of Egypt instead. If all else failed, Nero nursed the pathetic delusion that he could make a living as a harpist.

Now that all classes of society had abandoned him, he began hatching plans to kill the senators, burn down the city and sail to Alexandria. He dropped this hint in regard to his future plans: 'Even though I have been driven from my post as emperor, yet this little talent shall support me there.' He had truly reached the height of stupidity if he genuinely believed that he could last more than a moment as a private citizen – especially as a lyre-player.

Cassius Dio *History* 63.27

As soon at it became known that Nero was planning to abandon Rome, Rome abandoned Nero. Suetonius tells us that Nero awakened in the night on 8 June to find his bodyguard gone. Leaping from his bed he went to seek out his friends who were staying in the palace. Finding they had abandoned him, he called for his staff, who had also gone – taking the chance to do some discreet looting as they went. When Nero did find human company, he received the news that, led by Nymphidius Sabinus, the Praetorians had declared for Galba.

Nero fled the city to the villa of Phaon, one of his freedmen, where he heard that the senate had declared him a public enemy and sentenced him to death. By now it was evident, even to Nero, that the game was up.

He grabbed two daggers which he had brought along, and tested the tips. Then he threw them down again, insisting that he should not be premature. He begged Sporus to mourn his passing, and pleaded that someone of those with him should set an example by being the first to kill himself. He bitterly lamented his own cowardice, saying, 'Life has truly become ugly and vulgar.' Then again to himself, in Greek, 'You are doing no credit to yourself, Nero, no credit at all. Come on, pull yourself together!'.... Then with the help of his scribe Epaphroditus he stabbed himself in the throat.

Suetonius *Nero* 49

It is claimed that Nero's last words were, 'What an artist the world loses in me!' However, Suetonius reports that he said these words before the arrival of the cavalry sent to bring him back to Rome. The centurion in charge of that troop, mindful of his orders that the emperor should be taken alive, tried hard to staunch the dying Nero's wound with his cloak. 'Do you call this loyalty?' demanded Nero, and died soon afterwards.

CHAPTER 9

EPILOGUE

*'If the vast structure of our Empire could remain as it stands without a
single guiding spirit, I would have thought myself fit to restore the Republic.
As it is, we have been long reduced from that position.... Under Tiberius,
Gaius [Caligula] and Claudius, the Empire was, so to speak, the possession
of a single family. Now the family of the Julians and Claudians
has perished, and the choice of who to succeed them will be our substitute
for freedom.'*
(Extract from a speech by Galba, Nero's successor) Tacitus *Histories* I.16

One of the principal problems facing the emperors of Rome was that the
principate was an informal institution outside the constitution of the
Roman state. Therefore there was no constitutional mechanism for the
transfer of power from one emperor to the next, and nothing like a set of
recognized criteria as to what constituted an eligible candidate for emperor.
Augustus had tried to compensate for this by the 'overlap' system, by
which an emperor designated his heir early, and steadily increased the
powers of his intended successor until his position was unassailable. The
problem was that not all emperors endorsed the notion of a replacement
for themselves being conveniently at hand, and these (Gaius Caligula
and Nero among the Julio-Claudians, though others were to follow)
tended to be the emperors most in need of replacing. When they were
gone, potential successors had to throw their hats in the ring and hope
that their candidature was given 'ex post facto' constitutionality. Once
the successful candidate had been selected, his explicit or potential rivals
were either co-opted as successors or informally eliminated. (Or sometimes option one, followed soon afterwards by option two.)

Because Augustus laid the foundations of his power upon 'universal consent', there was also no procedure for what was to be done if the universal consensus broke down. Assassination was an option from the very start, and was a viable solution to the rule of disastrous emperors such as Gaius Caligula, but it also meant that the Romans tended to bump along with merely mildly unsatisfactory emperors such as Claudius, simply because the option for not doing so was so drastic.

The main constituencies which an emperor or prospective emperor had to consider were the senate, the people, the army and his own family. Because Nero and his predecessors had been so successful in eliminating their own family, after Nero's death there was something of a contest between the remaining constituencies as to which had the greater right to impose their choice on the Roman state. Here the precedent set by Julius Caesar and Augustus showed itself true a century later – in the absence of any candidate with an uncontested right to power, the person with the best army secured the job. When its social and philosophical trappings were stripped away, as they were after Nero's death, the principate was revealed as what it had always been – a naked military dictatorship.

Tacitus commented that the year AD 69 revealed a secret of Empire – that emperors could be made elsewhere than in Rome. He was commenting on the fact that Rome's eighth emperor, Vitellius (who briefly succeeded Galba in 69), was the choice of the Rhine armies, and the ninth, Vespasian (ruled 69–79), was chosen by the army in the East. The corollary of this discovery was that while the emperor could be removed by people, senate, army or family members, or more probably a combination of these groups acting in concert, the final choice of successor rested unequivocally with the army. Furthermore, because there was no recognized method of replacing emperors, it meant that any method which was practical could be used, and the candidate tested for acceptability only after his accession.

An important part of the job description of every Julio-Claudian emperor was to keep such internal contradictions inherent in the principate from becoming apparent. Important questions about the system of government established by Augustus were left in the air – until the death of Nero brought them crashing down. Arguably, the fundamental problem with the principate was that Augustus had left it as a work in progress. The groundwork laid by Augustus was a work of political genius. Augustus' successors, while more or less competent, lacked the capability to build on that foundation, and the resulting edifice was fatally flawed.

The ad hoc solution to the problem of the imperial succession was to regard the Roman state as a possession of the Julio-Claudian family. 'Under Tiberius, Gaius and Claudius we were the inheritance, so to speak, of one family,' said Galba, Nero's immediate successor. Because there were no formal criteria for eligibility for the post of emperor, the choice fell by default on the most suitable Julio-Claudian. Because the system for succession was equally ad hoc and had the one requirement that the current emperor be dead, the Julio-Claudian emperors rapidly established that it was in their personal interest to deplete the pool of available Julio-Claudian alternatives.

The point where there were no Julio-Claudian alternatives at all was reached in AD 68 with the death of Nero. Had Britannicus still lived, he would almost certainly have succeeded his step-brother, and probably well before 68, which is precisely why he was dead. Vindex, governor in Gaul, had nominated Galba as Nero's successor mainly because he had no hope of getting the job himself. Galba was well respected, and was Vindex's neighbouring governor in Spain. By throwing Galba into the same boat as himself, Vindex guarded his rear from assault while he faced the Rhine armies, and afterwards, since Galba had been proposed and no one could think of a good reason why not, Galba, like most of the Julio-Claudians before him, became emperor by default.

At the time of his succession, Galba had already passed his seventieth birthday. The Romans had great respect for age, and it further helped Galba's credentials that he harked back to the early years of Augustus' rule. In fact, though he came from the ancient and respected line of the Sulpician Servii, he had been adopted in his youth by Livia, the wife of Augustus. Later, Galba married a Lepida, of the family of Augustus' tri-umviral colleague Aemilius Lepidus, and, since the Lepidi also married into the imperial family, this gave Galba a slight imperial connection. Apart from the highly endangered Julio-Claudian clan, Galba was prob-ably the most distinguished Roman of his day. Nevertheless, such was the mystique of the Julio-Claudian clan that as soon as Galba abandoned any lingering republican sentiment and decided to bid for the principate, he began to call himself 'Caesar'.

As Caesar, Galba discovered the hard way how difficult the job actually was. He came to it at the end of a long and successful career in government, and was by far the most suitable candidate. 'He would have been perfect for the job of emperor, if only he had not ruled,' remarked Tacitus unkindly. As it was, within a few months Galba had alienated the Roman people, the aristocracy and, fatally, the army. In a final display of his lack of political nous, Galba declared the highly aristocratic Piso as his successor, dashing the hopes of Otho – whom we last saw as a courtier of Nero who was sent to Spain so as to give the emperor a free run at his wife Poppaea Sabina.

Otho changed from a strong supporter of Galba to an embittered conspirator who briskly organized a revolutionary cadre among his old contacts in the Praetorian Guard. On 15 January AD 69 the Praetorians killed the emperor they were sworn to protect, and for good measure dragged Piso from the temple of Vesta where he had taken sanctuary, and butchered him also.

Like Galba, Otho lasted two months in Rome. His brief rule (15 January to 15 March) was marked by efforts to placate senate, Praetorians and citizens; efforts which were in vain since the Rhine armies failed to recognize him as Caesar, and instead marched on Rome to install their own candidate, Vitellius. Though outnumbered, Otho used his forces to fight a canny campaign whilst he mustered his legions. But after defeat on 14 April at the battle of Bedriacum, it dawned on Rome's new emperor that the best service he could render the state was to avoid further bloodshed. On 16 April he killed himself.

It appears that the ambition which had propelled Vitellius to the imperial throne belonged more to his army than the new emperor himself. Vitellius was a political appointee who had little military experience, but who knew that once the army had saluted him as emperor he had either to make the salutation reality, or die in the attempt. Led by two capable lieutenants, Valens and Caecina, his army began its march on Rome while Galba was still emperor, and hardly broke stride on news of Otho's succession.

With Otho removed from the picture, Vitellius' march to Rome was unimpeded, and he arrived in late June or early July. His rule was marked by public moderation and private excess. Vitellius did not take the title of Caesar, but styled himself more modestly as 'consul for life'. How short that life might be was made brutally plain when the war-hardened army which had been suppressing the Jewish revolt in the East marched on Italy to impose its own choice – Flavius Vespasian.

There were signs that Vitellius was already unhappy with his elevation and would have cheerfully resigned in his rival's favour if he could have found a way of doing so. Vitellius' lieutenant Valens was ill, and Caecina tried to take his army to the Flavian side. However, his men opted to settle the matter in gladiatorial style at the battle of Cremona (also known as the second battle of Bedriacum) on 24 October AD 69.

When his forces were defeated, Vitellius did in fact resign the Empire. However, both his soldiers and the Roman mob insisted, amid scenes of near-anarchy, that he stand by his elevation. Consequently, the Flavian troops had to fight their way into Rome two days later. Vitellius was dragged from his hiding place, killed in the forum, and his body thrown into the Tiber as that of a criminal.

As AD 69, the Year of the Four Emperors, drew to a close, the senate passed the *lex de imperio Vespasiani*, officially designating Vespasian heir to the throne of the Caesars. Rome's new master was a cheerfully mundane, matter-of-fact character with none of the glamour or wild rumours of personal excess which so enlivened the rule of his predecessors. Some of the character of his reign can be seen from his reply to his son Titus, who complained that charging an entrance fee to public toilets was below the dignity of even a cash-strapped emperor, as Vespasian certainly was. Vespasian shoved a handful of coins under Titus' nose and demanded 'So? Do they smell?'

Vespasian ruled until AD 79, and in the process restored the stability – both fiscal and political – which Nero had so comprehensively overturned. One of the omens which marked the end of his reign was that the mausoleum of Augustus was opened, either by the doors springing open, or a large crack appearing in the walls. 'Ah', remarked Vespasian with his usual insouciance, 'that will be for Junia Calvina.' From this comment we can be reasonably sure that it was around this time that the last descen-

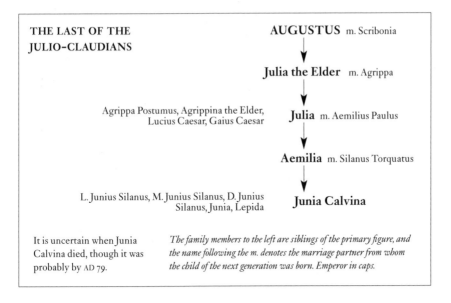

THE LAST OF THE
JULIO-CLAUDIANS

AUGUSTUS m. Scribonia

Julia the Elder m. Agrippa

Agrippa Postumus, Agrippina the Elder,
Lucius Caesar, Gaius Caesar **Julia** m. Aemilius Paulus

Aemilia m. Silanus Torquatus

L. Junius Silanus, M. Junius Silanus, D. Junius
Silanus, Junia, Lepida **Junia Calvina**

It is uncertain when Junia Calvina died, though it was probably by AD 79.

The family members to the left are siblings of the primary figure, and the name following the m. denotes the marriage partner from whom the child of the next generation was born. Emperor in caps.

dant of Augustus passed away. Junia Calvina was the great-great-granddaughter of Augustus. Like almost every female descendant of Augustus, she had been accused of sexual impropriety and exiled, though probably allowed to return to Rome by the easy-going Vespasian. She was either barren, or more probably considered that, for both herself and her offspring, the risks of reproduction hardly made it worthwhile.

She was the last flower of two of Rome's greatest families. Her passing marked the end of a line that stretched back to the foundation of the Roman Republic on the one hand, and to legendary Troy on the other. The Roman Empire would produce its own dynasties, from the Flavians to the Antonines and the Severans. None, in terms of antiquity, originality or style, came close to matching the standards laid down by imperial Rome's founding family.

Imperial Themes

From the start of their rule, the Caesars left an indelible mark on Rome. Their influence was both direct and indirect. The Augustan age of Rome saw an extraordinary flowering of the arts. This was in part a reflection of the fact that those with the ability to compose now had the leisure and tranquillity to do so, but also because the Caesars had pre-empted some of the more obvious forms of self-advertisement, leaving artistic patronage one of the few safe ways for the aristocracy to put itself in the public eye.

Horace, Livy, Virgil, Ovid and Lucan all wrote while the Caesars ruled. Martial, Tacitus, Josephus and Juvenal were born in the latter part of their reign. These names are among the most illustrious in Latin literature, and to them must be added the contribution of Julius Caesar himself.

Because the emperors had to prove that they were useful to the Roman state, and especially to the city of Rome, they made a massive architectural contribution to the city. It was a tradition of the Roman aristocracy to enhance their native city, and in this, as in many other ways, the Roman emperors conducted themselves as Roman senators writ large. If a Cato built a basilica, Julius Caesar and Augustus built entire forums. Pompey built a theatre, Claudius built a seaport. Nero, of course, attempted to rebuild the whole of Rome, but made the fatal error of seeming to do so in his own interest rather than that of the Roman people.

Yet the direct contribution of the Caesars to Rome was massively outweighed by their benefit to the Empire as a whole. Since their conquest by Rome, most of the provinces had previously known only war, corruption and ruinous taxation. Many of the wars involved either the internecine struggles of the Roman aristocracy or their efforts at self-aggrandizement, and high taxation and corruption were mainly the consequence of having to pay for their military or political struggles. The accession of the Caesars solved many of the problems of Rome's subjects at a stroke, since the Caesars muted and refereed the internal struggles of the aristocrats, not letting them enrich themselves at the expense of the provincials and certainly not letting their rivalries break into open warfare.

Most provincials had limited experience of anything other than autocracy. They had no republican inhibitions about hailing the Caesars as emperors, gods or whatever title they chose for themselves. Instead they threw themselves into the development of their civic life with such energy that within a few generations, provinces such as Gaul and Spain were as productive and cosmopolitan as Italy itself, and ready to assume their share of government. Under the Caesars the Roman Empire took its first steps to becoming an Empire shared by all its subjects.

It is this peace and prosperity created by relatively good government for which the Julio-Claudian emperors deserve to be known. The flamboyant excesses and cruelties of Nero and Gaius Caligula should not hide the fact that even these emperors spent a great deal of their time with the routine duties of government, meeting embassies, seeing petitioners and considering appointments to office, not to mention spending considerable time and effort in dealing, both formally and informally, with the Empire's fractious elites.

If we are to believe popular caricature, after Augustus, Rome was ruled successively by a sexual degenerate, a raving lunatic, a dribbling idiot and a murderous tyrant. Yet over the same period the Empire became steadily more prosperous, and the Caesars remained popular. It was almost exactly one hundred years from Augustus' victory at the battle of Actium to the death of Nero. If all the Caesars had been as genuinely incompetent as Nero in his later years, their government would not have lasted half as long. Yet as Nero's lingering support in the East demonstrated, the provinces' experience of even a bad Julio-Claudian was far more pleasant than (for example) the truly tyrannical oppression of the noble republican Brutus.

This is not to say that the Caesars set the Roman world completely to rights. Nero's debasement of the coinage started a trend which would not cease until Rome's currency was practically worthless. Even more fundamentally, the economic system of Rome had been built over half a millennium on the principle of relentless expansion and conquest. In the Empire this expansion slowed. Augustus was defeated in Germany. Britain under Claudius, and the annexation of some Eastern client kingdoms under Nero, marked the last permanent gains for the Empire. Under the Julio-Claudians, the boom created by peace, development and trade masked the loss of economic impetus provided by conquest, but the fundamental economic system of the Empire did not change, leaving problems waiting in the future.

Still, as Augustus was aware that he had not resolved all the problems of the principate, some problems could justifiably be left to posterity. Each Caesar had his own part to play, and as Augustus remarked on his deathbed, it was difficult enough to play even that well.

CHRONOLOGY

100 BC Birth of Julius Caesar. Marius consul for the sixth time

90 BC Start of Social War

87 BC Marius takes Rome

86 BC Death of Marius

84 BC Caesar marries Cornelia

82 BC Sulla takes Rome

79 BC Sulla resigns dictatorship

75 BC Caesar captured by pirates

73 BC Uprising of Spartacus

71 BC Crassus defeats Spartacus

70 BC Birth of the poet Virgil

67 BC Caesar marries Pompeia

65 BC Caesar elected Aedile

63 BC Caesar Pontifex Maximus. Catiline's conspiracy. Cicero consul

62 BC Clodius and the *Bona Dea* scandal

61 BC Caesar goes as governor to Spain

60 BC Formation of the first Triumvirate

59 BC Consulship of Caesar. Pompey marries Julia

58 BC Start of the Gallic Wars. Clodius Tribune

56 BC Triumvirate renewed

54 BC Death of Julia the Elder (Caesar's daughter)

52 BC Death of Clodius. End of Gallic War

49 BC Start of civil war. Caesar crosses the Rubicon

48 BC Battle of Pharsalus. Death of Pompey

46 BC Caesar in Africa. Death of Cato

44 BC Caesar made dictator for life. Caesar assassinated

43 BC Formation of the second Triumvirate. Cicero executed

42 BC Triumvirs win at Philippi. Birth of future emperor Tiberius

40 BC Antony marries Octavia

38 BC Octavian weds Livia Drusilla

37 BC Antony marries Cleopatra

31 BC Battle of Actium

30 BC Suicides of Antony and Cleopatra

27 BC First constitutional settlement

25 BC Julia marries Marcellus

23 BC Illness of Augustus. Second constitutional settlement

21 BC Julia marries Agrippa

20 BC Birth of Gaius Caesar (son of Julia). Parthia returns standards

17 BC Birth of Lucius Caesar (brother of Gaius). Augustus adopts both brothers

12 BC Death of Agrippa. Augustus (formerly Octavian) becomes Pontifex Maximus

11 BC Julia marries Tiberius who divorces Vipsania

10 BC Birth of Claudius

9 BC Death of Drusus the Elder (brother of Tiberius)

2 BC Banishment of Julia

AD 2 Death of Lucius Caesar

AD 4 Death of Gaius Caesar. Augustus

adopts Tiberius. Tiberius adopts Germanicus

AD 5 Banishment of Agrippa Postumus

AD 9 Varus and his legions are destroyed in Germany

AD 12 Germanicus consul. Birth of Gaius Caligula

AD 13 Tiberius has his Tribunician power renewed and gains the Proconsular Imperium in all provinces

AD 14 Augustus dies at Nola in Campania. Tiberius becomes emperor

AD 15 Tiberius becomes Pontifex Maximus

AD 16 Recall of Germanicus from Germany

AD 17 Sejanus becomes prefect of the Praetorians. Deaths of the historian Livy and the poet Ovid

AD 19 Death of Germanicus at Antioch

AD 20 War with Tacfarinas in Africa. Trial and suicide of Piso

AD 23 Drusus the Younger (son of Tiberius) poisoned

AD 27 Tiberius moves to Capri

AD 29 Death of Livia. Agrippina the Elder banished to Pandateria

AD 30 Drusus Caesar (son of Germanicus) arrested

AD 31 Sejanus becomes consul and is denounced by Tiberius

AD 32 Death of Drusus Caesar

AD 33 Agrippina commits suicide

AD 37 Death of Tiberius in Misenum. Gaius Caligula becomes emperor

AD 38 Death of Drusilla (sister of Caligula). Caligula marries Lollia Paulina. Claudius (his uncle) marries Messalina

AD 39 Execution of Gaetulicus and disgrace of Agrippina the Younger. Bridge

at Baiae built

AD 41 Assassination of Gaius Caligula. Accession of Claudius

AD 42 Revolt of Scribonius in Dalmatia. New harbour begun at Ostia

AD 43 Conquest of Britain begins. Claudius goes to Britain

AD 46 Birth of the biographer Plutarch

AD 48 Remarriage and death of Messalina

AD 49 Claudius marries Agrippina the Younger. Seneca recalled from exile

AD 50 Adoption of Nero

AD 53 Nero marries Octavia (daughter of Claudius)

AD 54 Death of Claudius. Accession of Nero

AD 55 Death of Britannicus. War with Parthia

AD 59 Execution of Agrippina

AD 61 Revolt of Boudicca in Britain

AD 62 Death of Burrus. Nero divorces, and later kills, Octavia. Nero marries Poppaea Sabina

AD 64 Great fire of Rome

AD 65 Suicide of Seneca. Death of Poppaea

AD 66 Start of the Jewish revolt

AD 67 Nero in Greece

AD 68 Rebellion of Vindex. Suicide of Nero. Galba becomes emperor

AD 69 Year of the Four Emperors

AD c. 79 End of the Julio-Claudian line

GLOSSARY

Aedile A magistrate with a functional rather than legislative role. Aediles were in charge of keeping the streets clean and the sewers working, of relegating eating houses, taverns and brothels, and staging the ever more extravagant games which took place on Roman holidays. An aedile who spent his own money while in office could easily regain his investment if the electorate appreciated his efforts.

Auctoritas Personal authority and ability to get things done. The degree of respect and fear from others by which elite Romans were judged.

Censor Not just in charge of civic morality, the censor also regulated the handing out of state contracts. As the name indicates, the censors were supposed to conduct a census of the Roman people, though the chaos that preceded the reign of Augustus meant that some censors were not even able to regulate the roll of senators – another important, and politically dangerous, task. The censorship was meant to come at the end of a long and distinguished career.

Centurion An officer in a legion. Though the name implies command of 100 men, the responsibilities of centurions varied immensely. Some centurions were of the minor aristocracy, and the idea that they were all hard-bitten NCOs has not withstood historical scrutiny.

Conscript fathers An ancient term for senators.

Consul One of the two chief officers of the Roman state. The holder was elected with a colleague and held office for a year (the usual length of Roman offices). Originally the consuls spent much of their time commanding armies, but later they spent most of the year politiking in Rome before going abroad as proconsuls – first as generals, and later as governors in the provinces. Under the Caesars it became customary for consuls to resign early and leave the (now mostly honorary) position for another 'suffect' consul.

Curia The meeting house of the senate. Not all meetings were held in the senate house, as any temple to a Roman god was deemed sufficient for the purpose.

Cursus honorum The order of advancement of an elite Roman through the elected offices of the state.

Delator Someone who was prepared to point out the enemies of the state to the proper authorities in return for a small fee.

Familia Nearer to a household than a family, the *familia* included slaves, various relatives, pets and certain items (called *res mancipi*) which the owner could not sell without the permission of the rest of his *familia*.

Fides Loyalty and trustworthyness.

Freedman On manumission (the formal freedom ceremony) an ex-slave was expected to take the family name of his former master and to remain under a deep obligation to him. Many freedmen were slaves who had a position of considerable responsibility which they continued to hold once freed.

Gens A loose family grouping, claiming to come from a common ancestor, and sharing a family name. Thus the Scipios,

284

Cinnas and Sullas were all part of the Gens Cornelia, and the Appians and Marcellans were part of the Claudian Gens. Membership of a Gens did not stop members taking opposite sides politically or being bitter personal enemies.

Imperial fisc The private resources of the emperor (often supplemented by bequests in wills, the expedient execution of those who refused to make such bequests, and the confiscation of what was left).

Legates These were generally senators or members of senatorial families who were appointed on the recommendation of a commander or governor to serve on his staff. They had greater independence than military officers, and were used in a wider variety of roles. Both Pompey and Caesar found that their political commitments made it impossible to rule their provinces directly, and so their legates were effectively governors of the provinces to which they were sent. In the imperial era the emperor directly commanded a large number of provinces, and sent a legate to govern each.

Military tribune A member of the entourage of a general, often a young aristocrat at the start of his career. Until the last days of the Republic it was essential for a young man to do extensive military service before starting into politics, and this tradition was to a large degree maintained even in the Empire.

Maius imperium (proconsulare) The power which elevated the emperor above provincial governors and effectively made him master of the Empire.

Patrician A caste within the senate. The patricians considered themselves the original aristocracy of Rome. At one time they would not marry outside their caste and had a special rite for marrying within it. Some priestly offices were reserved for patricians, as initially was the consulship.

Even later generations preferred to see one patrician and one plebeian as consuls. The Julians and most Claudians were patricians.

Pietas Showing respect and an awareness of one's obligations.

Plebeians Originally the poorer people of Rome, the plebs forced the patricians to share power, so that plebeian later came to mean 'a Roman who is not a patrician'.

Pomerium The sacred boundary of Rome. Generals in arms and kings were not allowed across the *pomerium*, nor were burials generally permitted within it. The *pomerium* was rarely extended, and only then with great ceremony.

Pontifex A member of Rome's priestly elite. Rome had a number of priestly colleges, such as the Arval Brotherhood, and far from separating church and state, the Romans gave their priests not just a constitutional but also a political role. Every Roman politician collected every possible priesthood. The ceremonial chief priest of Rome was the *flamen dialis*, who was surrounded by a host of rituals and superstitions, whilst the most powerful priestly office was that of Pontifex Maximus. In the best politico-religious Roman tradition, the Pontifex Maximus was elected by a popular vote.

Praetor The rank below a consul. Though praetors commanded armies, they also had a judicial role. In fact until the late twentieth century when the office was abolished, there were still magistrates called praetors handing out justice in Rome and the rest of Italy.

Proscription The very Roman idea that a reign of terror could be better organized if those due for summary execution knew who they were, so that the remainder could relax. The proscribed lost their money and land, which has led some historians to see it as a drastic money-raising technique as much as a political purge.

Provincials Non-Italians who did not hold the Roman citizenship (most Italians did after the Social War of 90 BC). Lightly – if sometimes brutally – ruled by Rome, provincials enjoyed taxation without representation until sufficient of their number entered the Roman army to have a very real say in Rome's choice of emperor.

Quaestor The most junior magistracy, which qualified the holder for a place in the senate. Quaestors usually worked with a more senior magistrate, and had administrative duties, mainly financial.

Toga The formal garb of a Roman citizen. It was utterly impractical for everyday wear, so the average Roman wore a tunic and kept his toga for weddings, funerals and appearances in front of a magistrate. The *toga praetexta* was edged in purple to show a senior Roman senator, and a young man received the *toga virilis* at his coming-of-age ceremony.

Treasury The official financial reserves of the Roman state. Since Rome supported a larger standing army than could be paid for by taxation and the occasional conquest, the treasury was dependent on large transfusions from the imperial fisc, and, from the time of Nero, judicious depreciation of the currency.

Tribune Elected only by the plebs, and having no power outside the city of Rome, tribunes were intended to protect the people against the abuses of the powerful. Tribunes could veto legislation, order prisoners released, or even arrest the consuls. This office was captured by the plebeian aristocracy, and though it was theoretically a college of equals, usually the most powerful aristocrat dominated his fellows.

Tribunician power The constitutional base for the emperor's power in Rome. The emperor sometimes shared this power with a potential successor.

Triumvir One of a group of three people in charge. In the Roman tradition, such groups of senior administrators were not uncommon, and the record shows triumvirs, duumvirs and decemvirs in charge of different departments, cities, or even of Rome itself.

FURTHER READING

G&R = Greece and Rome
JRS = Journal of Roman Studies
PBSR = Papers of the British School at Rome
TAPA = Transactions of the American
 Philological Association

Allen, W. 1941 'The political atmosphere of the reign of Tiberius', *TAPA* 72: 1–25.

Balsdon, J. 1969 'Fabula Clodiana', *Historia* 25: 198–204.

Barnes, T. 1981 'Julia's child', *Phoenix* 362–63.

Barrett, A. 1989 *Caligula: The Corruption of Power*. London: Batsford.

—— 1996 *Agrippina. Sex, Power and Politics in the Early Empire*. New Haven: Yale University Press.

—— 2002 *Livia, First Lady of Imperial Rome*. New Haven: Yale University Press.

Bauman, R. 1967 *The Crimen Maiestatis in the Roman Republic and Augustan Principate*. Johannesburg: Witwatersrand University Press.

—— 1974 *Impietas In Principem: a Study of Treason against the Roman Emperor with Special Reference to the First Century AD*. Munich: Beck.

—— 1992 *Women and Politics in Ancient Rome*. London: Routledge.

Bradford, E. 1984 *Julius Caesar: The Pursuit of Power*. London: H. Hamilton.

Braund, D. 1984 *Augustus to Nero. A Sourcebook on Roman History 31 BC– AD 68*. London: Croom Helm.

Breglia, L. 1968 *Roman Imperial Coins*. New York: Praeger.

Brunt, P. 1981 'The revenues of Rome', *JRS* 71: 161–72.

Campbell, J. 1984 *The Emperor and the Roman Army, 31 BC–AD 235*. Oxford: Clarendon Press.

Charlesworth, M. 1939 'The refusal of divine honours, an Augustan formula', *PBSR* 15: 1–10.

Chisholm, K. & Ferguson, J. 1981 *Rome: the Augustan Age*. Oxford: Oxford University Press.

Corbeill, A. 1996 *Controlling Laughter: Political Humor in the Late Roman Republic*. Princeton: Princeton University Press.

Dawson, A. 1969 'Whatever happened to Lady Agrippina?', *Classical Journal* 64.

Deutsch, M. 1928 'Caesar's son and heir', *University of California Publications in Classical Philology.* 127–48.

Eck, W. 2003 *Augustus* (trans. Schneider). Oxford: Blackwell Publishing.

Edwards C. 1993 *The Politics of Immorality in Ancient Rome*. Cambridge: Cambridge University Press.

Elsner, J. & Masters, J. (eds) 1994 *Reflections of Nero*. London: Duckworth.

Ferrill, A. 1991 *Caligula, Emperor of Rome*. London & New York: Thames & Hudson.

Fishwick, D. 1987 *The Imperial Cult in the Latin West: Studies in the Ruler Cult of the Western Provinces of the Roman Empire*. New York: Leiden.

Galinsky, K. 1996 *Augustan Culture*. Princeton, NJ: Princeton University Press.

Garnsey, P. 1970 *Social Status and Legal Privilege in the Roman Empire*. Oxford: Clarendon Press.

Gelzer, M. (trans. P. Needham) 1968 *Caesar: Politician and Statesman*. Oxford: Blackwell.

Gowing, A. 1992 *The Triumviral Narratives of Appian and Cassius Dio*. Ann Arbor: University of Michigan Press.

Greenhalgh, P. 1980 *Pompey: the Roman Alexander*. London: Weidenfeld and Nicolson.

Gruen, E. S. 1974 *The Last Generation of the Roman Republic*. California: Berkeley.

Griffin, M. 1984 *Nero: the End of a Dynasty*. London: Batsford.

Hallett, J. 1984 *Fathers and Daughters in*

Roman Society. Princeton & Guildford: Princeton University Press.

Holland, T. 2000 *Nero: the Man Behind the Myth*. Stroud: Sutton.

—— 2004 *Rubicon: The Triumph and Tragedy of the Roman Republic*. London: Abacus.

Hollemann, A. 1986 'The first Claudian at Rome', *Historia* 35: 377–78.

Jimenez, R. 2000 *Caesar Against Rome*. Westport: Praeger.

Kahn, A. 1986 *The Education of Julius Caesar*. New York: Schocken Books.

Kiefer, O. 1994 *Sexual Life in Ancient Rome*. London: Constable.

Kohne, E. & Ewigleben, C. 2000 *Gladiators and Caesars*. London: British Museum Press.

Kokkinos, N. 1992 *Antonia Augusta. Portrait of a Great Roman Lady*. London & New York: Routledge.

Levick, B. 1971 'The beginning of Tiberius' career', *Classical Quarterly* 21: 478–86.

—— 1975 'Julians and Claudians', *G&R* 22: 29–38.

—— 1976 *Tiberius the Politician*. London: Thames & Hudson.

—— 1985 *The Government of the Roman Empire: A Sourcebook*, London: Croom Helm (2nd ed. 2000, London: Routledge).

—— 1990 *Claudius*. London: Batsford.

Lewis, N. & Reinhold, M. 1995 vol. 2 'The Empire', from *Roman Civilisation*, 3rd ed. New York & Chichester: Columbia University Press.

Linder, A. 1987 *The Jews in Roman Imperial Legislation*. Detroit, MI: Wayne State University Press; Jerusalem: Israel Academy of Sciences & Humanities.

Meier, C. (trans D. McLintock) 1995 *Caesar*. London: HarperCollins.

Millar, F. 1967 *The Roman Empire and its Neighbours*. London: Weidenfeld & Nicolson.

Millar, F. & Segal, E. 1984 *Caesar Augustus: Seven Aspects*. Oxford: Clarendon Press.

Mitchell, R. 1990 *Patricians and Plebeians: the Origin of the Roman State*. Ithaca, NY: Cornell University Press.

Nicols, J. 1975 'Antonia and Sejanus', *Historia* 24: 48–58.

Nippel, W. 1995 *Public Order in Ancient Rome*. Cambridge: Cambridge University Press.

Patterson, J. 2000 *Political Life in the City of Rome*. London: Bristol Classical Press.

Pomeroy, S. 1975 *Goddesses, Whores, Wives and Slaves. Women in Classical Antiquity* New York: Schocken Books.

Price. S. 1984 *Rituals and Power: The Roman Imperial Cult in Asia Minor*. Cambridge: Cambridge University Press.

Raaflaub, K. & Toher, M. (eds) 1990 *Between Republic and Empire*. California: Berkeley.

Rajak, T. 1983 *Josephus: The Historian and his Society*. London: Duckworth.

Rawson, B. 1986 *Intellectual Life in the Late Roman Republic*. London: Duckworth.

Rawson, B. & Weaver, P. (eds) 1997 *The Roman Family in Italy: Status, Sentiment, Space*. Canberra: Humanities Research Centre; New York & Oxford: Clarendon Press.

Rudich, V. 1993 *Political Dissidence Under Nero: the Price of Dissimulation*. London & New York: Routledge.

Saller, R. 1979 'Men's age at marriage and its consequences in the Roman family', *Classical Philology* 21–34.

—— 1982 *Personal Patronage Under the Early Empire*. Cambridge: Cambridge University Press.

Sabben-Clare, J. 1971 *Caesar and Roman Politics 60–50 BC: Source Material in Translation*. London: Bristol Classical Press.

Seager, R. 1972 *Tiberius*. London: Eyre Methuen.

Scullard, H. H. 1959 *From the Gracchi to Nero. a History of Rome from 133 BC to AD 68*. London: Methuen & Co.

Shotter, D. 1992 *Tiberius Caesar*. London: Routledge.

Smallwood, M. 1967 *Documents Illustrating the Principates of Gaius, Claudius and Nero*. London: Cambridge University Press.

Syme, R. 1980 'No son for Caesar?', *Historia* 29: 422–37.

——1986 *The Augustan Aristocracy.* Oxford: Clarendon Press.

Talbert, R. 1984 *The Senate of Imperial Rome.* Princeton & Guildford: Princeton University Press.

Tatum, W. 1999 *The Patrician Tribune: Publius Clodius Pulcher.* Chapel Hill & London: University of North Carolina Press.

Thornton, M. 1986 'Julio-Claudian building programs; eat, drink and be merry', *Historia* 35: 28–44.

Thornton, M. & R. 1983 'Manpower needs for the public works programs of the Julio-Claudian emperors', *Journal of Economic History* 43: 373–78.

Treggiari, S. 1991 *Roman Marriage.* Oxford: Clarendon Press.

Wallace-Hadrill, A. 1982 'Civilis princeps: between citizen and king', *JRS* 72: 32–84.

——1983 *Suetonius: the Scholar and his Caesars.* London: Duckworth.

——1993 *Augustan Rome.* London: Bristol Classical Press.

Weaver, P. 1972 *Familia Caesaris: a Social Study of the Emperor's Freedmen and Slaves.* London: Cambridge University Press.

Wellesley, K. 1954 'Can you trust Tacitus?', *G&R* 1: 13–33.

Wiedemann, T. 1989 *The Julio-Claudian Emperors.* London: Bristol Classical Press.

Woodman, A. 1977 (ed.) *Velleius Paterculus: The Tiberian Narrative.* Cambridge: Cambridge University Press.

——1998 *Tacitus Reviewed* Oxford: Clarendon Press.

Yavetz, Z. 1969 *Plebs and Princeps.* London: Oxford University Press.

Zanker, P. (trans. A. Shapiro) 1988 *The Power of Images in the Age of Augustus.* Ann Arbor: University of Michigan Press.

CREDITS &
ACKNOWLEDGMENTS

All quotations are the author's own translations.

t = top, b = bottom, l = left, r= right;
BM = The British Museum, London; ML = ML Design

In-text illustrations

frontispiece The Walters Art Gallery, Baltimore; **map** ML; 1 Deutsches Archäeologisches Institut, Rome; 2 BM; 3 I Musei Capitolini, Rome; 4 BM; 5 Giovanni Caselli; 6 Staatliche Museen zu Berlin; 7 Castello Ducale di Agliè; 8 ML; 9 BM; 10 BM; 11 BM; 12 Nasjonalgalleriet, Oslo; 13 Staatliche Museen zu Berlin; 14 Bildarchiv Marburg; 15 Museo Arqueologico, Seville; 16 BM; 17 BM; 18 Deutsches Archäeologisches Institut, Rome; 19 akg-images/Peter Connolly; 20 Ny Carlsberg Glyptotek, Copenhagen; 21 BM; 22 Pompeii Museum; 23 Ny Carlsberg Glyptotek, Copenhagen; 24 Alinari; 25 BM; 26 akg-images/Erich Lessing; 27 BM; 28 Philip Winton; 29 BM; 30 Alinari; 31 BM; 32 BM; 33 Glyptothek, Munich; 34 BM; 35 Ny Carlsberg Glyptotek, Copenhagen; 36 Collection ESR, Zurich (Photo Leonard Von Matt); 37 Museo Nazionale delle Terme, Rome; 38 BM; 39 I Musei Capitolini, Rome; 40 BM; 41 Michael Duigan; 42 Kunsthistorisches Museum, Vienna; 43 akg-images/Erich Lessing; 44 BM; 45 Fototeca Unione; 46 Collection ESR, Zurich (Photo Leonard Von Matt); 47 Museum of El Djem, Tunisia; 48 ML; 49 Courtesy, Museum of Fine Arts, Boston; 50 Musée du Louvre, Paris.

Plate sections

1 I Musei Vaticani; 2 I Musei Vaticani; 3 Ny Carlsberg Glyptotek, Copenhagen; 4 Fototeca Unione; 5 Roger Wilson; 6 Giovanni Lattanzi; 7 BM; 8 Deutsches Archäeologisches Institut, Rome; 9 Kingston Lacey, Dorset; 10 Kunsthistorisches Museum, Vienna; 11 akg-images/Nimatallah; 12 Scala; 13 akg-images; 14 Museo Nazionale delle Terme, Rome; 15 Courtesy, Museum of Fine Arts, Boston; 16 Alinari; 17 Alinari; 18 BM; 19 Musée du Louvre, Paris; 20 Bibliothèque Nationale de France, Paris; 21 BM; 22 Deutsches Archäeologisches Institut, Rome; 23 BM; 24 Aphrodisias Archive, Institute of Fine Arts, New York; 25 Colchester and Essex Museums; 26 Bibliothèque Nationale de France, Paris; 27 akg-images; 28–30 Giovanni Lattanzi; 31 BM; 32 BM; 33 Staatliche Museen zu Berlin.

Acknowledgments

My thanks to all who attempted to guide me through the nightmarish ramifications of the Julio-Claudian family tree, to Barbara Levick for bringing her profound depth of knowledge to the project, and to Adrian Goldsworthy for his help and encouragement. Above all thanks to my wife Malgosia for surviving two years with the Julio-Claudians without losing her sense of humour. And finally my thanks to Melissa Danny for her tireless work and attention to detail, which has made this book a much more organized (and accurate) piece of work than it would otherwise have been.

INDEX